Performance Evaluation:

A Management Basic for Librarians

Performance Evaluation:
A Management Basic for Librarians

Edited by Jonathan A. Lindsey

 ORYX PRESS
1986

The rare Arabian Oryx is believed to have inspired the myth of the unicorn. This desert antelope became virtually extinct in the early 1960s. At that time several groups of international conservationists arranged to have 9 animals sent to the Phoenix Zoo to be the nucleus of a captive breeding herd. Today the Oryx population is over 400, and herds have been returned to reserves in Israel, Jordan, and Oman.

Copyright © 1986 by
The Oryx Press
2214 North Central at Encanto
Phoenix, AZ 85004-1483

Published simultaneously in Canada

Printed and Bound in the United States of America

∞ The paper used in this publication meets the minimum requirements of American National Standard for Information Science—Permanence of Paper for Printed Library Materials, ANSI Z39.48, 1984.

Library of Congress Cataloging-in-Publication Data

Performance evaluation.

Includes bibliographies and index.
1. Library employees—Rating of. 2. Librarians—Rating of. 3. Library personnel management. I. Lindsey, Jonathan A., 1937–
Z682.P34   1986   023'.9   86-42746
ISBN 0-89774-313-X (alk. paper)

Contents

Preface

Performance evaluation generates more anxiety in an organization than any other single event during the year. So many outcomes ride on appraisals. So much responsibility falls on the appraiser. The related issues are almost overwhelming. Now the legal side of performance evaluation is a major concern, too.

Does your stomach tighten up annually as you must confront the reluctance of supervisory personnel to deal with the weaknesses of staff whom they must evaluate? As you look over evaluation forms, does the human tendency to avoid the extremes confront you? This tendency, called the halo effect, lumps most performance into a middle group, thus making discrete reward decisions difficult.

Librarians, like so many other professionals, have tended to promote from within into administrative posts. Until the last decade or so, little attention was given to the supervisory responsibilities and skills involved in such administrative positions. The growth of personnel management and human resources management as disciplines in schools of business testifies to the rise of interest among all professionals in many of these issues. And the civil rights movements of the 60s focused many questions on the nature of performance evaluation as an industrial and individual issue. In addition, expectations of accountability have increased among all public institutions, including public libraries; accountability is the foundation on which such libraries are now operating.

To attempt to review every development in the area of performance evaluation over the past two decades would be a gargantuan task and one that would be productive in only an academic pursuit. As an administrator, responsible for the productivity, motivation, and performance of a diverse group of persons in an academic setting, I felt that more practical help was needed. Two resources seemed potent: *Library Literature* and *Business Periodicals Index.* A literature search of these two sources encompassing the past five years produced a number of citations. From reading this material, it became clear that librarians could profit from greater familiarity with basic management literature.

Also, when I was editor of *North Carolina Libraries,* some questions about performance evaluation were beginning to be addressed.

The Spring 1984 issue of *North Carolina Libraries* featured several articles which dealt with the question; I have included one article ("The Human Dimension in Performance Appraisal") from that issue in this book. Besides *North Carolina Libraries,* the only other attempt made to provide an overview of performance appraisal was in the work of Robert D. Steuart and John Eastlick in *Library Management,* 2d ed. (Libraries Unlimited, 1981). These two overview resources and the five-year literature search made up the basis of my research.

The purpose of this volume is simply to place in librarians' hands a body of literature that I have judged to be a management basic. In addition to the 20 "core" articles reprinted here, I have also included an annotated bibliography of additional articles. Between the articles which are reprinted here and the annotated bibliography, the reader should be able to gain a solid grasp on the most recent literature. Both the reprints and the bibliography point to sources beyond the scope of this publication. The aim of the annotations in the bibliography is to provide a stronger sense of balance for an important area of library administration.

Two conclusions can be drawn from a review of this literature, which, with three exceptions, is limited to the 1980s.

1. Broad interest in questions related to performance evaluation dates back to the late 1950s, with the publication of Douglas McGregor's "An Uneasy Look at Performance Appraisal" (*Harvard Business Review,* May/June 1957), now considered a classic. From this beginning has flowed a steady stream of research, publication, and review.

2. Regardless of the system used for evaluation of employees, certain common concerns emerge:
   — Adequacy of instrument/system to measure
   — Training and skill development for evaluation
   — Communication
   — Legal issues

The 20 articles that appear in this book address these concerns. The choice between reprinting an article and abstracting it was sometimes dictated by its length and degree of technical content, since a purpose of this publication is to appeal to a broad audience, including paraprofessional and support personnel. Also, I wanted this book to appeal to a wide range of library constituencies, including special libraries. Finally, I wanted the articles to meet some of the following criteria in providing information:

- theory and practicality;
- library-specific application of performance evaluation theory;
- variety of library types;
- issues affecting the evaluator and the evaluated;

- some relevant legal questions;
- a look at the appraisal process; and
- a sense of wholeness of perspective.

The articles grouped themselves somewhat easily. Because it would be impossible to reprint every relevant article here, the idea of an annotated bibliography was born.

As you read through the articles as they are grouped, I hope you will perceive the strongly human(e) issues which I feel are at the base of any examination of performance evaluation and at the base of performance evaluation itself. People—individual persons and their lives, their careers, their future—depend on the effectiveness of the institution's performance evaluation system. Change, the great stress creator, is also right there in the middle of performance evaluation. The compilation of articles begins with these two notes in mind.

The next two major issues in performance evaluation are communication and legal issues. Nearly all writers of performance evaluation tend to say something about communication and the need for it to be effective, offer advice about skill development and the need for it, or call for greater attention to be paid to the communication process. The legal issues which have an impact on performance evaluation have increased in their visibility in the past decade. For instance, civil rights, women's and minority issues, and unionization at production and professional levels all contribute to the legal questions to be faced. In each of the articles reprinted in these two sections, I have sought to provide theory and practice and point to a larger resource.

Performance appraisal is performed almost routinely in American libraries. In the "Types of Library Appraisals" section, the needs of school media specialists and academic librarians have been especially singled out because they have spoken most directly to the appraisal issue. However, the articles in this section address types of appraisals useful to all libraries.

The next section, "Appraisal May Be ...," addresses the question of what to do when you have an outstanding performer who continuously outperforms everyone else. The superior employee provides greater appraisal challenges than the average, mediocre, or poor performer. One article among all of the items addresses this question. Allied to it is the functional role of evaluation from the manager's perspective of both planning and motivation. This question is dealt with in a library-specific application.

Two final issues are dealt with in this book. First, the appraisal of performance evaluation, a sort of self-critical approach, is assayed. Articles in this section demonstrate the vitality of the personnel/ management issue. Finally, the last two articles in this book look toward the future of performance evaluation in libraries, again responding to the needs for specific application within libraries.

Since 1981, I have struggled with the implications of Daniel Yankelovich's articulation of a new ethic. I heard him at the ALA annual conference in San Francisco. I read *New Rules: Searching for Self Fulfillment in a World Turned Upside Down* (New York: Random House, 1981) and his summary by the same title in *Psychology Today* (15, April 1981, pp. 35–37ff). Yankelovich points to the implications of changes in the value system and ethical structure in "Let's Put the Work Ethic to Work." There he asserts that the American workplace was caught in a commitment gap. Other than the single citation, I found no mention in the literature I examined of the need for or role of commitment in performance evaluation. Yet, commitment seems to be a recurrent and underlying, although unarticulated, issue. The question of commitment is a thorny issue. It deals with relationships between employer and employee. It deals with the level of personal energy investments which employees can/should make in their jobs. It deals with career orientation among both production line and human services occupations. Theories X–Z and quality circles are based on a gestalt that recognizes commitment at their base.

By raising the question of commitment, I hope to contribute to the forthcoming dialog concerning performance evaluation. Further, by raising the question of commitment, I hope we shall move from process and procedure in a vacuum and deal even with these important aspects from a sense of philosophical wholeness.

Four titles from 1985 (listed in the bibliography) have influenced my thinking in this regard:

1. Berkeley Rice. "Performance Review: The Job Nobody Likes"
2. Ron Zemke. "Is Performance Appraisal a Paper Tiger?"
3. John E. Clewis and Janice I. Panting. *Performance Appraisal: An Investment in Human Capital.*
4. "Guidelines for Performance Evaluation of Professional Librarians." *The Newsletter* (California Library Association) 27 (November 1985).

From the perspective of commitment, performance evaluation seems to focus on the concerns articulated in these four pieces. The positive aspect of performance evaluation is that it is (or should be) mutually beneficial to both employer and employee. Each has needs. Each must be committed to the other for maximum mutual benefit. Without commitment as a base, appraisal will take place, but it will lack an essential ingredient.

Finally, this publication owes its existence to Jim Thomas and Jan Krygier, Oryx Press. Their patience and encouragement have been essential. To the faculty and staff of Baylor University Libraries, however, will go any monetary benefit of this publication, designated to a fund for faculty/staff development.

Some Initial Thoughts

The Human Dimension in Performance Appraisal

by Jonathan A. Lindsey

THE MANAGEMENT MENTALITY

Management is "in" these days. At the end of 1982, the top item in college bookstores was Garfield; in mid-November 1983, the top items were Kenneth Blanchard, *The One Minute Manager,* and Thomas J. Peters and Robert H. Waterman, Jr., *In Search of Excellence: Lessons from America's Best Run Companies.*[1] The change from the self-help volumes of a decade ago to the emphasis on management is a comment on cultural change and attitudes. More recently, getting the job done well appears to be of greater interest than the antics of a comic cat. Underlying this "management mania," as some might call it, is a tension in which libraries have been caught for generations, the conflict of attempting to evaluate objectively what is essentially a subjective experience. Service versus productivity is *the* polarity for libraries.

One element in the tension reflected by last fall's best sellers on management is not their emphasis on technologically based efficiency but their surprising acknowledgement of the human element in large, successful businesses. In many instances, Peters and Waterman describe the human relationships within the companies they studied— from hype to personal pride in products. But at the basis of the high performance of the companies in their study was a strong sense of the human dimension, the personal touch, the almost forgotten second-mile ethos of the work ethic. Their identification of "close to the customer," "productivity through people," "hands-on, value driven" as three of the eight attributes of excellence are people-based.[2]

Jonathan A. Lindsey is coordinator of library affairs, Baylor University, Waco, TX. "The Human Dimension in Performance Appraisal" is reprinted with permission of the author from *North Carolina Libraries* 42 (1) (Spring 1984).

Libraries have always experienced the tension which these management writers are now recognizing. Libraries provide service, yet much of the work of library personnel is production-oriented. For the past twenty years, libraries have been developing management systems focused on production. As librarians have grown into and become parts of expanding bureaucracies, management's requirement of accountability has been the motivation for performance evaluation. However, we now find ourselves in 1984 needing to look more carefully at the human dimension in management.

RECENT RESEARCH REPORTS

Not only has "management mania" taken hold in libraries in the past decade; the status of the employee in public agencies has also created the need for carefully defined documentation about the performance of personnel. Stanley P. Hodge has provided a fine treatment of the performance appraisal instrument that has been shaped by legislative and judicial decisions in the past decade of evolving equal employment opportunity requirements.[3] Hodge identifies seven functions for which performance appraisals are often used: facilitating personnel planning, making employment decisions, supporting job development, providing performance feedback to employees, eliciting feedback from employees, creating a base for modification of behavior, and establishing needs for training or coaching.[4] He traces the legal base for each of these characteristics and provides a sample of a document used at Texas A & M that could have general application throughout libraries.

Hodge appears to understand the advice of H. Rebecca Kroll, who sets out four criteria for any evaluation program.

1. Determine what the job is. (Define the goals.)
2. Establish a reasonable performance level. (Define the objectives in terms of quantity, quality, time spent.)
3. Measure the actual performance (by firsthand observation, viewing completed work, reading the employee's own report, and the like).
4. Compare the actual performance to the standards set.[5]

Both Kroll and Hodge follow the wisdom of Robert D. Steuart and John Taylor Eastlick, who have articulated five functions for a personnel evaluation program. These include measuring performance against job description expectations, documenting to justify termination, providing a base for positive personnel action, indicating an individual's capability and potential, and generating personal goals which support implementation of institutional goals.[6]

The bibliographies of these four writers direct the administrator to a selection of library, personnel, and federal sources written during the period between 1968 and 1982 but centering on the years 1977 to 1981. These sources, supplemented by N. K. Kaske's reviews of performance and appraisal that appear in the American Library Association *Yearbook,* 1976–81,[7] provide significant reading and a sampling of evaluation/appraisal instruments.

WHY PERFORMANCE EVALUATION MAY NOT WORK

Despite library management's ambivalence about performance evaluation, the phenomenon is not new, and it is here to stay. Regardless too of the mixed systems of management style, ranging from laissez faire to the latest adaptation of business school theorists, accountability in multiple copy is a fact of life to be faced, lived with, and worked through. Given these realities, the success or failure of any evaluation/appraisal experience depends upon the philosophy of the institution in which the evaluation is performed and the attitude of the person being evaluated toward the whole experience. The favorable attitude of the person being evaluated toward the event, the process, and the product of evaluation is essential to the effective implementation of any evaluative experience. If the individual fails to perceive value in the product, the process and the event are irrelevant. Saul Gellerman said this more compellingly when he commented that personnel would "want to correct the deficiencies in their performance if they *agreed* that they were deficient and if there appeared to be enough *advantage* in correcting them to justify the effort."[8]

At least four common causes of personnel dissatisfaction with evaluations focus on perceptions of the lack of effectiveness of the evaluation. These causes may or may not exist in fact, but if they are perceived to exist, trouble ensues:

1. if across-the-board raises always appear to occur;
2. if nonperformers appear to be promoted;
3. if supervisors always rate high (or low);
4. if fear of legal action mitigates evaluation.

Each of these is so common that they usually fail to be discussed in other than staff-room asides.

Steuart and Eastlick cite six pitfalls of performance evaluation which they credit to the Denver Public Library's *Manual for Performance Evaluation.* These are the errors of (1) the "halo effect"; (2) "prejudice and partiality"; (3) "leniency, softness, or spinelessness;" (4) "central tendency"; (5) "contrast"; and (6) "association."[9] Errors one and three are opposites and reflect attitudes of the evaluator. Error two refers to discrimination in any of its legally defined forms. Errors four and six refer to the middle of the range and sequential constancy in rating. Error five refers to the actual performance versus the rater's perception of potential. These "errors" are articulated for supervisors to remind them of their responsibility in the rating process.

PRE-EMPLOYMENT ANALYSIS

Good experiences with personnel evaluation begin before employment and are particularly important at the employment stage. The foundation for good personnel evaluation experiences lies in a clear articulation of the tasks to be performed, the skills required to perform the tasks, and matching persons with skills appropriate to the tasks. This kind of pre-employment analysis can facilitate the development of job descriptions and performance expectations.

For instance, who has not experienced the page who has no numerical acuity? Such frustration might be avoided by two pre-employment decisions. One decision is to determine that the primary tasks of pages require the skill of accurately placing books on shelves, reading shelves, and even performing inventory. The primary skill is the ability to perceive numerical sequences quickly. To achieve the match between task, skill, and personnel may require a simple numerical acuity examination, with minimum scores for employment and for increased levels of experience and responsibility.

In another instance, the pre-employment decision may be that the human needs of the library require a warm, "motherly" figure at the circulation counter. Certainly this primary public relations location in the library requires personnel that have more than minimal interpersonal skills. This question particularly needs to be considered as we increase the use of computer-based circulation systems that require combining a different set of technological skills with human response skills. A decision may have to be made that the human response skills are more critical at the circulation counter!

Consider the reference department, where skill is required in "negotiating the reference interview," the current jargon for being able to ask the kinds of questions which help the user define a need and provide the librarian with data to begin to help meet that need. Reference librarians in the past have been trained in bibliographical knowledge but have received little training in inquiry and search strategy. The Association for Clinical Pastoral Education[10] is a pioneer in the use of *verbatim reports* as a means of developing listening/ hearing skills. Their method could be adapted for use in library education after a careful description of the tasks, skills, and expected performance of reference librarians. Verbatim reports could also be applied in the library as a technique for evaluating reference skills. This would require preparation of reports of the reference interview from which a judgment could be made of the effectiveness of the reference librarian's interpretation of the question and initial search strategy.

Consider the performance evaluation from the perspective of a letter of reference. Letters of reference need to be specific, describe the candidate's skills with concrete examples, refer to career goals, and note limitation where appropriate.[11] Well-documented letters of reference are based on precise evaluation. This is especially important for students who may use library employment as references for their first professional jobs.

As stated at the beginning of this section, successful performance evaluation is based on decisions made by administrators before the employment of the person to be evaluated. Without careful, recurring analysis of tasks and skills refined to reflect the variety and changing functions of library service, effective performance evaluation will not occur. Many things can impede effective evaluation, but none can substitute for this level of preparation.

SO WHAT?

In 1984, with all of its inherent overtones and innuendoes, with the "management mania" which appears to have cultural endorsement, with the realistic need for accountability, and with the increased impact of technology on our lives, performance evaluation/appraisal is not going to fade into the sunset. This phenomenon of life in the bureaucracy is with us. If current speculations are accurate, that 67 to 75 per cent of the American work force will be information-related by the end of the century, and if the predicted rates of change in other employment sectors take place, careful pre-employment analysis is going to be necessary. Pre-employment analysis of functions, because of these changes, is going to require modification of tasks and skills required and the evaluation of performance. At the base, however, of any performance evaluation/ appraisal system is the attitude of the person being evaluated. If the individual places value on the product of evaluation, the individual will be willing to change behavior. If, however, the individual does not value the product, then the process will not provide positive individual benefit. Even "one minute managers" waste time and energy with persons who do not value the product.

REFERENCES

1. *The Chronicle of Higher Education* 14 (November 28, 1983): 2.

2. Thomas J. Peters and Robert H. Waterman, Jr., *In Search of Excellence: Lessons from America's Best Run Companies* (New York: Harper & Row, 1982), 13–15. Also see separate chapter treatments on each attribute.

3. Stanley P. Hodge, "Performance Appraisal: Developing a Sound Legal and Managerial System," *College & Research Libraries* 44 (July 1983): 235–244.

4. Ibid., 235.

5. H. Rebecca Kroll, "Beyond Evaluation: Performance Appraisal as a Planning and Motivational Tool in Libraries," *The Journal of Academic Librarianship* 9 (1983): 27.

6. Robert D. Steuart and John Taylor Eastlick, *Library Management,* 2d ed. (Littleton, Colorado: Libraries Unlimited, 1981), 97.

7. N. K. Kaste, "Personnel and Employment: Performance and Appraisal," *ALA Yearbook* (Chicago: American Library Association, 1976–1981).

8. Saul W. Gellerman, *Management by Motivation* (Chicago: American Management Association, 1968), 141.

9. Steuart and Eastlick, 98–99.

10. Association for Clinical Pastoral Education, 475 Riverside Drive, New York, New York 10027.

11. Stacy E. Palmer, "What to Say in a Letter of Recommendation? Sometimes What You Don't Say Matters Most," *The Chronicle of Higher Education* 27 (September 7, 1983): 21.

The "Ten Commandments" for Performance Appraisal Interviews

by Bernard S. Schlessinger and
June H. Schlessinger

Under the subject heading, Employee Evaluation in *Library Literature,* 1979–1983,[1] there is a relatively constant flow of articles, adding up to 45 listings over the five-year period. The 45 items, taken collectively, present a comprehensive picture of performance appraisal (needs, forms, rewards, standards, expectations, uses) in all types of libraries, but they deal only peripherally and superficially with the process of conducting the performance interview. Surprisingly, the same result is found in the business literature, in a search of *Business Periodical Index*[2] and a review paper by Cederblom.[3]

The authors, together representing close to 50 years of experience with employee performance appraisal in education (secondary and university), libraries, and laboratories, have found that conducting a performance appraisal interview is a critical element in successful performance appraisal. Over the years they have developed a set of procedures for conducting a performance appraisal interview, which are summarized in the following "ten commandments."

THE "TEN COMMANDMENTS" FOR PERFORMANCE APPRAISAL INTERVIEWS

1. *The supervisor will not conduct a performance appraisal interview without first reviewing the rationales for holding the interview.*

Bernard S. Schlessinger is a professor in the Department of Library Science, Texas Woman's University, Denton, TX. June H. Schlessinger is an assistant professor of English at North Texas State University, Denton, TX. Their article, "The 'Ten Commandments' for Performance Appraisal Interviews," is reprinted with their permission from *Texas Library Journal* 61 (1) (Spring 1985).

Supervisors exposed to the pressures of everyday administration can forget the reasons for performance appraisal. It is easy to recognize the process as necessary for providing for sound decisions in matters of promotion, tenure, salary changes, or retention. However, although these may indeed be the ultimate outcomes of evaluation, the basic rationale should be the discussion of expectations and how well they are being met and a clear statement of how the individual can become more valuable to the organization. This mutual understanding can best be achieved by face-to-face discussion, rather than depending on interpretation of the written word, which at best is an imperfect vehicle of communication.

2. *The performance appraisal interview will be conducted only on the basis of evaluations by both the supervisor and the employee.*

One of the most effective preparations for the interview is the filling out of the evaluation form by both the supervisor and the employee prior to the interview, with expectations and performance stated and evaluated. If the two agree, then the interview can be short. However, if they disagree the interview will be necessarily longer, and, in order to justify the time spent, must lead to a better mutual understanding of expectations and satisfactory performance levels.

3. *The performance appraisal interview will be conducted at stated periods, and the time allotted will be adequate.*

Perhaps the most-asked question in sessions held on this subject concerns the frequency and length of the interview. An answer is difficult, since, just as evaluation must be ongoing, so must appraisal interviews be ongoing. If a problem or an example of excellent performance is recognized, the employee should be made aware of the supervisor's perception of the problem or the supervisor's pleasure in a job well-done. In spite of their importance, these "spot interviews" usually are short and regardless of their frequency do not replace the regular, careful, written evaluations and resultant performance appraisal interviews. Probably the complete interview will be required only on an annual basis; however, if many problems emerge or if disagreement exists, a semiannual evaluation and interview should be held. As to time, no less than one hour should be set aside for the interview and schedules should be flexible enough to permit even longer periods if necessary, particularly since problems incompletely addressed will probably grow between interviews.

4. *Performance appraisal will be standard and mandatory, as will the interview and the resultant paperwork.*

   Although this is usually viewed as a documentation requisite and a protection for the supervisor, it is no less important to the employee. Very few employees are willing to be assertive enough to demand an appraisal or an interview if they are not stated requirements, and many may be very relieved if the process is not necessary. The same can be said about many supervisors. Mandatory appraisal and appraisal interviews remove the need for employee assertiveness and for a confrontational attitude that might accompany a requested interview session, rather than a required one. Standard forms and formats help in these matters. And a requirement that the employee and supervisor both sign the resultant paperwork, indicating agreement or disagreement, prevents many unpleasant situations from occurring later.

5. *The stage will be set to make the interview as effective as possible.*

   The physical setting of performance appraisal interviews is very often overlooked in planning. In addition to adequate time allotment noted above, attention should also be paid to other factors.

   a. The supervisor should insure that there will be no interruptions. There is nothing more unnerving for an employee than to be told that there is a serious problem with his/her work only to have the interview interrupted by a phone call and then have to wait while the supervisor settles a series of family or job problems in a prolonged conversation.

   b. The supervisor and employee should sit together in friendly fashion, without a desk interposed between them and without the supervisor seated in a position emphasizing authority.

   c. The setting should be physically comfortable. It should be private, with appropriate temperature, suitable light conditions, etc. Review of an employee's performance where other employees can hear, where either person is uncomfortably warm or cold, or where either person faces glaring light, can destroy an otherwise well-planned performance interview.

6. *Both positives and negatives must be included in the interview.*

   A performance appraisal interview should not be viewed as either an ego-builder or an ego-destroyer. A supervisor should be able to find examples of both strong and weak points to use in the interview. Our rule-of-thumb has been to begin with discussions of strengths, move smoothly into discussions of weaknesses and finish on a positive note. This should leave the employee neither devastated nor euphoric.

7. *Any topics that are raised should be discussed.*

Although, as stated above, the basic purpose of the interview is not to discuss promotion, tenure, salary, or retention, the interview format should not preclude discussion of any of these topics or anything else of concern to the employee or the supervisor. Both parties should regard the interview as a time to handle in an unhurried fashion any concerns that might affect the employee's future with the organization.

8. *The supervisor must not allow personality differences to enter the evaluation process.*

The supervisor may like or dislike an employee's personality. Although it may be difficult to separate personal feelings from objective interaction, these must be divorced from the conduct and content of the appraisal and the interview. A supervisor must conduct the interview without regard to personal feelings of like or dislike.

9. *The supervisor must be kind.*

Even though it may not be apparent, an employee, even the best employee, is apprehensive and uncomfortable during an interview. And frequently the supervisor must make statements which will reinforce the apprehension and increase the discomfort. Remembering to maintain a kind posture in this atmosphere will help enormously in conducting the interview.

10. *The supervisor must be honest.*

In an attempt to be encouraging sometimes the supervisor can be convinced that something less than honesty is required in the interview. Both the supervisor and the employee must steel themselves to confront a full appraisal and discussion of performances. Only honesty expressed by both sides can accomplish an effective performance appraisal interview.

Finally, the supervisor should find that the performance appraisal interview, conducted in accordance with the "ten commandments," can become a very important tool in effective management of the human resources in the organization.

REFERENCES

1. *Library Literature.* New York: H.W. Wilson, 1979–1983.
2. Business Periodical Index. New York: H.W. Wilson, 1979–1983.
3. Cederblum, Douglas. "The Performance Appraisal Interview: A Review, Implications and Suggestions," *Academy of Management Review,* 1982, pp. 219–227.

Dealing with Resistance to Change

by Joseph Stanislao and Bettie C. Stanislao

A great frustration is having the answer to a problem in the form of a proposed change, and being unable to get anyone to accept or carry out that change. This article handily surveys the reasons supervisors and workers resist change. Also, it offers some prescriptions for dealing with common resistances.

Change is inevitable if an organization is to survive in a world of developing technology and new consumer and employee demands. Maintaining the status quo is likely to stifle success, so managers at all levels must develop skills in changing people, procedures, methods, and machinery. But even with adequate planning, the manager is likely to encounter resistance to change in employees. Such resistance stems from fear; this fear is easier to prevent than it is to remove once it has developed.

According to Certo, the major factors when changing an organization are determining what should be changed, what type of change needs to be made, who will be affected by the change, and who will be the change agent. These factors and their interaction collectively determine whether the change will be successful.[1]

Since major technological changes are few relative to the number of day-to-day changes in product, process, and procedures, the following discussion devotes attention to these day-to-day changes.

Joseph Stanislao is dean and professor, College of Engineering and Architecture, North Dakota State University, Fargo, ND. Bettie C. Stanislao is a nutritionist and registered dietitian at the Fargo Diabetes Education Center, Fargo, ND. Their article, "Dealing with Resistance to Change," *Business Horizons* (July/August 1983): pp. 74–78, is reprinted with permission of the School of Business, Indiana University, Bloomington, IN.

1. Samuel C. Certo, *Principles of Modern Management Functions and Systems* (Dubuque, Iowa: Wm. C. Brown Company, 1980): 265.

When considering the people to be affected, it is useful to distinguish between the individual who has authority to accept or reject a change and the individual who has no voice in acceptance or rejection of the proposed change. If the latter is affected, he or she must cooperate in order for the change to be successful; both groups deserve separate analysis.

RESISTANCE TO CHANGE BY A PERSON HAVING VETO POWER

Any person with the authority to accept or reject a proposal may reject it for any one of the reasons outlined below.

Inertia. An innate desire to retain the status quo exists, even when the current situation is inferior. Inertia is the tendency to want to do things in the accustomed manner. Thus, a supervisor will oppose the new method merely because it is different from the accustomed one. This person will not "get around to doing" anything differently unless impressed with necessity.

Uncertainty or fear of the unknown. Regardless of how bad the existing method might be, at least how well it functions is known. Any deviation from the known procedure involves risk, and the proposed method offers no guarantee of better results. In this case, supervisors are unwilling to trade inferiority of which they are certain, for superiority of which they are uncertain. This fear or uncertainty can be eliminated by training programs in the new methods.

Insecurity and fear of failure. The individual who is to accept the new idea may see no need for any change and may resist because of the fear of possible failure. In this case, implementing the change on a trial basis may reassure the supervisor that success is possible. Change on a trial basis should reduce the fear of personal loss and will give the people involved an opportunity to get more facts about the change.

Ignorance. Even when individuals are not directly involved, their failure to understand the new system will produce cautiousness and resentment. Properly prepare the employees for change by providing as much information as possible about the change. Lack of knowledge may lead to imaginary problems in addition to the real problems of change. Do not underestimate the grapevine as a source of information to employees, and do not underestimate the grapevine's capability of providing misinformation if given nothing better.

Obsolescence. People are afraid of having a skill which is considered obsolete. One who has invested years of experience in building up a high level of skill, knowledge, and judgment for a specific activity may resist any new proposal. A fear of not being or not becoming proficient in the new system may cause apprehension and a resistance to change.

Personality. Personality conflicts between the proposer and the proposee can produce resistance to change. Maintaining a friendly relationship with and showing respect for everyone helps in eliminating personality conflicts.

Outside Consultants. Reliance on outside help can cause resentment. A change developed by outsiders may not be accepted by insiders. The implication, as the insiders see it, is that insiders cannot handle their own problems. Make limited use of outside consultants in dealing with employees.

Resentment of criticism. Criticism may erupt from the person who originated the present method, since changing the present method may be a threat to that person's security. Noncritical statements are sometimes construed as criticism, so beware of critical statements and of ones that might be taken as such. In reality, the resentment of criticism is probably more responsible for failure of change programs than is resistance to change itself.

Participation. When a change is proposed, staff members may be embarrassed at not having conceived an idea which, with hindsight, appears obvious. The importance of participation by all staff members from the start should not be underestimated. Student refers to "influence" as the focal element in any successful change process.[2] Having some influence as the change is being proposed will strengthen the support of people affected by the change. People are more likely to support what they help to create.

Tact. Sometimes a few right words can make the difference between acceptance or resistance to change. The manner of presenting the proposal should be friendly, and words should be chosen to show personal regard for the persons affected. Encourage full participation of supervisors in helping employees accept change.

Confidence. If the person who is to carry out the change doesn't perceive adequate experience and expertise in the person who proposed it, he or she will resist the change and think it is doomed to fail. The person selected to be the change agent should be someone who inspires confidence.

Timing. Timing of the proposal is essential. Many good ideas are rejected because people are emotionally or physically upset, or unusually busy, or because business is in a temporary slump or labor relations are strained. Select a time when the receiver is in a receptive mood.

---

2. Kurt R. Student, "Managing Change: A Psychologist's Perspective," *Business Horizons,* December 1978: 28–33.

RESISTANCE TO CHANGE BY A PERSON HAVING NO VETO POWER

Resistance to change reactions may come from individuals who have no direct voice in the acceptance or rejection of the proposal, but who are directly affected by it, for any of the reasons given below.

Surprise. Employees tend to resist change, especially when the change is unexpected, sudden, or radical in their view. People need time to evaluate change before it occurs. Those affected should be informed well in advance.

Lack of information about how the change will affect the employee's job. Uncertainty will bring resistance even if the current situation is not satisfactory. The desire to resist is greater when risk of unemployment is involved in the change, particularly when those affected don't know how the idea was formulated. The worker may feel that any change is a move toward replacing him or her.

Lack of training. Failure to understand the new method or policy arouses suspicion or an insecure feeling rapidly, but feelings are hidden from immediate supervisors or other management personnel. Training programs to teach employees necessary skills should be started well before the change.

Lack of real understanding. Ignorance is a major reason why workers resist change. Too often little or no explanation is given to the workers, sometimes with the attitude that this is none of their business. The employees' parts in the program should be explained thoroughly, and changes planned with their help.

Loss of job status. Reduction in the skill required, or the importance of the job, or the responsibility of the worker involved may arouse resistance of the worker to a new idea. Such reduction in status of the employee will lead to insecurity. To prevent this, the worker should be reassured of his or her worth to the organization. Questions related to power, prestige, responsibility, skills required, and hours of work should be answered honestly.

Peer pressure. The work group often resists new ideas even though the individual workers may not feel as strongly against the new idea as their group actions would indicate. Every work group has certain ingrained policies, some expressed and others implied, which can resist new ideas. A person's reaction to change is usually influenced by what he or she knows or anticipates that the group wants. Being accepted by the group may motivate the employee to participate in resistance to change. Obtaining group support of the proposed change would eliminate resistance due to peer pressure.

Loss of security. Fear of economic insecurity can cause an immediate resistance to new concepts, particularly if workers fear a reduction in earnings. Resistance to change may arise as a result of a reduction in job classification, a tightening of a time standard as a result of the change in question, or an inability to master the new method or to reach the level of proficiency that the worker had attained under the replaced method. Here again, reassuring the workers of their worth will be beneficial.

Loss of known work group. Alteration of social relationships, coupled with the fear that a closely knit work group will be replaced or eliminated, may cause resistance. Workers need reassurance that they will not be expected to betray friends.

Personality conflicts. Antagonism toward the person introducing the change may be a personal antagonism, or may be an antagonism toward the person's function, or may be toward management in general. Such hostility causes individuals and groups to resist almost any change that comes from management, referred to as resistance on general principles. The change agent, or person who tries to effect change, should be able to use behavioral science tools to influence the employees before and during the change. To be successful, the change agent must determine how much change the employees can withstand and should limit change to that amount. Changes must be made in such a way that employees who must change their behavior are given the opportunity to become ready to learn the new behavior, to try the new behavior, to make the new behavior useful, and to accept the new behavior as part of themselves. Lewin refers to these stages in the change process as unfreezing, changing, and refreezing.[3] The change agent must give ideas or innovations time to become acceptable.

Timing. Poor timing may cause maximum resistance to change. If the business has slack periods, changes should be made during these periods to minimize confusion. The proposed change should wait until all employees who will be affected by it have received accurate information about how the change will affect them and their jobs. If possible, they should participate in change-related decisions.

RECOMMENDATIONS

The following recommendations should be considered in planning the introduction of an idea and in modifying the idea to make it more saleable and palatable. First, one should convincingly *explain* the need for change to receivers, particularly the workers. Use straightforward, clear, well-organized language to assure that they understand the method or policy. Do not take for granted the importance of this understanding. Tailor the communication format to suit the particular receiver. Many

---

3. Kurt Lewin, "Frontiers in Group Dynamics: Concept, Method, and Reality of Social Sciences: Social Equilibria and Social Change," *Human Relations,* June 1947: 5–14.

change programs have failed because of the lack of mutual understanding about what the program is trying to accomplish.

Facilitate participation, or at least the feeling of participation, in the formulation of the proposal. In general, people are concerned about making their own ideas and recommendations succeed. The feeling of participation may be imparted by consulting with the workers, and by seeking their information, opinions, and suggestions. Above all, show real interest in what these people have to say. Seeking their advice will encourage their participation in the change. Whenever possible, include the worthwhile suggestions of others in the final report and give credit to the appropriate individuals.

Use a tactful approach in introducing the change proposal. Watch wording and mannerisms and avoid implying criticism. In attempting to gain adoption of an idea, avoid making the proposal when the recipient is upset or busy. Allow sufficient time for the recipient to think it over. Also, avoid introducing certain changes when labor relations are abnormally strained.

In the case of major changes, try to design the proposal to introduce the *change in stages.* The mere magnitude of some proposals or ideas may frighten people and arouse objections. Capitalize on the features which provide the most personal benefits.

A procedure of *planting the idea* in the recipient's mind is usually effective if it can be properly executed. The difficulty with this planting concept is that it is not easily done, nor are people generally willing to allow others to get credit for their ideas.

Management should *show that it supports* the proposed change. Publicize the benefits of completed changes which are of interest to employees. Share the benefits of changes with the employees.

The foregoing measures, concerning the minimization of resistance to a specific change, are no substitute for a long-range plan for change. These measures should be supplemented by a long-term effort to prepare personnel for changes in general. Such a conditioning process will involve both technical and psychological preparation. Before the change is introduced and when considering long-term effort, plan for technical training, so that personnel will feel capable of mastering the new ideas and managerial techniques. Education on the importance of change, the consequences of change, the role of competition, and the need for change is emphasized through the psychological phase of minimizing resistance to change. Maintaining a policy of fair treatment of employees affected by change concerning job retention, job replacement and job content is also part of the psychological phase.

In general, an effective long-term measure in minimizing resistance to change is the very awareness of the phenomenon itself. Then if employees are aware of the causes, manifestations, and frequency of this reaction, the employee or supervisor will be less inclined to resist change.

Communication Is Basic

Effective Communication in the Performance Appraisal Interview

by John F. Kikoski and Joseph A. Litterer

Performance appraisal appears to be a simple management tool. Yet experience demonstrates just the opposite. That members of an organization should know how they are performing is obvious. And that superiors should tell subordinates about their performance is equally obvious. Yet some superiors avoid this crucial task, while others experience anxiety and discomfort doing it.[1]

There has been considerable progress in improving the instruments of performance appraisal systems. The early, openly subjective judgment of personal traits has been replaced by decades of effort which strains toward today's more objective evaluation of job expectancies and performance. More traditional graphic rating scales, and rankings and checklists have been supplanted by field reviews, more sophisticated forced-choice questionnaires, and listings of critical incidents. More recently, assessment centers and management by objectives have come into use. Most recently, behaviorally anchored rating scales have come to be utilized.

Yet a paradox exists. A review of the literature indicates that much of the research and publications in this area have focused upon the empirical *means* by which to appraise performance—the development of the methodologies and the construction of the instruments by which to more objectively and validly measure employee performance. But despite considerable progress in a number of these areas, the delivery of performance appraisal still tends to be resisted, if not

John F. Kikoski is assistant professor of political science, Sacred Heart University, Bridgeport, CT. Joseph A. Litterer is a professor of management, University of Massachusetts, Amherst, MA. Their article, "Effective Communication in the Performance Appraisal Interview," *Public Personnel Management Journal* 12 (December 1983): 7–10, is reprinted with permission of the International Personnel Management Association, Alexandria, VA.

avoided by many managers. For the central source of difficulty still remains. This occurs when the manager sits down to review face-to-face his subordinate's performance. The appraisal interview itself is the Achilles' heel of the entire process.

This article is concerned with the delivery of the performance appraisal interview. It is divided into three parts of sequentially narrowing focus. We first treat the factors which have increased the use and significance of performance appraisals in the public management process. Next, we focus upon the general nature of the dialogue and relationship between superior and subordinate in the delivery of the performance appraisal itself; in it we examine four basic components for a successful performance appraisal interview. Finally, we propose six specific, structured and learnable skills to help make managers more effective in the actual delivery of the performance appraisal itself.

ENVIRONMENTAL PRESSURES INCREASING THE USE OF PERFORMANCE APPRAISALS

There are today a number of powerful pressures—some almost traditional, others novel—which are increasing the use and significance of performance appraisal systems today.

First, there is the perennial and general need for organizations to become more productive, more effective. This typically means better use of their chief resource—their human potential. In its developmental dimension, performance appraisal is a management tool of powerful potential which can link organizational need and individual capability.[2]

Second, in this era of reductions in government expenditures at the national level, of Propositions "13's" and "2½'s" at the state and local levels, when Buckminister Fuller's admonition, "Less is more," increasingly makes sense, and with the concept of "cut back management" becoming growing reality throughout the public sector performance appraisal becomes more appropriate and more necessary at every level of public management, not only to increase congruence between ability and position, but also to guarantee the future availability of seasoned, inhouse talent when it is needed.

Next, the growth of public unions, coupled with the spread of affirmative action and equal opportunity legislation are pushing public organizations to make their employment procedures more objective and rational. Promotion, pay raises, discipline and dismissals will require more grounding in objective, accurate and fair performance appraisals, for the coming decade will probably witness an increase in the number of court cases where the validity of performance appraisals will be a fundamental issue.[3]

Finally, the passage of the 1978 Civil Service Reform Act (CSRA) not only mandated linkage between executive performance and pay, but also established performance appraisal as the linchpin for its accomplishment. In 1980–1981, approximately 120,000 federal civil servants between Grades 13–15 converted to a merit pay schedule in which performance appraisal played a key role. Unfortunately, in the fall of 1981, the funds available for merit pay increases were reduced. This resulted in the announcement by Donald Devine, Director of the Office of Personnel Management that "all merit pay employees (except for special rate employees . . .) are to be granted the full 4.8 percent General Schedule adjustment."[4] Recent research indicates that while federal civil servants are deeply involved in implementing the CSRA, they also recognize its shortcomings.[5] On the state level, one study found there to be broad and deep receptivity among state employees and supervisors to a performance appraisal system,[6] even though another study found employee performance appraisal systems to be inadequate in most cities and states surveyed.[7] For these reasons performance appraisal can be expected to occupy an increasingly central and crucial role in both public and private organizations in the 1980's.[8]

Yet despite these strong pressures, managers are often reluctant and anxious about the appraisal interview.[9] They often dislike the face-to-face encounter and feel unskilled in performing the vital appraisal interview into which all prior efforts flow.[10]

There is a good reason for this. A review by this author of 351 recent journal articles related to performance appraisal found only a handful which focused upon the appraisal interview itself. Those which did tended to fall into one of two categories. Some sought to identify and measure the behaviors and dynamics of the appraisal interview according to empirical and statistical methods; the others typically took a general, vague and often contradictory "maxims" approach which offered little more than organized common sense to the manager who must conduct the actual interview itself.

In this paper we take a different approach. The next section identifies four dimensions or preconditions which are basic to a successful performance appraisal interview. They form the matrix for the discussion of the six more discrete and specific skills which follow in the final section of this paper.

THE FOUR DIMENSIONS OF SUCCESSFUL PERFORMANCE APPRAISAL INTERVIEWS

The Cognitive/Rational Dimension

Performance appraisal interviews may be conducted as if they were performance appraisal pronouncements: the superior has a message; the subordinate is there to receive it; the superior does the talking (or the bulk of it), while the subordinate does the listening (or the bulk of it).

It would be the rare employee who would not feel uncomfortable entering such a situation. The actions individuals take which lead to the outcomes under review—except in relatively simple types of work—are taken with many immediate contingencies in mind. An individual may have exceeded their budget but, given the circumstances at that time, may have kept the average from being much higher. The superior may or may not know of these contingency factors, but the subordinate will not feel he or she is being treated fairly—or be really willing to listen—until he or she feels that their performance is being assessed in its host context. In addition, a key ingredient for a successful performance appraisal interview has been found to be "ownership," that psychological concept of participation by the subordinate whereby they feel encouraged to speak and offer their views.[11] Establishing this understanding by the superior and participation by the subordinate can only come *through dialogue* not pronouncement.

Point one: *For an effective appraisal interview, there needs to be a genuine dialogue on the cognitive/rational level taking place between superior and subordinate.*

The Affective/Emotional Dimension

It is understandable that an appraisal interview is often charged with emotion. Guilt, fear, pleasure, regret and hope are only some of the emotions which are at work here. More than this, one's past performance is on display, one's future may be on the table in a sort of public "self-disclosure"—one of the most powerful, yet rarely-used of personal interactions. There is good reason for this, for with self-disclosure we are vulnerable.

The subordinate comes to the interview on edge, already somewhat apprehensive, even defensive, wondering what is about to happen to him. Superiors may also come on edge, wondering whether they will hurt the other person's feelings, wondering whether they will be called upon at some future time to explain or to justify their judgments possibly even in court, and not be able to do so adequately.

Experiencing the superior's tension, the subordinate may interpret this as "coldness" or "hardness" and begin to respond accordingly. The superior, sensing the subordinate's wariness, responds in kind. Without design the cycle continues, a relationship grows that may be detrimental to a good performance appraisal interview.

In emotionally-charged situations such as this, people can fail to hear clear mesages, distort others—and then create totally unanticipated meanings for the facts being discussed. The superior needs to be alert to this emotional setting, and the fact that an appraisal interview involves not only verbal and non-verbal communication of facts and ideas, but of attitudes and feelings as well.[12]

Point two: *For an effective appraisal interview, there should be a genuine dialogue on the affective, emotional level taking place between superior and subordinate.*

The Performance/Conscious Dimension

At best, many managers feel awkward and ill-at-ease in the appraisal interview. At worst, they are unskilled in this task. Given this, much good advice has been proposed to help them via the proverbs, or maxims approach. Not uncommonly, superiors are advised: (1) don't be judgmental; (2) take the other person's feelings into account; (3) be clear, be sure the other person knows what you mean; (4) don't talk about issues the subordinate can do nothing about, or are beyond his control; (5) be specific, talk in concrete terms, etc.

There is other good, but contradictory advice. As Smith and Brouwer put it: if a superior gives advice or explains, he may be telling his subordinate how to do it *his* way; if a superior attempts to reassure, he may undermine evaluation.[13] In addition, pleading is weak; ordering is one-way communication; while criticism may blunt initiative, and encourage mindless conformity. Advice available to a superior can be confusing and contradictory to a subordinate. How then to proceed?

The advice may be good, the insights insightful. But the weltering plethora of proverbs and contradictions may result in a fundamental lack of certainty in the superior's mind about *what* to do in the appraisal interview, *what* advice to apply and, most importantly, *how*?

Point three: *For an effective appraisal interview, the superior should possess more of a conscious awareness of what specifically to do and say in his performance of the appraisal interview.*

The Dyadic Dimension: The Relationship between Parties

An obvious, but basic point is that the performance appraisal interview takes place in a dyad, that is between two individuals. The nature of the relationship between these individuals is the fourth vital precondition for a successful appraisal interview.

The field of psychotherapy demonstrates the importance of the relationship between the individuals involved—therapist and client—

to the successful outcome of the work at hand. There are many approaches to psychotherapy—Freudian, Rogerian, Cognitive and Behavioral Therapies—to mention just a few. Each has its own systems, methods and claims for success. Research into which is best has shown that more important than *which* approach is used is the *quality of the relationship* between client and therapist. Effective treatment occurs when there is a good relationship between the parties—irrespective of which approach is used.[14]

We can expect similar conditions to hold in performance appraisal interviews. To conduct a successful interview may depend more upon the relationship between superior and subordinate than on the specific instrument used to appraise the performance now being discussed. An effective relationship in the appraisal interview is characterized by the subordinate feeling that he or she has been acknowledged as a person, that the conditions under which they have labored are understood, that they and their behaviors are accepted (if not necessarily approved), and that they have been listened to and understood. When such a relationship exists, complex and difficult matters can be handled with remarkable speed and efficiency.

Point four: *For an effective appraisal interview, for the superior to communicate and the subordinate to be open to change/be helped, an effective relationship is essential.*

To this point, we have identified four basic preconditions for a successful performance appraisal interview. They include: (1) a genuine dialogue on the cognitive/rational level; (2) a genuine dialogue on the affective/emotional level; (3) the superior's conscious awareness of what to do and say in his implementation of the appraisal interview itself; and (4) the establishment and maintenance of an effective relationship between superior and subordinate.

These four dimensions provide us with the general guidelines for conducting a successful performance appraisal interview. They are not simply "maxims," for specific and learnable skills have been identified which can be used to implement and realize them.

THE SIX SKILLS OF MICROTRAINING

For about fifteen years Doctors Allen Ivey, and now Joseph Litterer of the University of Massachusetts, Amherst have sought to clarify and structure the skills of face-to-face communication, most recently in the organizational setting. Their efforts have concentrated upon isolating and identifying the specific verbal and non-verbal skills, from the most basic to the most complex. Once identified, these skills can be learned one-at-a-time to most effectively open that dialogue and establish that relationship which lends to fullest communication, particularly in the appraisal interview.

This approach, termed "Microtraining," has been tested by more than 150 data-base studies conducted in a variety of group and organizational settings. The overarching finding is that microtraining is as, or more effective than any other approach in face-to-face communication.[15] What follows is a step-by-step exposition of the microtraining skills which have relevance in the performance appraisal interview.

Basic Attending Skills

To begin to build an effective relationship with a subordinate, a superior needs to "attend" to his or her subordinate. It is the superior who sets the tone for the appraisal interview. By consciously using those skills with which we are all unconsciously aware, the superior can more successfully involve the subordinate in the encounter. Recent research indicates the value of this. A number of studies indicate that employees are more satisfied with their appraisal interviews, and with their superiors who conduct them when they participate more in the appraisal process, more particularly in the interview itself.[16]

Attending behavior involves a set of interrelated subskills. The superior should verbally and non-verbally "attend" to the subordinate to comfortably encourage his or her participation in the appraisal interview.

The first such skill is non-verbal: *a slight, but comfortable forward lean of the upper body trunk* unconsciously encourages others to talk. We all have come to know the term "Body Language." Leaning forward, or leaning back can encourage or discourage a subordinate's participation. So may eye contact. *Maintaining eye contact* indicates you are paying attention; breaking eye contact, looking away, implicitly, but effectively indicates your disinterest and may inhibit the other individual. *Speak in a warm, but natural voice.* Your voice is part of your body language. Try to speak in as pleasant a tone as you can; don't let your voice trail off at critical points. *Use minimal encouragers.* Head nods, "Yes's," "I see's," and "Uh-huh's." The simple repetition of key words—"Compliance?" "Budget problems?"—also encourages the employee to go on in his or her explanations. Finally, *stay on the topic.* Exhaust a topic to your satisfaction before moving on. Don't topic-jump, or propose solutions before you know the problem as fully as needed. Verbally following a topic, and using the other attending skills will, by themselves, heighten a subordinate's participation in the appraisal interview and, therefore, his or her satisfaction with it.

Feedback

Essentially, the second skill, feedback, helps provide the subordinate with a set of channels for responses on his or her performance. It also helps provide the superior with a set of cues concerning how to approach discussion of the subordinate's performance so as to open up rather than close communication. As such, it serves the search for the more cognitively-oriented dialogue which is such an important part of the appraisal interview.

Feedback first involves *clear and concrete data.* In the appraisal interview, statements should not be vague, but precise.

Vague: "Your work with clients has been very good this year."

Concrete: "This year you've increased placements by 20%, while cutting complaints in half."

A second aspect of feedback is the *employment of a non-judgmental attitude.* Judgmental statements are not only vague, but emotion-laden, and may compel a reciprocal emotional response, even if it is not always voiced. Negative judgments, in particular, incline a subordinate toward defensiveness. When a superior uses a judgmental "attack" he evokes one sort of response from his subordinate. When he uses non-judgmental "analysis" he evokes another, more positive one. Simply, non-judgmental statements are more factual, matter-of-fact, and analytical, while providing insight and clarification for the subordinate.

Judgmental: "You're terrible in meetings with other people. Every time I take you, you foul it up."

Non-judgmental: "You seem too eager to me in meetings. Your behavior could be misinterpreted as pushiness, and be turning people off."

A third component of feedback is the *timely/present-tense statement.* While a performance appraisal deals with behaviors over time, more can be gained than lost by examining more recent problems, or casting comments in a present tense. To dredge up long-past incidents does little good; to choose the present over the past is a much more powerful tool for change.

Distant Past Feedback: "You've screwed up the budget for the past three years, and this time I've had enough of it."

Recent Past Feedback: "In reviewing the annual budgets last week, I found yours to be fouled up the worst. As usual."

Timely/Present-Tense Feedback: "Harry, I've just made some suggestions to you on how you can improve your budget. But you don't sound too enthusiastic about them. How can I help you become more effective in your budget preparation?"

Finally, *feedback deals with correctable items over which the subordinate has some control.* It may be of little good to ask a somewhat shy, but otherwise effective employee, "Why don't you spend more time with the gang, and become part of the group?"

Paraphrasing

A third microtraining skill is the paraphrase. A paraphrase is a concise restatement in your own words of the essence of what your subordinate has just said. Here again, the central emphasis is more upon the cognitive realm of fact than the affective realm of emotion. Effective paraphrasing clarifies for the superior, and indicates to the subordinate that you "understand," are "on the same wavelength," and therefore encourages them to go on. In addition, it is an excellent channel by which to explore issues in-depth, and to establish new linkage between issues.

The content of a paraphrase, again, should be non-judgmental and matter-of-fact. A paraphrase may begin with such items as "If I heard you correctly . . .," "You're saying that . . .," or "It seems that what you're telling me is . . . ." It may end with such stems which allow you to check the accuracy of your paraphrase as: "Is that close?" or "Is that what I hear you saying?"

Subordinate: ". . . So the regional office problem is why our caseloads are down."

Superior: "You're saying that the new Regional Director's staff shakeups have lowered their productivity. And that now it's spilled over to your office? Is that about right?"

Subordinate: "Yeah. And what's more . . ."

Reflection of Feeling

It is trite to point out that emotions play a fundamental role in our lives, that they channel and undergird the rational, cognitive part of ourselves. It is also trite to point out that it is often difficult to express our emotions, but that we "feel better" if we do, and more positively toward that person who appears to "understand." But a skill, an approach which would be cognizant of this reality, and which would encourage the expression of that emotion would not be trite. The reflection of feeling is such a skill.

It is appropriate that the reflection of feeling follow the paraphrase. For where the paraphrase concentrates upon cognitive, task-related information, the reflection of feeling focuses more upon the affective emotions of the subordinate seated in front of you.

This skill is of particular importance in an appraisal interview where pride and fear, trust and suspicion, openness and defensiveness are so much on the block. To bottle up, to deny these emotions is to inhibit and constrain communication, whereas, to recognize and reflect them is not only to free communication, it is to lend a new basis, a new depth to a relationship. For herein, a superior and a subordinate can establish a commonality, a bond which can reinforce the more cognitive areas.

Similar to the paraphrase, the reflection of feeling is a literal, matter-of-fact, and timely statement or question. There is a structure to it. First, one uses the subordinate's first name, or the pronoun, "You." There follows a stem, such as "It sounds like you feel . . ." or "I hear you expressing some . . . ." Next, comes the label for the emotion, concentrating always upon the subordinate seated in front of you. Thirdly, one mentions the context in which the emotion occurs. And finally if you wish, a checking, final stem such as: "Am I right?" or "Is that so?"

> — "Hank, I sense that you're really anxious about this interview. Would you like to talk about it?"
> — "Jane, you seem to be feeling frustrated right now about your performance in this area. Perhaps we could talk about it for a few minutes?"

Emotions are real. The entire performance appraisal process, appropriately enough for most of the cycle, tries to eliminate or minimize them. But to reflect emotions in the appraisal interview can help establish that closer rapport, that stronger relationship between superior and subordinate. This is one of the most powerful, yet difficult to use skills in the appraisal interview. Yet it may be worth the risk, for the identification and reflection of these hitherto covert emotions creates that relationship which is so fundamental, yet so elusive in human interactions.

Open and Closed Questions

Open and closed questions can help the superior stay on the topic, and verbally "follow" the subordinate to ensure fullest and most accurate information. Research indicates that the more the subordinate has the chance to talk in a performance interview, the more satisfied he is with it.[17] Open and closed questions (the open question in particular) offer to subordinates an "invitation to participate." But each type of question bears a different fruit.

Open questions are just that . . . open. They frequently begin with, "Could," "Would," or "Why." They encourage subordinates to talk, to share; for an open question offers an invitation to respond in more than just one, or a few words. When asked non-judgmentally, they encourage feedback, and can deepen understanding in both cognitive and affective realms. Open questions are particularly useful at the beginning of an appraisal interview, or where the superior seeks to understand a particularly ambiguous, or complex area. By their very length of response, they also allow the questioner a chance to think.

Closed questions are also useful. They often help to speed up an interview, to clarify, or to nail down specific points. Often they begin with such words as "Did," "Is," "Are," or "How many." They invite a response of one, or just a few words. Following the use of open questions to explore more complex areas, closed questions can help concentrate the interview upon selected major topics.

Open question: "How is that new budget coming along?"

Closed question: "Is your new budget in?"

Focusing

Special attention in the appraisal interview needs to be given to the focus skill. Briefly, this skill helps us identify five potential areas of organizational problems, and the direction a superior might fruitfully take in dealing with them. In short, the focus skill helps us decide what we should pay attention to, and thereby achieve the best results.

There are five focus areas: person, problem, other, context, and self. A situation where a subordinate comes to complain about the entire performance appraisal and development process provides us with our problem-example.

— A *person focus* concentrates upon the subordinate. The person's first name, or the pronoun, "You," can help a manager's effectiveness.

"John, you sound frustrated about this performance appraisal system."

— A *problem focus* deals with the issue at hand while trying to gain more information about it. A major concern could be the technical aspects to the problem.

"John, could you tell me of your complaint with the appraisal instrument we used this year?"

— Another person, or other people become the highlight in an *other focus.*

"How do your colleagues feel about the system?"

— With a *context focus* we are concerned with how the problem impacts upon the entire organizational system.

"John, do you realize that every civil servant in this state is evaluated using the instrument you object to?"

— In a *self focus,* attention is concentrated upon you, the superior. Here, the superior seeks information from his subordinate about the impact of his actions upon the subordinate.

"John, I'd like to know if I said, or did anything in this performance appraisal process to upset you so much?"

A final note on the acquisition of these microtraining skills. They are learnable one-at-a-time but, like other skills, some are more easily added to a repertoire than others. People should identify those skills with which they are most comfortable, and begin using them. Then add more challenging skills. Practice will soon make them a natural part of a person's repertoire of behavior, and permit them to be used spontaneously and naturally.

SUMMARY

Performance appraisal and development will come into more widespread use in the 1980's as public organizations, for a variety of reasons, are forced back upon their most fundamental resource—the effectiveness of their employees. Past research and publications have focused upon the identification, isolation, and objectification of the elements and relationships which comprise the performance appraisal instruments and interview. Little attention, beyond the commonsensical, often contradictory "maxims" approach, has been paid to aiding the manager and improving the quality of performance appraisal at the critical point of the interview itself. This article has addressed that need. It has identified the four basic dimensions—cognitive, affective, performance, and relationship—whose realization is essential for a successful performance appraisal interview. It has gone further, and provided a set of six skills which are congruent with these dimensions. The specific, structured, and learnable microtraining skills of attending, feedback, paraphrasing, reflection of feeling, open and closed questions, and focusing can make the manager more effective at the neglected and crucial interview point in the process where the appraisal itself is delivered and discussed. The awareness and employment of microtraining skills can lead to more effective communication in the performance appraisal interview.

NOTES

1. Douglas McGregor, "An Uneasy Look at Performance Appraisal," *Harvard Business Review*, vol. 35, no. 3 (May/June, 1957), pp. 89–94.

2. H. P. Smith and P. J. Brouwer, *Performance Appraisal and Human Development* (Reading, Massachusetts: Addison-Wesley, 1977), pp. 35–42, 87–103.

3. W. L. Kandel, "Performance Evaluation and EEO," *Employee Relations Law Journal*, vol. 6, no. 3, 1980 (Winter, 1980/1981), especially pp. 481–483.

4. U.S. Office of Personnel Management, *Federal Personnel Manual System: FPM Manual, Advance Edition Limited* (FPM 540–19, October 21, 1981), p. 1.

5. L. G. Nigro, "Attitudes of Federal Employees Toward Performance Appraisal and Merit Pay: Implications for CSRA Implementation," *Public Administration Review*, vol. 41, no. 1 (January/February, 1981), pp. 84–86.

6. N. P. Lovrich, Jr., P. L. Shaffer, R. H. Hopkins and D. A. Yale, "Do Public Servants Welcome or Fear Merit Evaluation of their Performance?" *Public Administration Review*, vol. 40, no. 3 (May/June, 1980), pp. 214–222.

7. K. J. Lacho, G. K. Stearns and M. F. Villere, "A Study of Employee Performance Appraisal Systems in State Governments," *Midwest Review of Public Administration*, vol. 13, no. 4 (December, 1979), pp. 247–259.

8. D. W. Brinkerhoff and R. M. Kanter, "Appraising the Performance of Performance Appraisal," *Sloan Management Review*, vol. 21 (Spring, 1980), p. 3.

9. R. D. Sylvia, "Some Potential Impacts of the Carter Reforms upon Agencies with MBO Systems," *The Bureaucrat*, vol. 9, no. 2 (Summer, 1980), p. 49.

10. R. J. Burke, "Why Performance Appraisal Systems Fail," *Personnel Administration*, vol. 35, no. 3 (May/June, 1972), p. 33.

11. M. M. Greller, "The Nature of Subordinate Participation in the Appraisal Interview," *Academy of Management Journal*, vol. 21, no. 4 (December, 1978), pp. 649–652.

12. N. Sigband, *Communication for Management* (Glenview, Illinois: Scott Foresman & Company, 1980), pp. 313–317.

13. Smith and Brouwer, *op. cit.*, pp. 9–10.

14. C. B. Truax and K. M. Mitchell, "Research on Certain Therapists' Interpersonal Skills in Relation to Process and Outcome," in A. E. Bergen and S. L. Garfield (eds.), *Handbook on Psychotherapy and Behavior Change: An Empirical Analysis* (New York: John Wiley & Sons, 1971), pp. 299–344.

15. A. Ivey and J. Authier, *Microcounseling* (Springfield, Illinois: Charles E. Thomas, 1978), pp. 334–347; A. Ivey and J. Litterer, *Face to Face* (Amherst, Massachusetts: Amherst Consulting Group, 1979).

16. M. M. Greller, "Subordinate Participation and Reactions to the Appraisal Interview," *Journal of Applied Psychology*, vol. 60, no. 5 (1975), pp. 544–49.

17. A. R. Solem, "Some Supervisory Problems in Appraisal Interviewing," *Personnel Administration*, vol. 23 (1960), pp. 27–35; K. N. Wexley, J. P. Singh and Gary Yukl, "Subordinate Personality as a Moderator

of the Effects of Participation in Three Types of Appraisal Interviews," *Journal of Applied Psychology*, vol. 58, no. 1 (1973), pp. 57–58; M. M. Greller, *op. cit.*, pp. 546–549; and W. F. Nemeroff and K. N. Wexley, "Relationships Between Performance Feedback Interview Characteristics and Interview Outcomes as Perceived by Managers and Subordinates," *Proceedings of the Academy of Management* (1977), p. 34.

How to Give Feedback

by Priscilla Diffie-Couch

Have you ever told your best joke only to have it met with a cool stare, or made your most eloquent apology on the phone only to be greeted with icy silence? In that brief moment, company presidents and kings alike can be reduced to less-than-common peasants. Feedback—particularly the lack of it—can have a powerful effect on human activity and interaction.

Why is feedback so critical to your success as a supervisor? That should become immediately clear as we consider what feedback is, what its distinguishing features are, and what research tells us about the value and impact of feedback.

FEEDBACK DEFINED

Feedback is any verbal or nonverbal element that facilitates or inhibits understanding, controls or influences the flow of messages and satisfaction in interactions, and enables us to adapt or adjust those messages. We cannot avoid giving feedback during an interaction. Refusal to talk is feedback. The icy silence or cool stare in the examples above are both kinds of feedback. They certainly control the flow and quality of those particular communication encounters.

Indeed, if we leave an employee who has asked earlier to see us in a hot, isolated, uncomfortable environment for 20 minutes, we are giving that person feedback before any words are even exchanged. If we choose our dowdiest or loudest blazer the day we are lunching with the chairman of the board, we are again giving feedback.

Priscilla Diffie-Couch is president, Productive Performance Systems, Dallas, TX. Her article "How to Give Feedback," is reprinted, by permission of the American Management Association, from *Supervisory Management* (8) August 1983 © 1983. [5 pp.] Periodicals Division, American Management Association, New York. All rights reserved.

If we ignore an employee who has been learning a new task for six weeks, we are abusing the potential that well-timed feedback can tap. If we nag and criticize an employee who has never received the proper training, we are setting ourselves up for the multitude of harms that can flow from negative feedback. If we make general comments about improving performance in a weekly staff meeting, we sacrifice the value that comes from personal, specific feedback.

FEEDBACK'S EFFECT

Employees want feedback because it helps them learn about themselves, helps them learn how they compare with others, helps them learn how they measure up to established standards, and tells them how they need to change and how they can implement that change. They will carefully watch nonverbal cues to get this information when verbal statements are not provided. And the conclusions they draw may not always be valid.

Effective feedback is immediate, clear, accurate, specific, and positive. Research on the subject has found that:

1. Verbal feedback is desired even when nonverbal feedback is positive and frequent. People like the reassurance that they are reading the nonverbal right. They want to know whether the pat on the back means, "You're doing great," "You're doing better than most beginners," or "Just keep at it—you'll catch up eventually." People want to know whether your smile means, "We're going to meet the deadline after all," or "We may miss the deadline, but it won't be because you're not trying."

2. Verbal feedback must accompany nonverbal to ensure complete clarity. No facial expression—no matter how encouraging—can substitute for verbal feedback. Contrary to the popular myth, silence is seldom golden. And it's more often the words we didn't say that we most strongly regret.

3. Immediate feedback is almost always more useful than delayed feedback. The exception to this rule can be found in the sage advice that one should count to ten before responding when one is angry. The danger here lies in assuming that it's better to wait hours, days, or months to resolve hostility. It festers as we know so well.

Even when strong feelings are not involved, people depend on immediate feedback as indicators of "appropriate action," "preferred methods," "accurate interpretations," and the like. Considering the ever-present communication barriers, the more immediate the feedback, the less likely receiver and sender of the message will misunderstand each other.

The longer you as a supervisor delay, the less important the employee assumes the matter to be. The longer you delay, the more mistakes he or she may make. The longer you delay, the more the employee will assume you are satisfied with what he or she is doing.

4. Negative feedback may be better than no feedback at all, but positive feedback produces the best results. It's better to express discontent over something than never to react at all. However, if your reactions are consistently negative over a long period, the recipient is likely to acquire an immunity and will write them off as "just the way you are."

A Few Feedback Dos and Don'ts

Though few rules in communication are to be followed under all conditions, these general guidelines are useful in most feedback circumstances.

Don't

Don't confuse inference ("The machine must be broken") with fact ("I count seven copies here") in your feedback.

Don't focus on things that can't be changed in your feedback.

Don't rush through vital feedback (for example, a two-minute performance review).

Don't rely exclusively on corrective feedback ("That was not the right way to ...") when growth-oriented feedback ("I'm sure you'll be up to 65 next month") may serve your actual purpose better.

Don't toss out cold data when comparisons can be more productive. Why say "You were three short of our goal," when you could say, "You were at the top in sales this month in this division"?

Don't use feedback as a weapon ("As I said twice already, you've got the poorest track record in the group so I've posted that in red for all to see"). You'll destroy feedback's attractiveness and usefulness.

Don't treat all feedback as directed toward correcting your message (a cough may be nothing more than a cough).

Don't rely exclusively on either verbal or nonverbal feedback. A grimace or puzzled expression may not be enough. Ask questions; paraphrase the speaker; check for understanding.

Don't assume that the absence of questions means that you've gotten your message through. Encourage questions. Invite interaction.

Do

Do exhibit willingness to give and accept feedback—both direct and indirect.

Do create conditions under which people feel free to provide feedback that is mutually supportive, warmly candid, and specifically accurate.

Do keep in mind the nonverbal behaviors that elicit defensiveness and avoid them. Review the patterns of thought, speech, and behavior that contribute to communication barriers and adjust to them.

Not only does negative feedback limit the *amount* of interaction between a supervisor and employee, it limits the quality of that interaction as well. It may alienate the employee and even cause him or her to believe that what needs to be done is more difficult than it actually is.

If your objective is to eliminate mistakes or help the employee enhance his or her performance, a more constructive, results-oriented approach needs to be taken. Assume some responsibility for the employee's efforts (through your verbal/nonverbal feedback). Demonstrate belief in the employee's opinions (through your feedback). Turn your pronouncements ("This is the worst seal job I've ever seen") into a problem-solving question: "How can we improve the quality of these seals?"

5. Undeserved praise does not produce positive results. The first few times people are flattered; they may be pleased. But continued when undeserved, such praise will not result in improved performance. Over time employees may ask themselves, "If I'm doing so great, why improve?"

Unwarranted flattery from you may cause you to lose your credibility with your subordinates. They will believe that you don't know quality performance when you see it, that they can't depend on what you say, and that your enthusiasm is insincere.

This is not to suggest that you shouldn't be diplomatic when giving criticism. You don't have to be brutally frank to get a sincere and accurate message across to an employee.

6. People need to be primed to be more receptive to later feedback. For example, if an employee knows exactly what is expected of him or her—what he or she should be doing, how well, and by when—the employee will listen more willingly to your feedback on his or her performance. On the other hand, if the employee hasn't been properly trained or hasn't participated in development of the standards by which he or she will be measured, that employee will get defensive when you give him or her feedback, no matter how diplomatic you are.

7. Employees tend to remember longest what they hear first and last in a message. Studies support the familiar saying, "You may never get a second chance to make a good first impression." What you choose to say first (verbal feedback) may hit an employee so hard that he or she won't be able to recover well enough to even hear the rest of your message—much less understand and absorb it. Or the scowl on your face as you approach (nonverbal feedback) may linger so long in the employee's mind that it may block out the rest of your message. And the employee may forget your earlier statements because of your final flippant remark about how "bad (the employee) makes the department look these days."

It is easier to get away with verbal and nonverbal blunders during the course of your conversation than it is at the start and end of the conversation.

8. If you want a subordinate to react to your feedback, you must direct it personally—in many cases, privately—to the subordinate. General statements to a group are easy to dismiss as having no personal application. We are often blind to our personal flaws.

If those instances in which we are certain the comments made to a group are really intended for us, we tend to react defensively—often with resentment. No one likes to be made an example of in public.

9. Low amounts of feedback cause low confidence and may result in hostility. Lack of feedback can be too easily interpreted as lack of concern. If the supervisor truly cared, the employee thinks, he or she would have something to say. The supervisor may not be communicating because he or she doesn't know how to respond. But the employee doesn't see it this way. If the supervisor won't communicate with the employee, the employee decides not to talk to the supervisor.

10. Absence of feedback also communicates approval of or agreement with ideas and behaviors. The employee assumes that the supervisor either doesn't care about the employee's message or agrees with it if the supervisor doesn't respond.

If a supervisor allows an employee to perform a job for weeks without providing feedback to the employee, the employee will assume that he or she is doing fine. In one case, a worker overheard a new employee mention a much simpler procedure than the one she'd been doing for five years. She reported her discovery to her supervisor. "Oh, yes, that's the way I always do it myself" was the supervisor's reply. "Why didn't you tell me?" the employee demanded. "Because I thought your way was about as quick and that you preferred it."

11. Until we read one another's minds, feedback is the only source we have for what others think or feel. Most of us have been involved in a situation similar to the one above. How much time have we wasted, [how many] frustrations have we created for ourselves, by waiting for the other person to provide feedback first?

Feedback is more than a reaction to someone else's efforts to communicate. It is a continuous part of the continuous process involved in human interaction.

Both verbal and nonverbal feedback can take on very structured forms. For example, performance feedback can occur in a written performance appraisal or a performance appraisal interview as well as in a conversation about performance at the water fountain or over lunch. Feedback can consist of largely facts, feelings, or behaviors—or some combination of all three. While it is virtually impossible to report facts without adding personal interpretations, we have to remain constantly alert to the resulting impact on feedback. Constant care must be paid to the words we choose and all the nonverbal elements that are within our control. As supervisors, we cannot afford to discount the effect of our feedback on the success of those we supervise.

Five Steps to Making Performance Appraisal Writing Easier

by Shelley Krantz

Do you dread having to write performance appraisals? Do you procrastinate? And, if you push yourself to write them, do you feel anxious that what you wrote was vague, inaccurate, or maybe even illegal?

Ring true? If so, you're not alone. Hundreds of supervisors in organizations throughout the country complain about writing performance appraisals. Most, in fact, suffer from a performance appraisal writer's block. Why is this so?

One answer has to do with the nature of the supervisory job and the nature of writing. Most supervisors are "action people." They are used to either getting the work done through others or doing the work themselves. The supervisory job moves quickly, is highly interactive, and very results-oriented. Writing, on the other hand, is not interactive. It usually does not move quickly, and one cannot always count on results. It's passive, not active; it's isolated, not people-involved. No wonder it's not easy for supervisors.

Any writing is difficult enough for the action-oriented supervisor. But when it comes to writing performance appraisals, the problems are multiplied. When you write a performance appraisal, you have additional, *legitimate* fears, such as:

"What I'm writing will be cast in stone. What if I change my mind? What if I misunderstood an employee—if I overlooked something vital in the appraisal? How can I be *sure* of my evaluation?"

Shelley Krantz is president, Shelley Krantz and Associates, Studio City, CA. Her article, "Five Steps to Making Performance Appraisal Writing Easier," is reprinted, by permission of the publisher, from *Supervisory Management* (12) December 1983 © 1983. [4 pp.] Periodicals Division, American Management Association, New York. All rights reserved.

"**My writing is awful.** I don't use proper grammar—I'm sure my punctuation is terrible! My own boss and perhaps his boss will be reviewing these—what if I misspell words? What will they think?"

What if I say something illegal? I can't keep up with all these affirmative action laws and the do's and don'ts. What if I've unintentionally really messed up?"

"**I can't remember all the back-up stuff.** I really believe I know how to evaluate my people—but I've forgotten so many of the specifics. Will my appraisals be O.K. without them? Will I need to invent fillers?"

While each of these concerns is valid, they can be overcome. What's needed is skill building through practice. Writing, like any other skill, gets better, easier, and faster the more one does it. By using the following tips in writing performance appraisals, you will also find that the process can actually become more satisfying and productive.

THE STEPS

Step 1—start smart. Ask yourself: How much time do I need to write these appraisals? How much time am I willing to spend? What are my time constraints? When do I really need to get started? When is the best time for me to write? Where's the best place for me to write? Is there anyone I can ask to look over my work or give me encouragement? What are the company's expectations and guidelines on what is to be written? Are there any exemplary samples of past appraisals that I can use as guides?

Know the answers to these questions before you begin. Make yourself a writing plan and stick to it.

Step 2—jot notes. Record your thoughts anywhere—on napkins, scratch paper, or a tape recorder if you think of yourself as a talker rather than a writer. Carry a small pad around with you. Relying on your memory just won't do. Make it a habit to *record* those ideas that pop into your head when you least expect them.

Don't analyze or critique, *just write.* Keep a critical-incident file. Critical incidents are those events that make an employee stand out, either positively or negatively. What you need are specific examples of why you feel the way you do—what was or was not done, chronologically, to the minutest detail.

You can draw from your notes and critical-incident file the information you need to make your writing task easier. It's much easier this way than sitting down and staring at a blank piece of paper.

Step 3—organize. Gather together your notes, your company's performance appraisal form, your documentation, your critical-incident file, and your company's performance standards. Consolidate your notes according to what is to be written on the form. If your form has space for paragraph descriptions of employee performance, organize your notes first according to the performance factors being appraised. If further division of the material is necessary, divide it by simply looking for a logical beginning, middle, and end.

Find the method that works best for you. Don't worry that no one else uses your method of organization.

Step 4—write. If you've completed the first three steps, the writing step should really be quite easy. Work from the organization that you created in step three. Don't ponder each word, just spill it out. Promise yourself that no one will see this first draft but you. When you write, be sure that you are as specific as possible in describing the performance.

To give you an idea of what "specificity" really means, here are a few phrases, taken from an actual appraisal, that are *not specific.*

> . . .maintains good cost records. . . shows excellent results. . . demonstrates professional results. . . established an effective schedule.

What are "good cost records"? Are they organized? Neat? Systematic? What are "excellent results"? Are they accurate? Logical? What are "professional results"? How do they differ from excellent results? What is "an effective schedule"? Is it flexible, creative, consistent? See the problem?

It's remediable by using specific words and examples when you write a performance appraisal. To illustrate the point, think of one of your employees. Look at the words listed below and select one word that describes that employee's performance on the job. (Note that the words are both positive and negative.)

> ambiguous, apathetic, capable, clear thinking, careless, disorderly, efficient, helpful, hostile, inventive, organized, precise, thorough.

Now that you've selected one word that describes this employee's performance, build a sentence around the word. For example, for the key word precise:

> Sondra is precise in 90 percent of her secretarial work. She proofreads her work thoroughly and can be counted on to get the work out on schedule on a week-to-week basis.

Notice that the use of exact numbers helped the above example and made it more specific. Many supervisors try to avoid using exact numbers because they fear committing themselves on paper; they want to take a safe middle ground. This does nothing to maximize the potential effect a specific and exact performance appraisal can have. Here are some other examples:

Instead of	*Why not use?*
Caused a significant loss	Caused a 53% loss
Has a good attendance record	Has a 96 percent attendance record
Sold a contract for a substantial amount	Sold a contract for $34 million

The more specific and exact the appraisal document is, the more helpful it will be to employees in formulating performance improvement plans. Being specific also protects you in the eyes of the law.

Step 5—edit. After you've written the performance appraisal, put it away for an hour or two, if you're pressed for time, or better yet for 24 hours. Give yourself a break. When you go back to the performance appraisal, your editing needs will be clearer to you. Just cross out any unnecessary words, cut the jargon, make sure that everything you have written is logical, specific, and easily understandable to anyone else who might read it. The test is to ask yourself: If another manager read this, would he or she be able to describe this employee's performance accurately?

THE PAYOFF

By practicing the five-step process described here, you can take the fear out of appraisal writing, and *you will see a payoff.* In the beginning, it may take you a little longer to write an evaluation than you would like, but *consistent* practice and logical application of these five steps will make the performance appraisal writing task (indeed, all of your business writing tasks) less painful and more satisfying. More importantly, writing specific, logical, well-documented performance appraisals will go a long way toward maximizing the potential impact that appraisals can have on employee job performance.

And Then There Is the Law

Legal and Ethical Issues in Performance Appraisals

by N. B. Winstanley

In 1980 more than 30 million workers in industry and government will have their performances formally appraised for pay, promotion, manpower development, or some combination of these purposes. These evaluations form the backbone of the reward and value systems of organizations using them. Unfortunately, as a measurement device this process contains many potential sources of error.

It is not astonishing, therefore, that those who have examined the research on appraisals have found any number of *non*performance factors that are correlated with or bias employee ratings. Personality and occupational factors are well known. Less well known are such variables as relative salary, hierarchical rank, purpose of the appraisal, mandatory feedback, business function, and length of service. Recent court cases have publicized a few more: age, race, and sex.

These court cases come as no surprise; over the years a number of respected authorities have pointed out that appraisals are troublesome and inaccurate.

For example, in 1957 Douglas McGregor condemned conventional appraisals as a personnel method and asserted that managers could not acquire the skill necessary to use them effectively.[1] In

N.B. Winstanley lives in Rochester, NY. He has been Compensation Research Manager, Xerox Corp.; on the Corporate Industrial Relations Staff, ITT; and on the faculty of the Graduate School of Management, University of Rochester, NY. His article is reprinted by permission of the *Harvard Business Review*. "Legal and Ethical Issues in Performance Appraisals" by N.B. Winstanley (November/December 1980). Copyright © 1980 by the President and Fellows of Harvard College; all rights reserved.

1. Douglas McGregor, "An Uneasy Look at Performance Appraisal," HBR May-June 1957, p. 89 (reprinted as an HBR Classic in September-October 1972, p. 133).

1974 W.W. Ronan and A.P. Schwartz concluded that ratings "do not give a true picture of actual performance" and should not be used.[2]

ETHICAL ISSUE

Under these circumstances, it is reasonable to conclude that the best that managers can hope for is to identify and categorize accurately only extremes of performance, where about 10% to 15% of the employee population is rated. Discriminations in the midrange of ratings (that is, between a three and four on a five-point scale) are largely due to chance and to the biasing factors I have mentioned.

In my experience, at least three-quarters of summary performance ratings fall in this range. In organizations where such ratings are used for administrative decisions on pay, promotion, and termination, the reaction of many subordinates rated "satisfactory" or "average" (that is, given a three) is resentment or dismay. Research bears this out. Here is one instance from my experience:

At a Christmas party, the wife of one of our engineering managers remarked that she and the children were expecting a grim holiday because of her husband Paul's "report card." On his annual performance appraisal he had received a rating of three. The shock carried over into the home.

When Paul offered to resign shortly afterward, his manager was as shocked as Paul. The manager said to me later: "My God, what do I have to do to keep these people happy? I told him he did a decent job, and I put my money where my mouth was. I gave him an 8% increase." (Paul and his family left 11 months later.)

In another company, I am told, an evaluation of average is regarded as "the kiss of death." Clearly, most individuals' occupational self-esteem cannot tolerate a label of average.

If the difference between a three and a four bears little relation to actual performance, is the procedure worth the potential harm to the organization and its competent employees?

It is indeed ironic that performance information designed to be fair and helpful is often inaccurate and punishing. Such practices, when continued unchecked, become an ethical issue for business.

---

2. W.W. Ronan and A.P. Schwartz, "Ratings as Performance Criteria," *International Review of Applied Psychology* (1974), vol. 23, no. 2, p. 71.

LEGAL ISSUE

An equally serious dimension is the potential legal exposure. Although biased and inaccurate appraisals are, of themselves, not illegal, they become so when their application results in adverse and disparate effects on minorities, women, or older employees.

A number of court cases make that clear. For example, in *Mistretta* v. *Sandia Corporation* (1977), appraisals were shown to have been the main basis of layoff decisions affecting a disproportionate number of older employees. Judge Mechem noted that the appraisal system was "extremely subjective and had never been validated." He concluded:

"The evidence presented [by Sandia] is not sufficient to prove or disapprove the contention that at Sandia performance declines with age, but there is sufficient circumstantial evidence to indicate that age bias and age-based policies appear throughout the performance rating process to the detriment of the protected age group."

The judge awarded Mistretta and others involved in the case double damages (salary and increases) plus all costs.

In another case involving layoffs, *Brito et al.* v. *Zia Company* (1973), Spanish-surnamed workers were ordered reinstated with back pay because the company had used an appraisal method of unknown validity in an uncontrolled and unstandardized manner. As a consequence, a disproportionate number of these workers were laid off.

Analyses of such cases have led to the conclusion that use of performance appraisals is inappropriate—and therefore potentially illegal—if, for instance, the method of appraisal is not job related, performance standards are not derived via careful job analysis, the number of performance observations is inadequate, ratings are based on raters' evaluation of subjective or vague factors, raters are biased, or rating conditions are uncontrolled or unstandardized.[3] Another study of court cases suggests that at least half the merit increases and promotions awarded by companies are based on discriminatory performance evaluations.[4]

Although legislation and recent court cases have recognized the need for employee protection, only certain classes of workers have recourse to independent administrative and judicial agencies when they think that their economic and/or career growth has been damaged through misuse of performance appraisals. Those employees

---

3. William H. Holley and Hubert S. Field, "Performance Appraisal and the Law," *Labor Law Journal,* July 1975, p. 423.

4. Thomas A. Basnight and Benjamin W. Wolkinson, "Evaluating Managerial Performance: Is Your Appraisal System Legal?" *Employee Relations Law Journal,* Autumn 1977, p. 240.

who do not belong to unions have no protection except for whatever measures are provided and administered by their companies.

In corporate headquarters, the legal and ethical implications of using appraisals in today's climate have not gone unnoticed. Most companies permit the employee to see and question the performance appraisal. In some, like Levi Strauss and Northrop, any disagreement between supervisor and employee about the evaluation may be appealed to a third party in the organization—usually the personnel department. Not many industrial organizations have formal grievance procedures for salaried employees, and very few use external mediation or arbitration.

In short, the typical aggrieved employee must be his or her own advocate; there is no due process.[5] Under these circumstances, only the brave and the bold dare complain. If that person is a member of a "protected class," the worker may take the complaint to an outside agency; others usually suffer in silence and perhaps ignore future appraisals from their supervisors.

EFFECTING IMPROVEMENTS

In view of this unhappy situation and the legal and ethical issues involved, it seems prudent to consider improvements in the way disagreements are aired and administered.

Since years of research in various appraisal methods have failed to yield much improvement in accuracy—and since corporations are unable or unwilling to partially compensate for that inaccuracy through extensive rater training—the fair and wise recourse is to vent any employee grievance before it produces difficulties. Obviously, such a process requires a great deal of structure and a truly impartial third party.

Theoretically it is possible to have an open-door policy or ask a personnel staff member to serve as an arbiter. Such approaches, however, ignore the realities of social distance and power in any hierarchy. Chances are good that those practices would not work well enough to satisfy the subordinate or even to reduce the heat level.

For salaried workers, a company review panel (of nonmanagement employees), expedited arbitration, or the use of an organization ombudsman can be very effective in raising the level of objectivity, ensuring a measure of justice, and enhancing perceptions of management's fairness. In view of the frequent opposition of management to the first two

---

5. For a discussion of due process in general, see Clyde W. Summers, "Protecting *All* Employees Against Unjust Dismissal," HBR January–February 1980, p. 132.

approaches, the ombudsman idea should be attractive. The added expense can prove to be a very wise investment.

One company employing a full-time ombudsman found that 25% of his time was spent on appraisal-related matters. (Interestingly, a number of managers were plaintiffs, so obviously this position had a high degree of acceptance.)

His case load covered the range of performance appraisals. In one situation, for example, he found that a manager had been lowering the ratings of a subordinate because, the manager said, the person was "too valuable to lose" via promotion. The ombudsman got the two of them talking, and months later the subordinate was promoted on the manager's recommendation.

Another manager had been rating a poor performer too high—an instance of the good-ol'-boy relationship. Everybody, including the manager, loved the subordinate—until a budget squeeze occurred. When that came, the manager decided to transfer or lay off the employee, who complained that his performance ratings did not justify such treatment. Ultimately, with the help of the ombudsman, he was transferred to a lower level that was more suited to his talents.

Predictably, managers in an environment where meaningful due process prevails will demand and get the necessary training in rating and feedback skills. They will probably also take their responsibility more seriously. Under those conditions, any potential for legal action will be sharply diminished. Moreover, the ethical content of the management process will be improved.

Unless such improvements can be made generally, it is reasonable to predict a further increase in the number of court cases, which could lead eventually to more intervention by the legislative and administrative arms of the federal and state governments. Our cultural and legislative history of the past 50 years supports this outlook.

Adding to the impetus will be agitation from the 10 to 15 million now unprotected employees who may want to be covered. As citizens they may insist that, in the matter of subjective performance appraisals affecting their economic and professional well-being, employees be given all their civil rights.

George Odiorne, a leading expert on MBO, the most popular method of appraisal, apparently has a similar view of this developing situation. He recently wrote:

"The genius of the U.S. Constitution will be extended more and more into the workplace, especially as charges and protestations of discrimination for various reasons such as sex, age, race, national origin and religion are stated more and more emphatically."[6]

---

6. George Odiorne, *MBO II: A System of Managerial Leadership for the 80's* (Belmont, Calif.: Pearon Pitman Publishers, 1979), p. 27.

It is not my intent to discuss here how to head off this so-called danger. Others have done well by pointing to the need for manager training and employee participation in all phases of the evaluation process. I would add simply that these improvements, combined with less ambitious use of appraisals and provisions for due process, could make the future of performance measurement and feedback systems much brighter.

Performance Appraisals: Developing a Sound Legal and Managerial System[1]

by Stanley P. Hodge

Largely because their development and application as functional management tools have been profoundly affected by legislative and judicial decisions, performance appraisal systems have recently become a primary focus of attention in human resource management. The current performance appraisal situation is reviewed in light of recent equal employment opportunity requirements and managerial developments. Guidelines and recommendations based on current criteria are provided in order to assess a library's existing performance appraisal system or as an aid in developing one that meets current standards. This paper also provides a tested method for developing an acceptable appraisal instrument for library classified staff.

Performance appraisal (PA) systems are often viewed by library managers as a necessary evil. There may be several reasons for this: the evaluation process may be considered as a chore that takes time away from more productive activities; employees may feel the process has little or no effect on quality of performance;[1] and managers or staff may be dissatisfied with the appraisal instrument itself, either because it is inappropriate for the given situation or incorrectly administered.

An effective performance appraisal system involves more than just a rating form. It includes such factors as an evaluator's judgments, job standards and criteria, organizational policy, legal requirements, and evaluator training. When properly developed and admin-

Stanley P. Hodge is chief bibliographer, Ball State University Libraries, Muncie, IN. His article is reprinted by permission of the American Library Association (Hodge, Stanley P., "Performance Appraisals: Developing a Sound Legal and Managerial System," *College and Research Libraries* 44 (4) (July 1983): 235–44, copyright © 1983 by ALA.

istered, a PA system can overcome many of the familiar criticisms and provide library management with a useful tool that may perform many functions in personnel decision making and improve employee effectiveness as well.

While there is little supporting empirical data to indicate the extent to which organizational functions are served by PA systems, there is consensus on seven general functions for which they are often used.[2] These are:

1. To assist in personnel planning;
2. To provide a basis for employment decisions, i.e. promotion, termination, merit pay, demotion, etc.;
3. To guide job development;
4. To provide performance feedback to employees;
5. To elicit feedback from the employee;
6. To serve as a basis for modifying or changing behavior;
7. To determine the need for training and coaching.

Because PA systems are often used as a primary basis for decision making in the personnel area and serve to link the employee behavior to organizational rewards, it is important that they provide an accurate reflection of job performance. When they do not, an organization not only subjects itself to charges of failing to comply with equal employment opportunity legislation, but also jeopardizes the progress of its employees and the achievement of its organizational goals. Recent surveys have indicated that many organizations' PA systems lag behind applicable federal guidelines.[3]

Any rating instrument that is used as a screening device for employee decisions is viewed by the Equal Employment Opportunity Commission (EEOC) and the courts as an "employee selection procedure" and thus is subject to Title VII of the 1964 Civil Rights Act or precedents set by a number of federal court cases. At the very least, a library should review its performance appraisal system to determine that its effect has not discriminated against those groups protected by Title VII of this act. If adverse impact* is shown by a plaintiff, the employer must show that its PA system is job related. When job relatedness cannot be demonstrated, "the court may render the employer liable for back pay, court costs, specific management training programs for and/or promotion of more female and minority employees as part of the settlement of the case."[4]

The following discussion briefly reviews the established legal requirements pertaining to PA systems and some recommended criteria to use as a basis for developing a system that will serve managerial goals and avoid legal liability. In addition, the findings will be

---

*Adverse impact occurs when a substantially different rate of selection in hiring, promotion, or other employment decision results in a disadvantaged position for members of a protected group.

applied in a methodology to design a performance appraisal form for library classified staff.

LEGISLATION AFFECTING PERFORMANCE APPRAISAL

Title VII is concerned with discrimination in all conditions of employment on the basis of race, color, religion, sex, or national origin.† Employment decisions include the training, rewarding, reassigning, promoting, demoting, retraining, and dismissal of employees. When performance appraisals used for making any of the above decisions result in adverse impact, they clearly fall within the purview of Title VII and subsequent sets of government guidelines on employee selection.[5] The EEOC was created and given the power to bring suit against certain types of employers found to be in violation of Title VII. Those employers include federal, state, and municipal agencies, educational institutions, and any organization with more than fifteen employees who work for more than twenty consecutive weeks.

In 1970, the *Guidelines on Employee Selection Procedures*[6] broadened the scope of EEOC's power to enforce compliance with Title VII. For instance, the definition of *test* was expanded to include all formal, scored, quantified, and standardized techniques assessing job suitability when these are used as a basis for any employment decision.[7] Under these guidelines, personnel decisions that result in adverse impact are subject to challenge by the EEOC when a disproportionate number of the minority or protected group is screened out. EEOC guidelines also require that employment practices, i.e., performance evaluations, be validated if any of the components are found to have an adverse impact on these protected groups.[8]

Because the 1970 guidelines defined tests to include any and all formally scored, quantified, or standardized techniques used for selection and appraisal purposes, many organizations abandoned formal systems in favor of informal, intuitive procedures. The 1978 guidelines[9] then redefined *test* to also include unstandardized, informal, and unscored appraisal procedures and were more specific than the 1970 version with regard to adverse impact, indicating that adverse impact should be calculated according to the "Four Fifths Rule."[10] Other approaches used by the courts in assessing adverse impact include: (1) internal comparisons made between percentages of minorities employed in high- and low-level positions; (2) labor-market comparisons of the percentage of employed minorities with the per-

---

†The Age Discrimination Act of 1967 and its 1978 amendment parallels Title VII and prohibits discrimination against workers between forty and seventy years of age.

centage found in the general population; (3) evidence that an employer intentionally or unintentionally restricted members of a protected group; or (4) evidence that an employer continued to seek applicants for a position when a qualified applicant was rejected.[11, 12]

LANDMARK COURT CASES THAT AFFECT PERFORMANCE APPRAISAL SYSTEMS

Four landmark cases[13,14] relating directly or indirectly to PA systems have had an early significant impact on current standards and requirements. In these cases, it was determined that some type of discrimination resulted from the defendants' biased or unstandardized use of a selection or appraisal system. Four fundamental legal implications based on these court decisions resulted.

1. In *Griggs v. Duke Power Company* (1971), it was ruled that employment criteria that adversely affect a protected group must be shown to be *job related.*

2. In the decision of *Rowe v. General Motors Corporation* (1972), *subjective criteria were suspect* and ruled to be considered as only one component of an overall process.

3. In *Brito v. Zia Company* (1973), performance appraisals were considered *tests, and subject to validation.*

4. In the decision of *Wade v. Mississippi Cooperative Extension Service* (1974), the court ruled that the defendant used an appraisal system based on personal traits that are subject to partiality and to personal taste, whim, or fancy of the evaluator and rejected the performance appraisal validation because it was not based on *formal job analysis.*

In more recent rulings[15,16] the courts considered performance appraisal instruments as if they were "tests," and applied the Uniform Guidelines when evaluating their validity. Personnel specialists within both the public and private sectors have examined these and the numerous other cases involving discrimination charges that resulted from performance appraisal. While there is no guarantee that any rating instrument or PA system design will prove successful in an employer's defense, certain steps may be taken by library administrators to develop a sound legal and managerial PA system that has a favorable chance of being successfully defended.

SUGGESTED CRITERIA TO USE IN DEVELOPING/ASSESSING AND APPLYING A PERFORMANCE APPRAISAL SYSTEM

In order to understand more fully the implications of this review, the findings are presented in a way that the librarian-supervisor may apply them in a practical situation. The following list summarizes the legislative, judicial, and managerial criteria that would constitute a strong foundation upon which a PA system might be built. The list is based on a review of the recent literature on the topic and reports the advisory findings of academicians, lawyers, and personnel specialists regarding how PA systems can meet the aforementioned criteria when they are developed, assessed, or when an established system is applied in practice. By using these criteria, it is possible to develop a PA system that would not only be more acceptable to the library administrator as a management tool but also to the courts as well in discrimination suits involving personnel decisions resulting from the application of a PA system. Likewise, the criteria might be used by plaintiffs as a principal basis for developing their arguments in a suit against an employer.

Criteria for Developing/Assessing a Performance Appraisal System

1. The system is devised using job analysis and the enumeration of critical elements defined in terms of job descriptions and annual performance goals. Job analysis involves describing the tasks, duties, and responsibilities associated with a job.

2. Employees are involved in setting criteria based on "critical job factors."

3. Performance standards or requirements for both critical elements and other important job aspects are set, either separately or within position descriptions.

4. There is an absence or minimum of evaluation of personal traits, e.g., those that may permit substantial subjectivity by the supervisor.

5. Precise, unambiguous language is used throughout the appraisal form.

6. The weight of each measure in relation to the overall assessment is fixed if the appraisal involves various measures of performance.

7. When validation studies are required due to adverse impact, they are preceded by formal job analysis.

8. Training programs for managers and supervisors on conducting effective performance appraisals are completed by all managers/supervisors.

Criteria for Application of the Performance Appraisal System

1. Performance expected of employees is communicated and goals and objectives of the ratee's job are made clear in terms of behavior and the results to be achieved.
2. The ratee is advised of the purpose(s) of the appraisal.
3. At least two levels of supervisors review an appraisal before an evaluation is presented to an employee, particularly when it results in an "unsatisfactory" rating.
4. Persons completing the appraisal base their ratings on a personal knowledge of the ratee's performance and contact with the ratee.
5. Problems that may be hampering job performance are discussed with the ratee.
6. An opportunity is provided for the evaluatee to voice opinions during the appraisal process.
7. Procedures exist for employees who disagree with any aspect of an evaluation to appeal to higher management or a review committee.[17-21]

WHICH FORMAT TO USE?

A review of the literature indicates that there are numerous types of performance appraisal systems used in libraries. Among the most popular are the Graphic Rating Scale, Management by Objectives (MBO), Written Essay, Behavioral Observation Rating Scale (BORS), Ranking, Forced Choice, and Forced Distribution methods. The EEOC has not specified that any rating instrument is safe from litigation, and no single system is necessarily advocated. (It is not the instrument or process that is illegal but rather the consequences of the process.) Each has its advantages and drawbacks, and a library is advised to develop one that meets its own particular needs as a managerial tool.

An example of how the librarian-manager may develop a PA instrument that would meet the above-mentioned criteria is described below. In this case, the objective was to design a performance rating form for library classified staff engaged in technical services work. Some specific objectives of this form to assist library's management were:

1. To aid personnel decisions, i.e., merit pay, promotion;
2. To assess the need for job development and further training;
3. To provide performance feedback to the employee.

The instrument selected as an example for development was the Behavioral Observation Rating Scale (see appendix A). This consists of a number of related behavioral statements that are grouped into categories. Employees are observed and rated on a five-point Likert scale ranging from unsatisfactory to outstanding to describe how well an employee demonstrates those behaviors. The categories or behavioral statements may be weighted and the results quantified for a total average score, although this is not essential. Only five ratings are used for each behavior item because research shows that there is little gained by adding scale values beyond five.[22] Since in this case the appraisal form was developed to assess classified staff performing several different functions, some statements may not always be applicable, and the supervisor is given the option to indicate so by not rating on some items. (For instance, some staff may not perform supervisory functions.)

APPLICATION: DEVELOPMENT OF A BEHAVIORAL OBSERVATION RATING SCALE

Description of Organization for Whom the Appraisal Form Was Developed

The technical services functions at the library for which the appraisal form was developed consist of acquisitions, circulation, interlibrary services, processing, and resource development. Eighteen librarians and eighty-five classified staff are employed in these activities. Of the eighty-five classified staff, twenty are library assistants who have supervisory functions. Classified staffs' salaries range from about $8,000 to $16,000 per year. Their educational level ranges from a high-school diploma through a master's degree. Although a high turnover is characteristic of the lower-level positions in some divisions, several staff have seniority of fifteen to twenty years. Ninety-one percent are women.

Methodology and Results

The technique described below was not difficult to carry out; however, the cooperation of staff who provided and ranked the critical incidents in their jobs was instrumental in obtaining a valid and reliable list of characteristic job-related behaviors. A frequently used job analysis technique for developing a BORS is to develop a list of critical or important incidents of behavior. Supervisors and those whom they supervise are asked to provide observations about the critical requirements of the job. Generally, *effective* incidents are requested before *ineffective* incidents. This is done so the participant does not jump to the conclusion that the information is being sought to demote or terminate an employee.

Survey questionnaires (appendix B provides an example) were developed to elicit responses from the three categories of personnel (librarians, library assistants, and clerks/secretaries) about what they thought were the most important, critical job-related behaviors for their own jobs and for the co-workers within their divisions. Librarians were asked to list important job-related behaviors for library assistants and clerks/secretaries; library assistants for themselves and the clerks/secretaries; and clerks/secretaries for only their own category. All were also asked to list examples of unacceptable job-related behavior.

A representative sample of 25 percent of the personnel was desired for the survey. This would consist of 25 of the 103 total positions. Positions selected to survey were based largely on the distribution of job levels within each division.

Permission to conduct the survey was first obtained from the library's assistant director, the head of personnel, and each division head whose staff were to be surveyed. Division heads were asked to select experienced personnel from their division whom they felt had both a good grasp of responsibilities and the ability to verbalize critical behaviors. The survey questionnaire was tested for clarity of purpose with one division. No problems in comprehending what information was being sought were encountered by those initially surveyed. The procedure in administering the survey was to gather each separate division's staff together, distribute the survey, and briefly describe what they were being asked to do and why. They were told that they were a "select group" whom their division head felt would be able to provide significant insight into what was important in fulfilling their job responsibilities. They were told to indicate important job-related behaviors that they felt *made the difference* between doing a superior or poor job. They were asked to read over the form and to ask any questions.

Twenty-three of the twenty-five survey forms were returned. Over 250 job-related behaviors were supplied by the respondents. Many of these were very specific and duplicative. In addition, the undesirable behaviors were converted to be consistent with desirable ones, i.e., "Employee is consistently late for work" was converted to "Reports to work on schedule."

The reason for following the above procedure was to adhere to what researchers in this field believe satisfies the requirements of the Uniform Guidelines to allow employees to participate in identifying the critical elements of their job. Also, to promote their acceptance by employees, it is wise to proceed participatively when appraisal systems are developed or revised. The rating scale is thus developed from a systematic job analysis supplied *by* employees, *for* employees. This method helps to minimize the possibility that the behaviors described are too vague or are inappropriate to the job. It also results in an appraisal instrument that is *content valid.*

Since library staff usually perform a large and diversified number of tasks, the assessment of each would not be practical. Consequently, the 255 observations were matched and synthesized into thirty-six more-general statements. With the assistance of the library's head of personnel, those thirty-six behavioral observations were further refined, and divided into eight general performance areas. This procedure helped to reduce the appraisal instrument to a manageable size and to structure it into logical performance areas that could facilitate the rating and counseling process. The general performance areas were: supervision, job knowledge, work habits, responsibility, quality and accuracy of work, relations with supervisor, human relations/cooperation, and social behavior. In addition, when the individual responses from the original 255 were divided into thirty-six behavioral observations, they were tallied as to whether they were mentioned by a librarian, library assistant, or clerk/secretary to ensure that a generally proportional distribution among the staffing levels was obtained.

Reliability and Validity

Two additional steps were taken to assure reliability and content validity. First, the list of thirty-six behaviors was distributed to all twenty-three subjects who participated in the survey. They were asked to check what they thought were the two most important behaviors in each category and also to indicate one in each category that they thought was the least important. (Relations with supervisor was an exception since there are only two behaviors in this category.) Reliability means "dependability," "stability," or "consistency." The purpose of this second survey was to test how consistent respondents were in indicating the degree of importance placed on the various behaviors. Would, for instance, those behaviors that were most frequently suggested in the initial survey still be ranked as very important now that respondents would see behaviors they may have initially failed to mention?

The results of the second survey confirmed the reliability of critical behaviors listed by respondents in the first survey. For example, "trains staff patiently and thoroughly and informs them of updated procedures" was initiated by ten respondents on the initial survey. On the second survey, when twenty-three persons sampled were made aware of this behavior, it was listed as being one of the two most important in the supervision category by fourteen respondents, and as the least important by only one. Hence, the reliability or consistency of this behavior is demonstrated for the BORS instrument. Another behavior, however, "determines and assesses job priorities and delegates them to appropriate staff" received a low reliability rating. Table 1 illustrates the behaviors arranged by rank order of reliability within each category for the general performance area of "work habits." When determining the behaviors to be included on the BORS, those with the lowest reliability would be subject to deletion in the final edited version of the appraisal form. (Appendix A lists the twenty-eight considered most important of the original thirty-six.)

TABLE 1
Work Habits Behavior Arranged by Rank Order of Reliability

Item No.	1st Survey No. Times Mentioned	2d Survey Most Important	2d Survey Least Important
14	10	10	1
11	5	8	0
12	8	11	2
16	3	7	3
15	1	2	5
13	4	1	9

Item No.
14. Organizes work schedule and uses time efficiently.
11. Follows through on assignments.
12. Gives prompt attention to priority responsibilities.
16. Able to perform in absence of close supervision.
15. Adequately documents work so steps are not duplicated or omitted.
13. Maintains work area in a well-organized manner.

Second, content validity of the instrument was further tested by selecting a representative group of job descriptions for ten of the survey participants. The characteristic duties and responsibilities and personal qualifications listed on each job description were compared to the behaviors on the instrument and matched when possible. Matches between performance requirements and the behaviors were possible on twenty-seven of the thirty-six items. The omissions could have been the fault of the job descriptions more than the critical behaviors listed by the employees. It should be noted, however, that those items categorized as "social behavior" are not the type of thing traditionally indicated in job descriptions. The results further confirmed the content validity already inherent through the procedure applied in gathering the behavior statements. (These had been described as being critical elements of the job and critical for job performance.)

Additional Factors in a PA System

To assist the library's management in meeting the three objectives of the performance appraisal, a series of questions is developed that require a narrative response (see appendix A). It is also recommended that the ratee be provided with an opportunity to agree or disagree in writing regarding the appraisal statements and to comment if needed.

The training and instruction provided to the supervisors and raters is integral to the appraisal system. Research has indicated these will improve the reliability and accuracy of performance ratings.[23] In addition, the importance of a supervisor's review and counseling session with the library staff member cannot be overstressed. This "discussion provides the opportunity for clarifying any differences in perceptions concerning the employee's performance which cause the person to feel that the rating on a particular statement may not accurately reflect actual performance."[24] It is highly recommended that any newly developed PA system be tested and evaluated, on a small scale, separately or concurrently with one already in use by the employer.

CONCLUSION

A library's performance appraisal system that fails to incorporate current standards may have several negative consequences. It may not only trigger litigation when adverse impact results against protected groups, but it may also impede employee and managerial effectiveness as well. This paper has provided some checklists that library administrators may utilize in evaluating their present PA systems or to develop alternatives that adhere to current standards. A procedure was demonstrated that can yield a job-related performance appraisal instrument adhering to recent recommendations of professionals in the field of human resource management. Although the example is specifically related to classified staff in library technical services, the methodology may be generalized to a wide variety and level of tasks in other organizations.

REFERENCES

1. G. Edward Evans, "Another Look at Performance Appraisal in Libraries," *Journal of Library Administration* 3: 61–69 (Summer 1982).

2. Eileen K. Burton, "Measuring the Effectiveness of a Performance Appraisal System" (Ph.D. dissertation, Univ. of Washington, 1979), p. 9.

3. Hubert S. Field and William H. Holley, "Relationship of Performance Appraisal System Characteristics to Verdicts in Selected Employment Discrimination Cases," *Academy of Management Journal* 25: 392–406 (June 1982).

4. William H. Holley and Hubert S. Field, "Will Your Performance Appraisal System Hold Up in Court?" *Personnel* 59: 59–64 (Jan./Feb. 1982).

5. Lawrence D. Kleiman and Richard L. Durham, "Performance Appraisal, Promotion and the Courts: A Critical Review," *Personnel Psychology* 34: 103–21 (Spring 1981).

6. U.S. Equal Employment Opportunity Commission, "Guidelines on Employee Selection Procedures," *Federal Register* 35, no. 149: 12333–36 (Aug. 1, 1970).

7. Ibid., p. 12334.

8. The EEOC recommends that appraisal instruments be content valid; that is, they reflect important dimensions of job performance. Content validity is concerned with representativeness and relevance of the behaviors described within a rating instrument in terms of the critical elements of the job. Content validity is also concerned with whether the instrument adequately measures the behaviors considered critical for effective job performance. The courts also stress the importance of this issue. See Dena B. Schneier, "The Impact of EEO Legislation on Performance Appraisals," *Personnel* 55: 24–34 (July/Aug. 1978).

9. U.S. Equal Opportunity Commission and others, "Uniform Guidelines on Employee Selection Procedures," *Federal Register* 4, no. 166: 38290–38315 (Aug. 25, 1978).

10. The "Four Fifths Rule" is a rule of thumb and not a legal definition used by the EEOC for determining adverse impact. Hiring and promotion rates for minority groups which are less than four-fifths or 80 percent of the rate for the group with the highest hiring and promotion rate are regarded as evidence of adverse impact. See D.A. Cutchin, *Guide to Public Administration* (Itasca, Ill.: Peacock, 1981), p. 43.

11. Kleiman and Durham, "Performance Appraisal," p. 106.

12. Schneier, "The Impact of EEO Legislation," p. 26.

13. U.S. Office of Personnel Management. *Equal Opportunity Court Cases* (Washington, D.C.: Govt. Print. Off., 1979).

14. *Wade v. Mississippi Cooperative Extension Service* 12 FEP 1031 (1974).

15. *Watkins v. Scott Paper Co.* 12 FEP 1191 (1976).

16. *United States v. City of Chicago* 16 FEP 908 (1978).

17. Burton, "Measuring the Effectiveness," p. 171–73.

18. William L. Kandel, "Performance Evaluation and EEO," *Employee Relations Law Journal* 6: 476–83 (Winter 1980/81).

19. Patricia Linenburger and Timothy J. Kearny, "Performance Appraisal Standards Used by the Courts," *Personnel Administrator* 26: 89–94 (May 1981).

20. Gary L. Lubben and others, "Performance Appraisal: The Legal Implications of Title VII," *Personnel* 57: 11–21 (May/June 1980).

21. Jule Sugarman, "Some Realistic Criteria for Appraisal Systems," *Management* (U.S. Office of Personnel Management) 1: 16–21 (Spring 1980).

22. Gary P. Latham and Kenneth N. Wexley, *Increasing Productivity through Performance Appraisal* (Reading, Mass.: Addison Wesley, 1981).

23. H. Bernardin and C.S. Walter, "Effects of Rater Training and Diary-Keeping of Psychometric Error Ratings," *Journal of Applied Psychology* 62: 64–69 (Feb. 1977).

24. George Rosinger and others, "Development of a Behaviorally Based Performance Appraisal System," *Personnel Psychology* 35: 75-88 (Spring 1982), p. 82.

APPENDIX A: BEHAVIORAL OBSERVATION RATING SCALE DEVELOPED FOR LIBRARY TECHNICAL SERVICES STAFF

CODE: 1 Outstanding   2 Meritorious   3 Satisfactory

4 Needs Improvement   5 Unsatisfactory   N/A Not Applicable

SUPERVISION

1. Trains staff patiently and thoroughly and informs them of updated procedures.
2. Accessible to staff for answering questions and solving problems.
3. Handles problems impartially and provides those supervised with constructive suggestions.
4. Monitors and controls workflow in assigned area and anticipates problems.
5. Monitors quantity and quality of staff performance; evaluates and treats assigned staff fairly.

JOB KNOWLEDGE

6. Understands assigned responsibilities and their relationship to end product.
7. Learns and applies procedures and policies and knows where to find them.
8. Periodically reviews procedures and suggests changes/improvements.
9. Accurately interprets information available in work tools.

WORK HABITS

10. Organizes work schedule and uses time efficiently.
11. Follows through on assignments.
12. Gives prompt attention to priority responsibilities.
13. Able to perform in absence of close supervision.

RESPONSIBILITY

14. Takes initiative in performing job and handling minor problems.
15. Readily accepts suggestions and is receptive to new ideas and methods of accomplishing objectives.
16. Willing to accept added responsibilities when required.

QUALITY AND ACCURACY OF WORK

17. Thoroughly investigates and attempts to solve problems before referring them upward for resolution.
18. Checks own work for accuracy and completeness.

RELATIONS WITH SUPERVISOR

19. Requests assistance when appropriate.
20. Maintains and fosters communication channels with supervisor.

HUMAN RELATIONS/COOPERATION

21. Conveys helpful, cooperative, and friendly attitude when dealing with library patrons and staff.
22. Interacts well with co-workers to perform assigned responsibilities.
23. Conveys a positive attitude toward work and co-workers.
24. Resolves problems with co-workers and patrons in a mature manner.
25. Participates in resolving divisional problems and contributes positive suggestions.

SOCIAL BEHAVIOR

26. Reports for work on schedule and has good attendance record.
27. Avoids excessive socializing or disrupting others with noise.
28. Avoids abusing telephone or office equipment for personal use.

OTHER CONSIDERATIONS

29. What are this employee's major strengths?
30. What specific steps may the employee take to improve performance?
31. What job training or development programs are recommended to help further employee's progress?
32. Other comments by supervisor.

APPENDIX B: INSTRUCTIONS FOR LIBRARY ASSISTANTS

Think about the specific jobs you and your clerks/secretaries perform. What are the most important job-related behaviors required by you and your staff in your division? Some may be general behaviors that are important for all within the division. Others may apply more directly to those just within your unit. A representative sampling of desirable and important behavior relating to jobs within your division is requested. These should consist of simple, brief statements. Examples might be:

1. Checks and monitors quality of work for clerks under supervision.
2. Attempts to resolve problems with library users or staff before turning them over to a supervisor.
3. Checks work for accuracy before submitting it for further processing.

Advice: Try to begin the statements with a verb, i.e. knows, prepares, trains, delegates, completes, etc. This may not always be possible, however.

I. IMPORTANT JOB-RELATED BEHAVIORS FOR LIBRARY ASSISTANTS (list minimum of five):

II. IMPORTANT JOB-RELATED BEHAVIORS FOR CLERKS/SECRETARIES (list minimum of five):

Types of Library Appraisals

Peer Review for Librarians and Its Application in ARL Libraries

by Judy Horn

Abstract. As academic libraries and the responsibilities of librarians have become more sophisticated, they have sought a method of performance evaluation more suitable than previous reliance on evaluation by a single individual. Peer review is one such evaluation method. After a definition of peer review and conditions necessary for its success, the results of a survey on the utilization of peer review in ARL libraries are described. The responses indicate that some type of peer review is practiced in 67% of ARL libraries and that while librarians with faculty status are more likely to have peer review, those with professional status more frequently use it for annual evaluations as well as promotion and tenure decisions. There is no trend away from the use of peer review.

Keywords and Phrases. Association of Research Libraries, Peer Review, Performance Evaluation

INTRODUCTION

Performance evalution of librarians and the determination of appropriate rewards for this performance is an important part of our professional life. As the role of librarians has grown increasingly complex, we have sought to provide evaluation methods which are as equitable as possible. One evaluation method used by many academic libraries is peer review.

Judy Horn is head, government publications department, University Library, University of California, Irvine, CA. Her article, "Peer Review for Librarians and Its Application in ARL Libraries," is reprinted by permission of the American Library Association from *Academic Libraries: Myths and Realities.* Eds. Suzanne C. Dodson and Gary L. Menges. Chicago: ACRL, 1984.

Although the literature abounds with information on the status of librarians, studies focusing on the use of various evaluation methods are sparse. To date, there has been no overall survey of the use of peer review for librarians in academic libraries. After a brief scenario of developments leading to peer review, this paper discusses the utilization of peer review at large academic libraries. The data that are presented were gathered from a questionnaire that I sent to Association of Research Libraries (ARL). The purpose of the questionnaire was not to evaluate peer review as an evaluative method, but to examine its use in large academic libraries. In the course of this investigation, some unexpected myths and realities emerged.

HISTORICAL SCENARIO

Once upon a time, and not so very, very long ago, the director of an academic library was a sage, omniscient person who had a finger on the pulse of every activity within the library. This library director not only had complete knowledge about the intricacies of the heating system and could quote the titles of the new books added to the collection during the previous week, but was aware of the level of performance of each librarian at the institution be they catalogers, bibliographers, or reference librarians. Furthermore, this director was similarly familiar with the professional development activities of each librarian. The librarians understood that this director was obviously qualified to conduct performance reviews and to dispense just rewards. Few objected to such a system.

Today this has the elements of a mythical situation. Libraries, as we all know, are now far more sophisticated than those of yore. The duties and responsibilities of librarians have become increasingly complex and they routinely participate in a wide range of activities undreamed of by their predecessors.

By no stretch of anyone's imagination can today's library director be fully informed about the activities of the staff. In most instances it is also impossible for individual supervisors to evaluate all the various facets of a librarian's performance. A supervisor may have a good knowledge of a librarian's contribution in certain specified areas, however, more often than not the supervisor does not directly observe the work. Think for a moment about the number of activities in which you participate either in the performance of your professional responsibilities or in professional development. How frequently does your supervisor observe your performance or share the unique expertise that you possess?

As the role of librarians changed, they questioned the equity of a reward system determined by a single individual. More information drawn from a variety of sources was needed. Librarians sought other means by which each individual's performance could be competently, knowledgeably, and fairly rewarded and which would improve the quality of performance. An evaluation method which appeared to meet these criteria was peer review.

DEFINITION OF PEER REVIEW

Peer review or peer evaluation is defined as "the process of having members of a group judge the extent to which each of their fellow group members has exhibited specified traits, behaviors, or achievements."[1] Peer review as an assessment method dates from the 1920's but little research was done on it until after World War II.[2] Researchers agree that peer evaluation is most effective when it is only one segment of an evaluation system that is composed of several compatible and mutually supporting parts;[3] in other words, when there is input not just from peers, but also from a variety of other sources and levels. Various studies have validated the reliability of this method in general and have found that review by peers contributes to a more accurate perception of an individual's performance.[4]

Research indicates that peer evaluation is more effective in some organizational settings than in others. Its most successful use has been in situations in which certain conditions exist. These conditions are:

1. The existence of peer groups whose members are afforded unique views of salient aspects of each other's behavior;
2. The existence of peer groups whose members are capable of accurately perceiving and interpreting the salient aspects of each other's behavior;
3. A perceived need to improve the effectiveness with which some characteristic or characteristics of peer group members are being assessed.[5]

Peer review is used in a number of different situations by varying groups, each of which to some degree meets the above conditions. The military, the nursing profession, industries, certified public accountants, government agencies, faculty and librarians have successfully used some form of peer evaluation. Peer assessment used by these groups varies in purpose, method, and procedure. For example, it is used in the military to determine potential officers, by CPA firms to assure quality control, and by government agencies, such as the National Science Foundation and the National Institutes of Health, in awarding research grants.[6] Faculty and librarians both use peer review in the evaluation of past performance and in the determination of rewards for such performance. However, the methods and procedures used by these two groups are quite diverse.

The faculty review system has provided the model for academic librarians. The push for an equitable review process which includes participation by colleagues played an important role in the effort to gain faculty status. In reality, although the faculty environment meets the first two conditions for peer review, that is, group members who have the opportunity to observe the behavior of others and group members who are capable of accurately perceiving and interpreting the behavior of others, research indicates that systematic peer evaluation may not be as widely used by the faculty as is commonly believed. The literature on faculty evaluation contains numerous references to the lack of uniformity to be found in the review process and the proliferation of methodologies.[7]

The conditions for peer review likewise exist for librarians, possibly to even a greater extent than for faculty because of the daily opportunities for observing the performance of colleagues. The ACRL "Standards for Faculty Status for College and University Librarians" (1972) stipulate that a necessary element of the review process for librarians is "appraisal by a committee of peers who have access to all available evidence."[8] Several studies have been conducted on the status of librarians in academic libraries and on the criteria by which librarians are evaluated. These reports generally focus on a state, a particular area, or an individual institution.[9] Some of these articles have included a brief mention of peer review.

PEER REVIEW AT ARL LIBRARIES

To gather some information about how widely the ACRL Standards have been adopted in large academic libraries and to determine what relationships exist, if any, between peer review and the personnel status of librarians, I sent a brief questionnaire to U.S. academic libraries that are members of the Association of Research Libraries (Appendix A). ARL libraries were selected because they constitute an identifiable group of manageable size with similar attributes. For purposes of this survey, all seven University of California campuses which are members of ARL were considered one institution as were the three SUNY member libraries. This was done since the variables involved are consistent throughout each of the two systems. This reduced the number of ARL institutions included in the survey from 90 to 82.

The brief one page questionnaire included a question about the status of librarians at the institution. Two categories were designated: faculty status and professional status. I adopted the definitions used by Thomas English in his article "Librarian Status in the Eighty-nine U.S. Academic Institutions of the Association of Research Libraries: 1982" for this questionnaire.[10] The term "professional" denotes the various categories of librarian status not designated as "faculty," such as "academic," "administrative," and "classified."

One of the major questions was "Do librarians have peer review in performance evaluations?" The term "performance evaluation" was meant to include any evaluation of librarians, including salary increases, promotion, tenure, or contract renewal. This question created some confusion for those institutions which consider annual performance evaluations and promotion/tenure reviews as two different processes. A small test group failed to detect this potential area of confusion and the term was not defined in the cover letter. A misinterpretation of this question was usually revealed in the answers to other questions and adjustments were made in the responses, as necessary. For example, if the response to question three asking if there was peer review for performance evaluations was "no" and the institution answered under question five that it used peer review for promotion and tenure only, this institution was counted as having peer review.

Respondents were asked to indicate how peer review is conducted and if it is used for annual evaluations including merit and salary increases or if it is used only for promotion, tenure, or retention decisions. The year in which faculty status was achieved and the year peer review was first utilized were also requested. Libraries were asked about the type of review process that exists if peer review is not utilized. Data derived from this question are not included in this discussion. A final question designed to detect if there might be a possible trend away from peer review asked, "If librarians do not now have peer review, did they have it at any time in the past?"

Of the 82 institutions, 67 returned the questionnaire for an 82% response. The response indicated that even among ARL libraries there exists a wide variation in evaluation practices and terminology.

In the 67 responding institutions, 32 have faculty status and 35 have professional status. Forty-two of the responding libraries were state institutions and 25 were private institutions. This is close to the ratio of questionnaires that were sent: 50 state institutions and 32 private institutions (Table 1).

TABLE 1. Responses to Questionnaire

	Number	Percent
ARL Institutions surveyed	82	
Responses returned	67	
Return rate		82%
State Institutions	42	63%
Private Institutions	25	39%

The results of this survey replicate English's finding that librarians at state ARL institutions are more likely to have faculty status than are their colleagues at private ARL institutions. The findings in the English study, which included all U.S. ARL libraries, revealed that 61.4% (35) of the state institutions and 18.7% (6) of the private institutions have faculty status. The statistics in this survey show that 64% (27) of the state institutions and 20% (5) of the private institutions have faculty status. To state these figures in another way, 84% of the librarians with faculty status at ARL libraries are at state institutions (Table 2).

TABLE 2. Status of Librarians in ARL Libraries

Institutions	Faculty	Professional
State	27 (64%)	15 (36%)
Private	5 (20%)	20 (80%)
Total	32 (48%)	35 (53%)

Peer review of some type is practiced in 45 (67%) of the libraries. Three-fourths of these libraries are state institutions. Librarians at 28 of the libraries have faculty status and 17 have professional status. This figure for peer review at ARL libraries (67%) is higher than that reported in the literature for academic libraries in specific regions. A study of academic librarians in Ohio (1980) reported that 23% of the librarians in that state have peer review,[11] while a similar study on the status of academic librarians in Texas (1978) revealed that only 21% are evaluated by their peers.[12] Yet another study of academic librarians in New York (1983) found that 46% of the librarians undergo peer review for promotion.[13] The first two studies include peer review for annual performance evaluations while the third specified promotion only. These three studies indicate an increasing use of peer review with time.

The majority of the 45 institutions practicing peer review use it only for promotion and tenure decisions. Only 8 out of 20 libraries with faculty status utilize "full" review which includes merit or salary evaluations as well as promotion and tenure. Librarians with professional status are more likely than those with faculty status to be reviewed by a committee of peers for annual performance evaluations as well as for promotion and tenure. Of the 17 institutions in which librarians have professional status and peer review, 10 have peer review for annual evaluations and merit increases and 7 use it only for promotion and tenure decisions (Table 3). By a narrow margin, more librarians with professional status than with faculty status are in compliance with the ACRL standards that the performance of each librarian should be "regularly" reviewed by a committee of peers.

One conclusion that might be drawn from these statistics is that librarians with faculty status are reviewed according to the review system used by the faculty at that institution and that a large number of faculty are reviewed by their peers only for promotion or tenure. Four libraries in which librarians have faculty status did not indicate that any type of peer review is utilized.

TABLE 3. Peer Review in ARL Libraries

Libraries with peer review	45	(67%)
Libraries without peer review	22	(33%)
Libraries with Peer Review (45)		
State Institutions	35	(78%)
Private Institutions	10	(22%)
Faculty Status	28	(62%)
Promotion/tenure only	20	(71%)
P/T and annual reviews	8	(29%)
Professional status	17	(38%)
Promotion/tenure only	7	(41%)
P/T and annual reviews	10	(58%)

The use of peer review by ARL libraries appears to have been strongly influenced by the adoption of the ACRL standards. The earliest definite date supplied for the beginning of the peer review process was 1959 and the latest 1982. By far the majority of insitutions began the peer review process between 1971 and 1979 (Table 4).

TABLE 4. Date Peer Review was First Used

		(36 Responses)
Before 1960	1	
Between 1961–1965	2	
1966–1970	8	
1971–1979	22	
1980–1982	3	

This is also the time span in which the majority of institutions were granting faculty status to librarians. Of the 25 institutions responding with a definite date to the question regarding the year faculty status was achieved, 15 indicated the years between

1966–1977. However, 8 institutions received faculty status before
1960 (Table 5).

TABLE 5. Date Faculty Status was Granted

		(25 Responses)
Before	1950	5
Between	1951–1960	3
	1961–1965	1
	1966–1970	9
	1971–1979	6
	1980–1982	1

The time span between the beginning of faculty status and the
adoption of peer review in the evaluation process also varies. On
some campuses, peer review began the same year that faculty status
was granted but a period of time ranging from 3–20 years is more
common. Three institutions indicated that librarians had peer review
before attaining faculty status. Two were state institutions and the
third was a private institution.

The procedures used to conduct peer review in libraries are very
diverse. The one common denominator is that peer review is only a
part of a larger evaluative process that also includes evaluation by
supervisors, department heads, deans, vice chancellors, and provosts.
As stated earlier, this is viewed as the most effective type of peer
review. The data gathered from this part of the questionnaire are
imprecise because of the number of variables and non responses.
Only a general summary of some of the major components of peer
review as indicated in the responses to the questionnaire will be
presented here.

The most prevalent type of peer review is done by a committee
composed of librarians, reviewing evaluative information submitted
by the review initiator. This information may also contain data
submitted by peers. Twenty-six out of the 36 responses to this question indicated that this method is utilized. The second most frequently mentioned peer group was a university committee. Occasionally, the evaluation is reviewed by both a library and a university
committee. Four libraries indicated that peer review is carried out for
each librarian being reviewed by others with equal or higher rank. At
two of these institutions, librarians have faculty status and at the
other two, professional status.

There does not appear to be an appreciable trend away from peer
review. Only three responses indicated that peer review was used in
the past and is not currently being used. Librarians at one of these

institutions have faculty status, and at the other two professional status. One of these three libraries is continuing peer review (peer input) but with a less complex procedure. In the other two libraries, one used peer review from 1971–76 and the other indicated that peer review was dropped in 1979. Dissatisfaction by librarians and a general consensus that the process was more time consuming than it was worth were cited as reasons for ending peer review. In contrast, 5 libraries have begun using peer review since 1979. These were all libraries in which librarians have professional status.

CONCLUSION

The librarian environment is one which meets the conditions for peer evaluation. However, at ARL libraries only about 67% of the librarians have peer review. It is more prevalent among those institutions which have granted librarians faculty status and at state institutions. The figure for peer evaluation at ARL institutions is higher than any yet noted in the literature.

If we assume that the four institutions with faculty status which reported that they did not have peer review answered the question correctly, then the commonly held view that librarians with faculty status always have peer review is a myth. This challenges a basic belief. Further investigation is necessary before such statements can confidently be made. The literature on faculty use of peer review, although lacking precise statistics, is such that faculty status without peer review appears to be a distinct possibility.

Since the ACRL "Standards for Faculty Status for College and University Librarians" was "drafted by a committee of the Association of American Colleges, the American Association of University Professors, and ACRL,"[14] it appears that these groups endorsed "full" peer review for librarians with faculty status. This being the case, it was expected that a larger number of librarians with faculty status would have regular performance reviews by a committee of peers. However, the reality is that librarians with professional status are more likely than those with faculty status to have peer review for annual evaluations as well as for promotion and tenure decisions.

Although two libraries have discontinued peer review, there does not appear to be a move away from such practices. On the contrary, although a shift away from granting faculty status to librarians appears to be occurring,[15] institutions with professional status are continuing to adopt this method of review.

Overall the literature on the status of librarians and the findings of this survey indicate that libraries are striving for the most effective means of dispensing rewards. The variation in review methods, even amongst those utilizing peer review, is very interesting and unexpected. The majority of ARL institutions have found that review of a librarian's activities by colleagues offers the best chance for achieving accuracy and equity in today's libraries. Whatever the weaknesses inherent in peer evaluation, and they are a legitimate source of concern, review by colleagues has become the norm. If there ever was the wise and benevolent administrator who alone dispensed rewards and encouraged improved performance, that person will never reappear.

ACKNOWLEDGEMENTS

Part of the research for this project was supported by a grant from the Librarians Association of the University of California.

REFERENCES

1. Jeffrey S. Kane and Edward E. Lawler III, "Methods of Peer Assessment," *Psychological Bulletin* 85: 555 (May 1978).

2. Ibid., p. 556.

3. Kane and Lawler, "Methods of Peer Assessment," p. 584; Richard Klimoski and Manual Landon, "Role of the Rater in Performance Appraisal," *Journal of Applied Psychology* 59: 445–46 (August 1974).

4. Andrew S. Imada, "Social Interaction, Observation, and Stereotypes as Determinants of Differentiation in Peer Ratings," *Organizational Behavior and Human Performance* 29: 397–98; 412–13 (June 1982). See also Klimoski and Landon, "Role of the Rater in Performance Appraisal," p. 446.

5. Kane and Lawler, "Methods of Peer Assessment," p. 556.

6. R.G. Downey and others, "System for Predicting Subsequent Promotion of Senior Military Officers," *Journal of Applied Psychology* 61: 206–09 (April 1976); E.P. Hollander, "Buddy Ratings: Military Research and Industrial Implications," *Personnel Psychology* 7: 385–93 (Autumn 1954); Stephen Cole and others, *Peer Review in the National Science Foundation: Phase One of a Study* (Washington, D.C.: National Academy of Sciences, 1978); Margaret A. Loscalzo, "What is Peer Review All About?" *Journal of Accountancy* 148: 78–82 (October 1979).

7. Pamela J. Eckard, "Faculty Evaluation: the Basis for Rewards in Higher Education," *Peabody Journal of Education* 57: 94–100 (July 1980); Kala M. Stroup, "Faculty Evaluation," *New Directions for Higher Education* 41: 47–62 (March 1983); Peter Seldin, *How Colleges Evaluate Professors* (Croton-on-Hudson, N.Y.: Blythe-Pennington, 1975).

8. Association of College and Research Libraries, "Standards for Faculty Status for College and University Librarians," *College and Research Libraries News* 33: 210–11 (September 1972).

9. Greg Byerly, "The Faculty Status of Academic Librarians in Ohio," *College and Research Libraries* 41: 422–29 (Sept. 1980); Marjorie A. Benedict and others, "Status of Academic Librarians in New York State," *College and

Research Libraries 44: 12–19 (Jan. 1983); JoAnne Hawkins and others, *The Status of Status: The Status of Librarians in Texas Academic Libraries* (Austin: University of Texas at Austin Libraries, 1978), Ed 178 024; Russ Davidson and others, "Faculty Status for Librarians in the Rocky Mountain Region: A Review and Analysis," *College and Research Libraries* 42: 203–13 (May 1981); Robert G. Sewell, "Faculty Status for Librarians: The Rationale and the Case of Illinois," *College and Research Libraries* 44: 212–22 (May 1983).

10. Thomas G. English, "Librarian Status in the Eighty-nine U.S. Academic Institutions of the Association of Research Libraries: 1982," *College and Research Libraries* 44: 199–211 (May 1983).

11. Byerly, "The Faculty Status of Academic Librarians in Ohio," p. 427.

12. Hawkins, *The Status of Status,* p. 9, 31.

13. Benedict, "Status of Academic Librarians in New York State," p. 116.

14. Association of College and Research Libraries, "Membership Endorses Joint Statement on Faculty Status," *College and Research Libraries News* 33: 209 (Sept. 1972).

15. English, "Librarian Status in Eighty-nine U.S. Academic Institutions," p. 207.

APPENDIX A

Questionnaire on Peer Review

1. What is the personnel status of the majority of librarians at your institution?
   ___ Faculty status
   ___ Professional/academic status (also includes such terms as classified, staff, administrative)
2. If librarians have faculty status, what year was this status achieved? _____
3. Do librarians have peer review in performance evaluations?
   ___ YES ___ NO
4. Is peer review carried out by:
   ___ Promotion and review committees within the library composed of librarians
   ___ All librarians of equal or higher rank serve as peer group
   ___ University faculty committee
   ___ Written documentation submitted by colleagues in the library, university faculty, and in the profession without committee review
   ___ Other (please specify) _____
5. Is peer review conducted for:
   ___ Promotion or tenure (indefinite appointment) only
   ___ Merit increase, promotion and tenure
6. What year was peer review first utilized?

7. If librarians do not have peer review, what type of a review process exists?

___ Automatic salary step increases

___ Evaluative letter from supervisor/department head with approval by the Library Director

___ Form prepared by supervisor/department head with approval by Library Director

___ Other (please specify) _____

8. If librarians do not now have peer review, did they have it any time in the past?

___ YES   ___ NO

If yes, when? What was the reason for the change?

Evaluating the Performance of the School Media Specialist

by Margaret Ehrhardt

Evaluating the performance of the school media specialist (librarian) is never an easy task for the principal or for the district media coordinator. Many administrators have felt that if their choice of a media specialist was a good one and the person was well qualified then evaluating the performance of this person on a regular basis would be unnecessary. It has been only within the last ten years that the literature has mentioned any evaluation of librarian performance in general, and, specifically for school librarians or media specialists, within the last five years. In 1974, the Kansas State Legislature passed a bill requiring that each district have a personnel policy for evaluating all certified personnel, and this, of course, included librarians.

One of the difficulties in evaluating the school media specialist would be "What evaluation instrument could be used?" The traditional teacher evaluation forms are not applicable. Some of the questions are not relevant to the duties of this person and many media specialists feel that they exhibit different skills from teachers and should be evaluated by other instruments. Questions should be asked which would cover their duties more specifically.

In 1973, Robert N. Case directed the School Library Manpower Project for the American Library Association. The purpose of this project was to identify the job functions for school library media personnel. One of the publications growing out of this project[1] attempted to group tasks performed into seven categories: human behavior, learning and learning environment, planning and evaluation,

Margaret Ehrhardt is library consultant, South Carolina Department of Education, Columbia, SC. Her article, "Evaluating the Performance of the School Media Specialist," is reprinted from *The South Carolina Librarian* 23 (Spring 1979): 3–5. Used by permission of *The South Carolina Librarian*, official journal of the South Carolina Library Association.

media, management, research and professionalism. Teacher evaluation forms do not include the majority of these tasks.

Some of the evaluation methods which have been used for evaluating the performance of school media specialists have been on-site evaluations by administrators or supervisors, observations by fellow staff members, work sampling, rating, scales, management-by-objectives or mutual goal setting techniques, and by self-evaluation. Each of these methods has disadvantages which may make the findings unreliable.

The on-site evaluation by an administrator or supervisor may be made at an inopportune moment at the time before an exciting activity was to take place or just after a particularly productive session with a class. To a large extent the services which the school media specialist renders are controlled, not by this person, but by the clientele. Then much depends on who makes the evaluation. On-site evaluations call for a judgement on the part of the evaluator. He should be one who is well versed in all phases of the media program.

Observations by fellow staff members are somewhat more reliable since more than one person makes the evaluation, which is done on a day-to-day basis. Some type of opinion survey may be needed. However, it may be difficult for some to evaluate objectively because of personal bias, or one staff member may influence the thinking of others on the evaluation team.

There are inherent dangers in using rating scales. Some rating scales do not ask job related questions. They may include such general terms as "quality of work" or "knowledge of resources" which would be difficult to evaluate fairly. Then, too, the person performing the evaluation may have difficulty in being objective, or he may have a tendency to give average scores rather than scores at either end of the scale. He may also misunderstand the characteristics being rated and score the person incorrectly. The chief value of the rating scale seems to lie in the fact that it is administered on a regular basis.

The management-by-objective[s] approach rates the person's performance by comparing achievement with a pre-established set of goals. In this instance it is important that the goals be set by the individual being evaluated or in consultation with him. This method does have the advantage of offering an opportunity for dialogue between the media specialist and the administrator, and results in a better understanding of the media program.

Self evaluation, if done honestly, can offer the media specialist an opportunity for professional advancement or for correcting problem behavior, behavior of which he may not be aware. Some persons, however, using this method may be reluctant to recognize weaknesses or have a glorified opinion of their performance.[2]

In an effort to determine whether media specialists are being evaluated and what evaluation methods, if any, are being used in South Carolina schools we conducted a survey of fifteen school districts in the State. Twelve media coordinators and three directors of instruction who have the responsibility of coordinating the media program for the district were contacted by telephone. The assumption was made that districts having media coordinators or other district level personnel coordinating the media program would be more likely to evaluate the performance of the media specialist than would the other 77 districts.

All persons contacted indicated that some evaluation of media personnel was being done in their district, if only on-site evaluations. Fourteen districts indicated that written forms of some type were being used for this purpose. Some districts used a combination of several methods.

Ten districts indicated that the principals evaluated the media personnel in their schools, using identical forms for media specialists and teachers. The media specialists in one district have adapted their teacher evaluation form to apply more directly to media personnel.

In four districts the media coordinators have devised new evaluation forms using the job descriptions included in the State Department of Education publication *Media Programs: an Evaluation Guide.*[3]

One district uses a self-evaluation form, but there are not personal interviews to discuss the self-evaluation with the media personnel. Two districts, however, are using the personal interview methods.

Two districts are moving toward the management-by-objectives concept and are beginning to evaluate the performance of the media personnel with regard to mutually established goals. This concept is growing in popularity.

In 1976 the state of Texas adopted a competency based certification program for media specialists. According to their publication *Competencies for Learning Resources Specialists,* "Both in education and in jobs there has been an increasing demand for reliable indications of an individual's competency."[4]

None of the persons contacted in the survey indicated that any type of formal peer evaluation was being used.

All persons contacted indicated that they would welcome an effective instrument for measuring the performance of the media specialists; one coordinator even volunteered to serve on a committee to formulate such an instrument.

Personnel evaluations can make a useful contribution to the improvement of media programs. In an article in *Library Trends,* July 1971, Ernest R. DeProspo suggests that the goals method of evaluating personnel would provide impetus to staff development and growth.[5]

One district in Connecticut (Groton) is using performance evaluations as a method for making human resources more productive. Also the job targets selected by media specialists and teachers are used as a basis for in-service education. The basic components of performance evaluations: job descriptions, job targets, implementing objectives, monitoring techniques, assessment of data and conference follow-up are all directed toward improving instruction. This plan requires close cooperation between the principal, the media coordinator, and the building-level media specialist. The evaluation of personnel is secondary in importance to the improvement of the media program.

Media coordinators would find the *Behavioral Requirements Analysis Checklist*[6] already mentioned useful in identifying 75 functions of the school media center and the competencies necessary for effective performance. This publication would be useful for districts attempting any evaluation of media personnel.

We may conclude, then, that good evaluation methods are needed. Whether districts develop their own evaluations or use some standard forms would be of little consequence if the results served the district purpose—that of improving media programs in the district.

REFERENCES

1. *Behavioral requirements analysis checklist; a compilation of competency-based job functions and task statements for school library media personnel,* ed. by Robert N. Case. American Library Association. 1973.

2. Chisholm, Margaret E., and Ely, Donald P. *Media personnel in education; a competency approach.* 1976.

3. Ehrhardt, Margaret, and Griffin, Mary F. *Media programs: an evaluation guide.* South Carolina Department of Education. 1978.

4. Texas Education Agency. Instructional Resources Division. *Competencies for learning resources specialists.* The agency. 1979. p. III.

5. DeProspo, Ernest R. "Personnel evaluation as an impetus to growth." *Library Trends* (July 1971).

6. Op. cit.

A Practical Model for a Developmental Appraisal Program for School Library Media Specialists

by Fred C. Pfister and Nelson Towle

INTRODUCTION

We believe that there is a serious lack of communication between library media specialists and principals in many schools about the job the media specialist could and should be doing. This problem occurs even though a formal performance appraisal is conducted once or twice a year in virtually every school. Media specialists and principals are generally dissatisfied with the performance appraisals used, and properly so. Most school systems use the wrong kind of appraisal process to start with and compound the error by using an inappropriate appraisal instrument. This article will discuss problems with current practice, describe the field study that developed an improved performance-appraisal model, present conclusions, and give recommendations for applications of the model.

Fred C. Pfister is professor, Department of Library, Media, and Information Studies, University of South Florida, Tampa, FL. Nelson Towle is Director of Media Services, Sarasota School System, Sarasota, FL. Their article, "A Practical Model for a Developmental Appraisal Program for School Library Media Specialists," is reprinted from *School Library Media Quarterly* 11 (Winter 1983): 111–121. Used with permission of *School Library Media Quarterly*.

PROBLEMS WITH CURRENT PRACTICE

The Appraisal Process

Management literature tells us that the purpose of a performance appraisal can be either developmental or judgmental in nature— intended to evaluate for purposes of merit pay, promotion, transfer, or retention.[1] Our field study and other discussions indicate that what generally happens is that a form with a list of traits, behaviors, and results is developed by one or more district-level officials. This is provided to principals for the annual performance review of the media specialist and other instructional staff. It is viewed by many as a mandatory exercise to be completed as quickly as possible and laid aside until next year. Most school media specialists and their principals consider this process a useless waste of time because *none* of the purposes of the judgmental evaluation apply to them, and the principal and the library media specialist both know it. There is no merit pay, they have no real promotion opportunities, nor does it affect transfers. The one exception, of course, is where the library media specialist is not yet on tenure or continuing contract and is concerned with retention. On the other hand, the process in a developmental performance-appraisal system provides help for individual improvement in performance as well as other secondary benefits. It involves cooperative identification of job dimensions and priorities by the appraiser and the worker being appraised. In the case of the school media specialist, it would require that goals, objectives, and ways to meet those objectives be spelled out and agreed upon by the principal and the library media specialist. This process, which is so important for reducing role ambiguity and improving motivation and performance[2] is widely recommended in management literature.[3] This method of goal setting, known as management by objective (MBO), is described by McConkie as:

> A managerial process whereby organizational purposes are diagnosed and met by joining superiors and subordinates in pursuit of mutually agreed upon goals and objectives which are specific, measurable, time bounded, and joined to an action plan; progress and goal attainment are measured and monitored in appraisal sessions which center on mutually determined objective standards of performance.[4]

Research on management by objectives has indicated that this approach can improve performance and satisfaction in a number of ways.[5] When employees are involved in setting goals, their understanding of what is required on the job increases.[6] This involvement in the goal-setting process can also lead to the setting of higher goals than is the case where the supervisor sets them unilaterally.[7] In addition, when supervisors and employees together analyze problems and decide on acceptable courses of action, team building is fostered.[8] Other authors have determined that the mutual discussion of problems that may be hampering a subordinate's job performance and working toward solutions have an immediate and positive effect on productivity.[9] In addition, Burke, Weitzel, and Weir found a positive correlation between improved performance and the amount of thought and preparation spent by employees analyzing their job responsibilities, the problems encountered on their job, and the quality of their work. The employees who took this time were those who perceived that organizational rewards were contingent on the results of their performance.[10]

As early as 1972, the National Association of Secondary School Principals endorsed management by objectives for evaluating principals and other school personnel and pointed out that MBO is generally useful: "This approach, if handled intelligently and positively, has a way of becoming an all-pervasive force in an organization. Administrators at different levels of responsibility who begin to operate in an appraisal system characterized by management by objectives develop patterns of mutuality, which in turn establish better communication, smoother lines of organization, and common agreement. Participation or involvement is an essential ingredient in this method."[11]

Developmental appraisal for librarians has also been advocated for many years. An excellent early essay on the topic is DeProspo's 1971 *Library Trends* article entitled "Personnel Evaluation as an Impetus to Growth."[12] And the advocacy of developmental appraisal continues. Hilton, in the November 1978 *Special Libraries,* concluded, after reviewing the performance-appraisal literature: "There is growing agreement that performance appraisal . . . should concentrate on job objectives. These should be agreed on by supervisor and employee, being continually reviewed and reset as necessary."[13] The implications of these general statements for school media specialists are brought into focus by M. Donald Thomas, Salt Lake City, Utah, superintendent of schools. In his 1979 Phi Delta Kappa publication entitled *Performance Evaluation of Educational Personnel,* Thomas stated that:

> Today performance evaluation of educational personnel is receiving attention from school districts, legislative bodies, and the education profession in general. . . . A common theme is that quality education is dependent on quality performance of educators. Further, current performance evaluation programs are based on *performance standards* rather than traits, skills, product analysis, awards, or contributions. . . . Performance evaluation based on performance standards may be described as an MBO (management by objectives) system.[14]

Specifics on our model for a developmental appraisal process for school library media specialists will be presented later. First, however, let's look at some of the problems with appraisal instruments.

The Appraisal Instruments

Since most evaluation instruments currently in use are judgmental, they are subject to the problem of vague or nonexistent objectives that was discussed in connection with developmental appraisals. There are three additional problems with most current appraisal instruments. They are not job specific, they are not perceived as valid, and they rely heavily on traits for evaluation items.

Not Job Specific. A problem with most current performance-appraisal instruments used for school media specialists is that they are too general. As Kearney points out, it is not enough to have performance-appraisal items that apply to a broad class of employees. Instead, those items should be job specific.[15] The most obvious example of this problem is found in those schools where library media specialists are evaluated with the same form used for classroom teachers. These forms have many items that do not generally apply to media specialists. To illustrate this point, here are a few examples from actual copies of library media specialist evaluations done on a teacher evaluation form. Each was marked as "Not Applicable" by the principal doing the evaluation: evaluates pupil progress in fair and conscientious manner; uses classroom time wisely; promotes effective classroom interaction and mutual respect; thorough in preparation of lessons, including written plans; uses problem-solving techniques, effective questioning, and teacher-pupil planning. What is even more important is the fact that the standard teacher evaluation forms do not speak to specialized functions that media specialists *should* be engaged in.

Even districts with one specially designed evaluation form for all library media specialists have an inherent problem with job specificity. Think, for example, of two media specialists in the same system. One is in a kindergarten-first grade center. The other is in a vocational technical center. A single set of evaluation items that will be useful to both situations (and to the wide range of school conditions between the extremes) must be very comprehensive indeed. Even where a comprehensive form includes enough items to encompass the scope of all library media centers, the evaluation process followed generally makes no allowance for the priority or emphasis that should be placed on a given item in a given school.

Not Perceived as Valid. Another problem has to do with the validity of the appraisal items on media specialist appraisal forms. The behaviors called for or the results expected are generally based on professional standard statements such as *Media Programs: District and School.*[16] The underlying assumption is that building-level library media specialists and their principals will consider items for such standards to be essential. Recent research in Florida on essential competencies,[17] earlier research in Texas on perceptions of ideal roles and functions of school media specialists,[18] and other research on media specialist roles and function[19] make it clear that school-based personnel often disagree with professional leaders on what is essential. The essential competency study, for example, found that only twenty-one of the sixty-two media specialist competencies drawn from professional standards were considered essential by a stratified random sample of Florida classroom teachers, principals, and building media specialists.[20] This does not mean that the forty-one "rejected" competencies should not be used as evaluation items, but it does indicate that some explanation, discussion, or even selling may be necessary for evaluation items that ask principals to rate roles or functions that are not generally perceived as basic, or even as appropriate.

Rely Heavily on Traits. The third major problem is that many of the evaluation forms that have been specifically developed for library media specialists consist primarily of a list of key traits. Words such as *commitment, creativity, loyalty,* and *initiative* are so ambiguous that they are not easily defined in terms of observable, employee job behaviors. Appraisal items need to be defined in behavioral terms so that library media specialists and their supervisors have a clear understanding of the scope of the job and of performance expectations.

Evaluations based on traits have another serious problem. The courts have specifically condemned evaluation procedures based on trait scales. Title VII of the 1964 Civil Rights Act states that it is against the law to discriminate against a person in all phases of employment on the basis of race, color, religion, sex, and national origin. Educational institutions were covered by this law with the passage of the Equal Opportunity Act of 1972. The results of performance evaluations can affect an individual's salary and job tenure as well as training and promotion opportunities. Court decisions have, as a consequence, subjected performance evaluations to close investigation so that discrimination might be eliminated.[21]

As we have just seen, there is broad agreement among writers in management, librarianship, and education on the need for an effective performance-appraisal system that has been tailor-made to the requirements of a specific job. Such an appraisal system would increase employee productivity and satisfaction, would be useful for both developmental and comparative purposes, and would satisfy legal requirements. Nevertheless, little has been done thus far to use existing research findings and modify them in a practical way to develop an appraisal system for school library media specialists.

THE MODEL PERFORMANCE EVALUATION STUDY

General Background

The problem of providing more effective performance appraisals for school library media specialists was addressed by seeking answers to two basic questions:

1. What performance items and evidences of performance are appropriate for evaluating media specialists in schools of different levels and different sizes?
2. What procedures should be followed to successfully involve media specialists, principals, and district-level personnel in the evaluation process?

To get the answers, the following project was carried out. During 1981–82, district administrators, principals, and library media specialists in fourteen schools in four Florida school districts cooperated in a project to develop, try out, and revise several sets of empirically based job-duty statements and associated performance measures for evaluating building-level media specialists. Support and encouragement for the project was obtained from several sources. The Florida Educational Research and Development Corporation provided funds for travel to the field sites and for clerical help. The school districts—Sarasota County, DeSoto County, Seminole County, and Polk County—were cooperative, as was the University of South Florida (USF).

The Florida Association for Media in Education (FAME) supported the project as one facet of the work of the FAME Committee on Evaluation of Media Programs, on the assumption that evaluation of library media center personnel was an integral part of program evaluation. Since FAME is the major professional association for Florida media specialists, official backing from this organization was very helpful when school districts were asked to participate in the project.

Dr. Joyce Vincelette, assistant professor, USF College of Business, supported and encouraged the project from its early stages. As the work progressed, she participated in some facets of the project and agreed to coauthor the final report. That report has been sent to the Florida Educational Research and Development Corporation for review by the board of directors for possible publication and/or submission to the ERIC system.

Sarasota County

This section is an account of the events in Sarasota County as perceived by the county's district media supervisor. It outlines the needs perceived initially, the development of a solution, the field test of what was developed, and the outcomes of the field test.

Need. The need for a description of the job of a school library media specialist became apparent when several symptoms of an overall problem were identified. Thirteen of these symptoms are described to give the reader a basic comparison with his or her own situation.

1. Many Sarasota County school library media specialists have commented that they feel isolated from other media specialists. In most cases, schools are staffed with only one, or at the most, two media specialists. Daily contact with other media specialists is not possible, except by phone. Media specialists seem, therefore, to be a lonely bunch.

2. Services offered by media specialists to faculty and students differ from school to school. Many library media specialists were not knowledgeable about what services were being offered at a nearby school.

3. Many school principals could not describe, in detail, what the job of the library media specialist should be. This lack of understanding on the part of some school principals carried over into being unable to describe what the media specialist actually did each day.

4. Many district administrators and school-board members wanted, even demanded, quality media programs in the school but could not describe, operationally, what these programs should be.

5. Library media specialists were evaluated yearly by principals using the traditional teacher evaluation form, which did not include media-related tasks and evaluation items. Both principals and media specialists complained.

6. Because the library media program was not well understood by many people (including some media specialists), it was very difficult to justify the financial needs of the media program. On the other hand, it was sometimes very difficult to refuse unneeded equipment or furniture purchased by PTA fund-raising efforts (e.g., an expensive component stereo system for the media center when filmstrip projectors were really needed).

7. It was even more difficult to justify financial requests presented to the school board because they did not understand the objectives and operation of school library media programs and the job of the media specialist. (Do you recognize any of these as symptoms that exist in your school district? There are more.)

8. Many media specialists were uncertain as to the expectations of the district media coordinator other than to get book orders and inventory reports in on time.

9. Some library media specialists were uncertain as to what their principal expected and had no systematic way to discover those expectations. This was especially true where the principal and media specialist did not meet more than once a year to discuss the media program.

10. There were few, if any, discussions between curriculum coordinators and library media specialists, between teaching teams and media specialists, between guidance counselors and media specialists. The discussions that did occur were generally "ad hoc" in nature, with no need for follow-up. Undefined media programs and indefinite job descriptions did not promote good planning with other school staff.

11. In general, library media specialists reacted to situations instead of being *proactive* in presenting their media program. This resulted in trying to "catch up" rather than having a time line for activities.

12. In this time of generally decreasing or potentially decreasing financial resources, library media specialists need all the friends and supporters they can get. The lack of well-defined job descriptions for media specialists seemed to cause some teachers to think "I wish I were a media specialist—it looks like an easy job." If this attitude is prevalent, support for media program needs is difficult to obtain.

13. Some new and some not-so-new technologies were being neglected in some school library media programs through oversight of the media specialist or because no clear need was described by the objectives of the media program.

Development. The process of identifying solutions to these problems led to the need to develop a job description for the school media specialist. The need for strong school library media programs must be evident to the decision makers, and this evidence must be identified through evaluation of media programs. For Sarasota County schools, the most expedient way to evaluate media programs continues to be to evaluate library media specialists. The overall need was then further identified to be the lack of a job description and an accompanying evaluation form. This need for a job description was identified by both school library media specialists and district administrators.

The school media specialists, through their informal organization, appointed a committee that was charged with the responsibility of "developing a job description for media personnel to clarify and to establish the responsibilities of the media personnel in the schools and at the district level." During the 1978–79 school year, this committee met several times to organize and further define the committee responsibilities. A report from the committee in late spring 1979 indicated the hope to develop a job description for discussion during the 1979–80 school year.

Throughout the 1979–80 school year, sample job descriptions were received from other school districts and adapted from close examination of what library media specialists do each day. But it was not until the spring of 1981 that a job description deemed worthy of discussion was presented by the committee to the organization of media specialists. One point of discussion related to "Are we going to evaluate the person or the program?" At that meeting as well as at subsequent meetings when this discussion arose again, the conclusion was "We must evaluate the media specialist."

Field Test. This first version was pilot tested in five schools during the 1981–82 school year. It was also in the fall of 1981 that Sarasota County began to participate in the project to develop and test a model performance-evaluation process and instrument.

Copies of the job description were sent to the five principals and library media coordinator. During the meeting, each item on the job description was discussed to determine its application in that school, and a simulated evaluation of the media specialist was conducted on each item. This version of the job description described about thirty job activities that were based on data from *Identification of Specialization Competencies for Florida School Library Media Specialists.*[22] The job description underwent several revisions before and during the field test in the 1981–82 school year. Some principals asked for ways to evaluate whether or not a library media specialist was really doing the job as described. As a result, sample evidence was provided for each activity on the second version of the job-performance description. The three-point evaluation scale was also adopted in order to more closely parallel the new teacher evaluation system being developed at the same time.

During the spring of 1982, all thirty school library media specialists and their principals used the then-current version of the evaluation form to evaluate the media specialist performance for that year in a more comprehensive field test. The district media coordinator attended each evaluation session between principal and media specialist to facilitate discussion. After the evaluation portion of the meeting was completed, each principal/media specialist pair was asked to choose at least three items on the job-performance form to become high priority objectives for the media specialist for the 1982–83 school year.

End-of-project interviews were also arranged and conducted by Dr. Fred Pfister in Sarasota County (and in the other participating schools) in April 1982. The purpose of his interviews was to get participant reaction to the new evaluation procedure and suggestions about how to introduce it into other schools or school districts. Space limitations prohibit extensive quotes from those interviews, but information from them underlies the general "Conclusions" and "Recommendations" sections of this article.

Outcomes. There have been some important outcomes of this project. First, the job-performance descriptions initiated nontrivial discussions between the principal and media specialist. This improvement in communication proved to be one of the outcomes most valued by both media specialists and principals. Communication between the district media coordinator and principal and between media specialist and district media coordinator was also enhanced. Needs for in-service training, additional resources, planning, and support were identified easily and without blame or degradation of any of the participants.

The planning activities accompanying the evaluation procedure were also important outcomes. For the library media specialist to demonstrate several of the job-performance activities, planning with the principal was a prerequisite.

Expectations of the media specialist by the principal, and vice versa, were obviously more realistic than before the use of the library media specialist job description. The job description is intended to be flexible enough to be used by library media specialists at all levels, K–12. The principal and media specialist can negotiate the degree to which each performance item is applicable to their situation and therefore raise or lower expectations through discussion.

A fourth outcome, unexpected though important, is the usefulness of the job description in interviewing prospective library media specialists. The principal now has a guide for questioning and requesting evidence from a candidate as to his/her effectiveness as a media specialist.

Beyond that of good evaluation of media specialists, these four outcomes—improved communication, better planning, more realistic expectations, and an interviewing aid—have been nearly as important as the evaluation procedure itself. The present version of the media specialist job-performance description was adopted as the official evaluation instrument by the Sarasota County School Board in the fall of 1982. Nearly four years of work paid off in an evaluation system developed by school media specialists for school media specialists.

We will now turn from these specific outcomes in Sarasota County to the general conclusions drawn from the entire study.

CONCLUSIONS

Procedures for Evaluating Media Specialists Are Inadequate

Current procedures for evaluating library media specialists are inadequate in Florida and elsewhere in the U.S. The problem is more pronounced, although less likely to be recognized, in districts with no district-level media supervisors. Even though principals and media specialists both want to do a good job, they often do not come to grips with the specifics of how the media specialist and the library media program should be contributing to the desired outcomes of the school. They just do not talk to one another in an organized way about the media specialist's job in many schools.

Use of the Models Can Improve Performance Appraisal of Media Specialists

The models and the process described for using them represent significant improvements over what is currently being used to evaluate media specialists. Many current forms incorporate trait items that are difficult to justify as job related. In most cases there is no opportunity for the setting of goals or priorities. In many cases library media specialists are being evaluated with an instrument designed for classroom teachers. In these cases many of the evaluation items are not applicable to media specialists. In addition, often neither the media specialist nor the principal is aware of the full scope of the job because the critical job activities have not been identified. The models developed during this study have the potential to make improvements in all of these areas. Where traditional evaluation instruments are in use, the models still have the potential to provide useful input to the official evaluation.

The Models Have Uses Other Than for Performance Appraisal

In some school districts union contracts or other constraints dictate the formal performance-evaluation instrument that will be used for library media specialists. Even in those districts, the process developed in this study can be useful. It can improve communication and thus provide clearer expectations that will reduce role ambiguity. The model process can also be used for developmental purposes and can help in setting goals and priorities. The statement of expected job performance developed for a given district can also help to select the best available library media specialists when vacancies occur.

Improving Communication and Reducing Role Ambiguity. This study has demonstrated that communication between the media specialist and principal generally improved during the development of the evaluation instrument and during its use. Not only did the school principals gain a better understanding of the role and functions of a library media specialist and the problems they encounter, but the media specialists learned about the principal's job including some of the problems and limitations. In addition, by gaining a clear understanding of their principal's expectations and goals, library media specialists experienced less role ambiguity.

Developing Employees. Information obtained during this study indicates that the models have potential for developing media specialists. Proper use of the process described in the models will identify areas of strengths and weaknesses in performance. Areas of strength can be positively reinforced to encourage future occurrences of the desired behavior. Employees can also be counseled and training suggested in areas where performance deficiencies exist.

Planning and Goal Setting. In addition to their usefulness in facilitating communication, developing employees, and reducing role ambiguity, the models are also useful for planning and goal setting. This conclusion stems from statements such as the one that follows from the interview with John Zoretich, principal of the Sarasota County School Center. He said:

> I think, too, that this county is very weak in the evaluation procedure presently used. . . .Something like this, the Model Evaluation, is very helpful. It will give people direction and keep them on task. It's a reminder of major directions during those times when day to day pressures might make us lose sight of them.

Selecting New Personnel. Performance-evaluation models such as those developed in this study can be useful in the personnel selection process when new media specialists are hired. Knowing the critical elements of the job would enable the interviewer to ask better questions and be better able to evaluate a candidate's background and responses.

The Models Are Congruent with Current Management Trends

All the models developed in this study represent significant progress toward a more adequate appraisal system than is generally in use to evaluate library media specialists. The models developed in this study are all different in appearance, but each is a practical adaptation of the MBO and BARS techniques discussed in the management literature. This is particularly true of the model developed in Sarasota County and the DeSoto County adaptation derived from it.

In each of the Florida counties participating in the study, there were groups of media specialists, supervisors, and principals who worked together to decide on the critical dimensions to be evaluated as well as the items of sample evidence. Trait items are not included on any of the instruments developed. The critical job activities are all behavioral in nature and explain behaviors the library media specialist must exhibit to adequately perform the job. In addition, the systems were designed to include periodic goal setting between the library media specialist and the school principals to determine high-priority job activities that help to focus energy and allocate time.

RECOMMENDATIONS

The recommendations are based on the study and its conclusions, but are organized according to their major intended audiences rather than to parallel the conclusions.

Recommendations to Those Attempting to Implement a New Evaluation Instrument for Media Specialists

Adapt the Models. Schools or school districts interested in improving the performance-evaluation instruments presently being used for library media specialists or other classes of school personnel can use the models as a base or as examples. They must, however, be cautious in adopting new models. Preconstructed evaluation instruments should not be adopted "as is," but they can be used as a basis for local discussions. Personnel in the school or school district must understand and agree with the items included on the form. Each school and district has different facilities, different grade levels, etc., and the evaluation instruments developed must be specific to where they will be used.

Provide Leadership. Leadership for improvement should logically come from district-level media supervisors in those districts that have them. Media specialists, principals, or district-level administrators in districts without a library media supervisor may also wish to improve the performance-appraisal process in their schools. It is recommended that personnel in these districts contact the state department of education's school media consultant (or analogous office) to identify possible sources of outside assistance. Such assistance might then come from the state department of education, other school districts, universities, or other sources.

Get Support. Media supervisors or others attempting to implement a new evaluation instruction should seek initial support for the idea from strong people who can be expected to support this kind of change—people who would not be threatened by a more detailed appraisal of their performance.

Establish a District-Wide Time Frame. A time frame for accomplishments should be established. Unless a time frame is established, schools generally take too much time in the development process. Time goals need to be set for developing an initial model, for pilot testing the model, for district-wide implementation, and for a subsequent reassessment and revision of the model.

Establish Building-Level Review Policies. Each school should plan to reassess the model whenever there is a change in the library media center staff or in the school administration that does the performance evaluation. Reassessment is also needed when changes, such as the grade levels served or the addition of new equipment such as a microcomputer, cause the media specialist's job to change.

Improve the Models. Two ways to improve the models developed in this study are recommended. First, we recommend that consideration be given to the inclusion of a statement of resources or other support needed to accomplish each job duty. If a library media specialist is to be held responsible for goal accomplishment, he or she must have the resources, support, information, etc., to accomplish the goal. Several media specialists in Florida voiced concern that they would be evaluated on things that were not within their control. The addition of a statement of resources needed should ease this concern.

A second way to further develop the models would be to develop behavioral anchors or examples to help overcome the problem of judging the level of goal accomplishment. One might start with the major goals (high-priority objectives) established for the year and develop behavioral anchors for each point on a scale to illustrate degrees of goal accomplishment. This variation of the BARS technique discussed in the management literature is a practical alternative that provides a method of eventually developing anchors for each major dimension.[23] These behavioral anchors will more clearly define expectations for goal accomplishment and will also reduce role ambiguity.

Consider Other Uses for the Models. The models can be used even if a school system is unionized and the contract dictates that another formal evaluation instrument must be used. The models presented in this study can be used to create input for an existing evaluation system as well as for planning purposes, selecting and developing employees, increasing communication, and channeling energy into high-priority areas.

Recommendations to Those Responsible for Performance Appraisal in School Districts

Examine the Needs of All School Personnel. In the interviews with school principals and library media specialists, the need for improved performance evaluations for other classes of school personnel, such as guidance counselors and music teachers, was mentioned several times. If such needs exist, then steps should be taken to address the problem.

It is helpful, but not essential, to start with a base document, as we did in our research. Starting with a base document reduces the time involved considerably and makes the process a more manageable experience. If an area has nothing analogous to the essential competency information for media specialists, the process used in this study can still be paralleled. This would be done by having raters and ratees (e.g., principals and guidance counselors) create a local set of essential job dimensions to use as a starting point.

Provide In-Service Training. We have concluded that the evaluations used for library media specialists and other school personnel need improvement. In addition to using a better instrument and process, we believe it is also possible for many who are involved in the appraisal process to improve their techniques. Such techniques would include observation and recording skills, use of critical incident techniques, identifying rating errors and associated problems, and goal setting and feedback techniques.

We believe that considerable progress toward improvement could be made by using current research as a base for individual study. Much of this research is summarized in two recent books that would be useful to anyone doing further study on this topic. The first of these books is *Increasing Productivity through Performance Appraisal* (1981) by Gary P. Latham and Kenneth N. Wexley.[24] This volume is part of the Addison-Wesley series on Managing Human Resources. It gives thorough coverage of the legal aspects of performance evaluation, the development and validation of appraisal systems, and the motivational aspects of performance evaluations. This book also includes numerous examples and illustrations of performance-appraisal formats.

A second useful source for additional information is *Performance Appraisal and Review Systems: The Identification, Measurement, and Development of Performance in Organizations* by Steven J. Carroll and Craig C. Schneier.[25] In addition to covering many of the same topics as Latham and Wexley, this book provides extensive coverage of feedback techniques and management by objectives. Both of these books provide up-to-date, useful references on the topics discussed in this research report.

Examine the Reward Structure. Rewards for the library media specialist, such as money, recognition, etc., should ideally be related to both goal accomplishment and the performance of the job activities established as essential. The present lockstep salary schedule used in most school systems does not address this problem. There should be opportunity for merit at all levels. Even if this cannot be done for teachers and library media specialists, merit pay for principals is possible. The evaluation and subsequent rewards of school principals should take into account how well they develop and utilize employees. Do they conscientiously work with the library media specialist to set goals and provide support for the accomplishment of these goals? Are they getting good value for the money spent on the media program by using that staff to the best advantage? These and similar questions need to be asked about principals if we are to come close to getting maximum benefit from our library media programs.

SUMMARY

What we have attempted to develop in the model performance-evaluation project is an evaluation that will look at results, rather than traits or behaviors. As library media specialists, we should be actively involved in describing our outcomes and explaining them to the principals, teachers, students, and parents who need to understand what we do in order to support us. This study has reinforced our assumption that we have not taken advantage of the performance-evaluation process as a way to communicate with principals, and by extension, with the rest of the population we serve. We believe the models can be useful for this purpose.

REFERENCES

1. William J. Kearney, "Performance Appraisal: Which Way to Go?" *MSU Business Topics* 25: 58 (Winter 1977).

2. Bette Ann Stead and Richard W. Scamell, "A Study of the Relationships of Role Conflict, the Need for Role Clarity, and Job Satisfaction for Professional Librarians," *Library Quarterly* 50: 310–23 (July 1980); also Mary Van Sell, Arthur P. Brief, and Randall S. Schuler, "Role Conflict and Role Ambiguity: Integration of the Literature and Directions for Future Research," *Human Relations* 34: 43–71 (Jan. 1981).

3. For example, see Herbert H. Meyer, Emmanual Kay, and John R. P. French, "Split Roles in Performance Appraisal," *Harvard Business Review* 43: 123–29 (Jan.-Feb. 1965); John M. Ivancevich, "Changes in Performance in a Management by Objectives Program," *Administrative Science Quarterly* 19: 563–74 (Dec. 1974); and Gary P. Latham and Gary A. Yukl, "A Review of Research on the Application of Goal Setting in Organizations," *Academy of Management Journal* 18: 824–25 (Dec. 1975).

4. Mark L. McConkie, "A Clarification of the Goal Setting and Appraisal Process in MBO," *Academy of Management Review* 4: 29 (Jan. 1979).

5. Latham and Yukl, "A Review of Research," p. 26; also David A. Kolb and Richard A. Boyatzis, "Goal-setting and Self-directed Behavior Change," in David A. Kolb, Irwin M. Rubin, and James M. McIntyre, eds., *Organizational Psychology: A Book of Reading* (Englewood Cliffs, N.J.: Prentice-Hall, 1971).

6. McConkie, "A Clarification of the Goal," p. 30.

7. Gary P. Latham, Terence R. Mitchell, and Dennis L. Dossett, "Importance of Participative Goal Setting and Anticipated Rewards on Goal Difficulty and Job Performance," *Journal of Applied Psychology* 63: 163–71 (April 1978).

8. John R. Hinrichs, "An Eight Year Follow-up of a Management Assessment Center," *Journal of Applied Psychology* 63: 596–601 (Oct. 1978).

9. Norman Raymond Frederick Maier, *The Appraisal Interview: Objectives, Methods, and Skills* (New York: Wiley, 1958).

10. Ronald J. Burke, William Weitzel, and Tamara Weir, "Characteristics of Effective Employee Performance Review and Development Interviews: Replication and Extension," *Personnel Psychology* 31: 903–19 (Winter 1978).

11. Robert E. Greene, *Administrative Appraisal: A Step to Improved Leadership* (Washington, D.C.: National Association for Secondary School Principals, 1972).

12. Ernest R. DeProspo, "Personnel Evaluation as an Impetus to Growth," *Library Trends* 20: 60–69 (July 1971).

13. Robert C. Hilton, "Performance Evaluation of Library Personnel," *Special Libraries* 69: 433 (Nov. 1978).

14. M. Donald Thomas, *Performance Evaluation of Educational Personnel* (Bloomington, Ind.: Phi Delta Kappa Educational Foundation, 1979).

15. Kearney, "Performance Appraisal," p. 60.

16. American Association of School Librarians and Association for Educational Communications and Technology, *Media Programs: District and School* (Chicago: American Library Assn., 1975).

17. Fred C. Pfister, *Identification of Specialization Competencies for Florida School Library Media Specialists* (Bethesda, Md.: ERIC Document Reproduction Service, ED 198 805, 1980).

18. Fred C. Pfister and Karen Alexander, *Discrepancies between Actual and Ideal Roles and Functions of Texas School Librarians as Perceived by School Superintendents, Principals and Librarians* (Bethesda, Md.: ERIC Document Reproduction Service, ED 134 188, 1976).

19. For an interesting survey report, see Judy M. Pitts, "A Creative Survey of Research Concerning Role Expectations of Library Media Specialists," *School Library Media Quarterly* 10: 164–69 (Winter 1982).

20. Pfister, *Identification of Specialization Competencies,* p. 9.

21. For two examples, see *Albermarle Paper Company* v. *Moody,* 95 S Ct. 2362, 45 L Ed 2d 280; and *Wade* v. *Mississippi Cooperative Extension Service,* 372 F. Supp. 126 (1944), 7 EPD 9186.

22. Pfister, *Identification of Specialization Competencies.*

23. For example, see Gary P. Latham and Kenneth N. Wexley, *Increasing Productivity through Performance Appraisal* (Reading, Mass.: Addison-Wesley, 1981).

24. Latham and Wexley, *Increasing Productivity.*

25. Steven J. Carroll and Craig E. Schneier, *Performance Appraisal and Review Systems: The Identification Measurement and Development of Performance in Organizations* (Glenview, Ill.: Scott, Foresman, 1982).

Appraisal May Be...

Evaluating the Superior Employee

by T.J. Halatin

Most supervisors know that the greatest benefit they can provide the truly superior employee is an outstanding evaluation. Although rewards like time off, a flexible work schedule, improved working conditions, and recognition are important, it is the outstanding evaluation that is going to help the person get a pay raise, transfer, promotion, or bonus.

The formal evaluation creates a permanent record of outstanding performance and in that way brings the performance to the attention of others who might be involved in making personnel decisions. An evaluation is also a motivational tool that gives an employee both congratulations for a job well done and a guide for future improvement.

Most evaluations consist of some type of rating scale and a space for supervisor's comments. Superior performance earns the employee a very high or even the highest rating on the scale. Rating systems, however, often introduce problems for the supervisor who wants to single out outstanding performance. Some organizations, for instance, worry about the phenomenon of evaluation inflation in which nearly every employee receives a very high rating. Where this is true, the superior employee becomes just one of the crowd and a rating of excellent loses its meaning.

High ratings can also cause motivational problems when a person who has received a high rating is not rewarded with a promotion, a desired transfer, or some other expected benefit. The supervisor's evaluation then means little, and motivation may decline.

T.J. Halatin is assistant professor of management, Southwest Texas State University, San Marcos, TX. His article, "Evaluating the Superior Employee," is printed, by permission of the publisher, from *Supervisory Management*, December 1981 [3pp.] © 1981 AMACOM, a division of American Management Association, New York. All rights reserved.

With such problems in mind, management now places greater emphasis on the supervisor's comments to differentiate among employees who have the same or similar ratings.

PREPARING THE GROUND

Before the evaluation, know your people and what they do. Preparation for the evaluation of any superior employee begins well in advance of the date for the formal review. It involves documenting activities, conditions, and specific events that are noteworthy. For example, when the supervisor compliments an employee for superior performance, he or she should make a memo for the record that can be used in support of an outstanding appraisal.

As a supervisor, you should be able to document each person's performance and the conditions under which the job is carried out. You can expect each employee to be aware of the relative contributions made by others in the department, and their awareness leads the employees to form opinions about what constitutes a fair evaluation of each contributor. Departmental morale and the supervisor's credibility with management can be damaged when people receive ratings that are too high, too low, or out of line with what has been performed. Giving an outstanding rating when it is not really earned is just as damaging as failing to give an outstanding rating that has been earned.

Maintain your credibility with those who will review your evaluation. Your reputation for giving accurate appraisals enhances the value of the outstanding evaluation.

LOYALTY TO YOUR STAFF

Some organizations experiencing evaluation inflation attempt to offset the problem with certain policies and directives. An organization may establish a quota system, for instance, under which a supervisor is limited to the number of high ratings that can be given. Or the organization may promote the practice of limiting new employees to a less than outstanding evaluation so that improvement can be encouraged over a longer period of time. Such practices for reducing evaluation inflation can have a damaging effect on a person's career and can be disastrous if they are only temporary policies that affect just certain individuals.

Employees who have earned an outstanding rating should not be limited by company policy or deprived of what they have earned. If one, several, or all of your employees are superior in performance, then you should be able to evaluate them accordingly. If your organization is presently involved in a program to try to combat evaluation inflation, be prepared to present your case to your superior. Your personal credibility and the performance of your employees may win support from upper management. Even if you do not win the support on this present decision, it is possible that you will enhance your image with your employees when they realize that you are the type of supervisor who goes to bat for them.

Alert your superiors that you are planning to give an outstanding evaluation before the fact. An informal discussion of the coming outstanding evaluation can help you gain support ahead of time and resolve any potential areas of conflict.

WRITING SUGGESTIONS

A good deal of effort, thought, and concentration go into writing an outstanding evaluation. First, organize your thoughts in an outline. The outline permits the writer to rank an individual's strongest points so that they are placed in order of prominence. This keeps the most important factors from being hidden among the less important. In addition, the outline also serves as a checklist of points to be recorded in the evaluation. A quick review often identifies thoughts that may be missing and should be included in the evaluation.

Write a rough draft. Like the dress rehearsal of a stage performance, the rough draft is an opportunity to see how well all the parts fit together. The rough draft often reveals discrepancies that are not immediately evident and that should be corrected in the final draft.

Describe the performance of the superior employee in positive terms, deemphasizing possible weaknesses that might detract from the positive statement. A qualification or mention of a weakness might be highlighted in the review of an otherwise outstanding evaluation when the evaluations of several employees are being compared to determine who gets a promotion.

Carefully review the final copy. Remember that this document will remain in the employee's folder for many years and may affect the employee's future. It must be free of any errors that will distract a reader. Therefore, it is important that the supervisor make the final effort of proofreading and correcting errors that might create any negative impressions about the person under evaluation.

FOLLOWUP

Don't forget to review the evaluation with the employee. Such a meeting gives the employee an opportunity to respond to the evaluation that is going into the personnel records. When it is an assessment that both you and the employee should be proud of, take advantage of the time to thank the employee for past performance.

Remember to remind the employee that an outstanding evaluation is no guarantee that a certain personnel action will take place. Although you and the employee may hope that it leads to a pay raise or a promotion, don't hint that the evaluation will bring such a result.

Check with your superior to be sure that the evaluation has been received for review. The reminder can serve as a progress check and to alert management to an outstanding performer.

Finally, hang on to your supporting documentation. If your superior wants to discuss the high rating that you've given to the superior employee, be prepared to present the evidence.

Preparing an evaluation that makes an employee stand out as the best of the best requires time and effort. But the formal evaluation is one of the few direct rewards that a supervisor can give to the superior employee, and the supervisor should take advantage of the opportunity.

Beyond Evaluation: Performance Appraisal as a Planning and Motivational Tool in Libraries

by H. Rebecca Kroll

Performance appraisal for academic librarians can be more than a paper game. This article discusses types of performance appraisal now in use, their relative strengths and weaknesses, and how performance appraisal can be put to other uses, including long-ranging planning and employee motivation, which are of benefit to both the library and the librarian.

The current popularity of performance evaluation in management literature and practice, combined with increasing financial pressures on libraries of all types, is encouraging more serious consideration of performance appraisal as a worthy expenditure of time and effort on the part of all levels of library staff. Where performance appraisals once might have been limited to the production line and to junior management in the business world, and to clerical positions in the world of libraries, the application of the appraisal process in one form or another is becoming increasingly common for library faculty and professional staff. DeProspo noted that "librarians have tended, until very recently at least, to regard themselves as unique in the field of personnel administration."[1] In many ways this was particularly true of academic librarians, frequently caught between the rigors of a rapidly changing profession and the pressures of newly acquired

H. Rebecca Kroll is management/economics librarian, Lockwood Library, State University of New York at Buffalo. Her article, "Beyond Evaluation: Performance Appraisal as a Planning and Motivational Tool in Libraries," is reprinted from *The Journal of Academic Librarianship* 9 (1) (March 1983): 27–32. Used by permission of *The Journal of Academic Librarianship*.

faculty status, which brought with it the right to peer review in addition to review by a single supervisor.

This article is aimed specifically at the application of performance evaluation to faculty in academic libraries. To date there has been a relative dearth of discussion on this topic in the library literature. A recent article by Berkner gives an excellent overview of some types of performance appraisal and their application, but treats librarians throughout as professionals, rather than as faculty members, with all of the accompanying pomp and problems.[2]

There are many justifications for a performance evaluation program, but the focus of this article is on the uses of the evaluation process as a means of planning for the future while reviewing the past, and at the same time as a means of stimulating the library faculty to develop their talents in ways which will benefit themselves and the institution.

WHAT IS PERFORMANCE EVALUATION?

Performance evaluation and performance appraisal (used interchangeably here) are terms frequently used, albeit mostly in conversations regarding clerical staff, but the images conjured up by these terms may vary widely from library to library. While there is no single, "best" evaluation type, an evaluation program on any level should contain at least these four basic steps:

1. Determine what the job is (define the goals).
2. Establish a reasonable performance level (define the objectives in terms of quantity, quality, time spent).
3. Measure the actual performance (by first-hand observation, viewing completed work, reading employee's own report, etc.).
4. Compare the actual performance to the standards set.

Performance evaluation, then, can be defined as a method for formally measuring the output of an employee against a preestablished set of criteria, whether these criteria are dictated by a supervisor or are mutually agreed upon by the supervisor and the employee.

REASONS FOR PERFORMANCE EVALUATION

The academic library, like any other organization which is not completely self-sufficient, is constantly attempting to retain control and to minimize uncertainty. Thompson describes uncertainty as "the fundamental problem for complex organizations," breaking it down into three sources: generalized uncertainty, or lack of understanding of the macro-environment (the entire political, economic, and social climate), contingency, dependence on elements of the external and therefore noncontrollable environment on the part of the organization (such as State and Federal funding), and the interdependence of components within the organization (internal uncertainty) such as staffing changes due to attrition.[3]

Performance appraisals help reduce uncertainty within the organization, and when combined with other programs may help to reduce externally related uncertainty as well. Most performance appraisals, however, are used to accomplish basic informational tasks which benefit both the organization and the employee being evaluated. In a January 1978 article in *Personnel Journal,* Haynes describes the purposes of a performance appraisal program as providing management information to the organization and providing feedback to the employees.[4] As far back as 1957, McGregor pointed out that performance appraisals were also being increasingly used as a basis for counseling by the supervisor.[5]

For the organization, an ongoing performance appraisal program can provide instantaneous information for decisions on promotions, pay increases, bonus plans and internal reorganizations. It can also provide clues to the attitudes of managers toward their subordinates; no evaluation system is ever entirely free from bias, and much can be learned about the evaluator by noting the collective results of all the evaluations he/she produces.

A further benefit to the organization is the knowledge that evaluations will take place and be used as a basis for personnel decisions to help maintain control by stressing accountability. Evaluation also provides feedback to the organization as to whether the normal training and placement methods are succeeding, or need to be revised.

For the employee being evaluated, the performance appraisal program should ensure exact information as to expectations, as well as feedback on how well those expectations are being met. A good performance evaluation is not possible unless the employee knows what he is supposed to do, how his performance will be measured, and against what standards. Thus, uncertainty reduction takes place for the employee as well as for the organization, since the simple existence of the evaluation program guarantees at least a minimum level of knowledge. Uncertainty is further reduced when the employee is formally told how his performance is viewed. There are many ways of evaluating performance, and as many ways of communicating the results of the evaluation, not all of them beneficial. Any kind of performance appraisal program seriously carried out, however, provides at the very least some useful information to both the organization and the employee, regardless of the setting.

Some of the problems in evaluation for librarians are caused by the dichotomy between quality and quantity in library work. This is particularly dangerous because sometimes librarians are being evaluated not on their ability, but on how well they follow institutional philosophy. For example, should they catalog a few books perfectly, to meet exacting standards, or get a lot of books pushed through and get them onto the shelves where they are accessible? In other cases, there may not be a conflict between quantity and quality, but there may be no connection either: the number of reference questions answered by one librarian in one hour at the reference desk can be measured, but neither a very high nor a very low figure necessarily indicates high quality service. Nor is patron satisfaction always a safe indicator of the quality of service given.

It is relatively easy to record the quantity of work performed in a library situation: titles cataloged, orders placed, questions answered, interlibrary loan requests filled. Much more difficult is the estimation of the quality of the work performed: did the cataloging provide the best access points, was the best use made of the collection development budget, did patrons at the reference desk get the answers they needed? In many cases the evaluating librarian ends up making a judgment call as to the level of work performed.

For this reason, it is important to have a job description which spells out very clearly the expectations of the supervisor, the library, and the university, and to provide an opportunity to discuss the contents of the evaluation and its implications.

Thus far we have considered performance appraisal mainly as a review of the past, whereas it has equally strong potential for looking to the future. In *Performance Appraisal and the Manager,* Keil lists additional purposes for performance evaluation beyond informing employees of the standards being used and how they are meeting them; he adds coaching employees on how to perform the job better, and encouraging them to work harder.[6] At the same time, however, Keil notes that an appraisal system is valid only if the employee *can* control the quality and quantity of his output, i.e., if his performance is not affected by environmental or organizational variables. A reference librarian should not be penalized for failure to successfully answer all questions if the real source of the problem is an inadequate reference collection. While this holds true at some levels of evaluation, many academic librarians would agree that the ability to cope with those extraneous variables is a very important part of their overall performance, particularly for those in public services positions where they represent the library to the rest of the academic world. The ability to deliver creative and cheerful reference service despite a limited collection may distinguish between an adequate reference librarian and a first-rate one.

TYPES OF PERFORMANCE EVALUATION

The procedure for performance evaluation varies from simplistic to extremely complex, as does the goal-setting process. Performance evaluation types can be classified either by the format used for the evaluation, or by the degree of participation of the employee being evaluated. To some extent the two classification schemes parallel each other, in that the more complicated formats tend to allow for more employee involvement. Simply adding more pages to a prepared form, or more dimensions to the overall review, however, does not guarantee participation. Likewise, an extremely short and simple form, if used as the basis for a friendly and wide-open discussion, can result in a very high degree of input from the employee.

Classification by Format

Evaluation procedures can be roughly grouped into two major types: those methods which focus on some form of rating system, and those which concentrate on objectives. The rating system methods work on the principle of comparison; the employee's work may be compared to an absolute standard set arbitrarily by the company, to a predetermined rate of output established by precedent or by exhaustive time-measurement projects, or to a standard as abstract and complex as the criteria for tenure at a particular academic institution. In this sense, tenure review for academic librarians comes as the ultimate performance evaluation. Unfortunately, some librarians arrive at the measurement of actual performance step described above without ever having had the opportunity to define the goals or the objectives clearly.

The "publish or perish" syndrome has been cited so often that it has lost most of its meaning. On many university campuses, however, it is the simple truth, and applies to all members of the faculty. Librarians' contributions to research and education do not take the same form as the contributions of the professorial faculty, but too often, a campus-wide personnel review panel composed entirely of non-library faculty will expect the tenure dossier of a practicing academic librarian to equal in every respect the dossier of a professor of library science. Regular performance evaluation for academic librarians can help in many ways: it can document professional growth, give timely warning of weakness or inadequate development in critical areas, and show excellence in strong areas. All three of these—excellent job performance, proof of professional growth, and a well-rounded display of competence—are beneficial during tenure review.

Relative Ranking System

Another form of comparison is the relative ranking system, in which employees are compared with each other rather than to an absolute standard. Whether the employee is compared with fellow workers or judged against a separate standard, however, there is usually a rating scale on which to build the comparison. The simplest rating scale is a one-dimensional global evaluation, for which the supervisor must combine all performance of an individual into a single point on a scale. The actual format for this type of evaluation may be a scale of numbers (e.g., one to ten, where one is the lowest and ten is the highest level of performance), or a series of tersely described categories such as "unsatisfactory," "needs improvement," "above average." The advantage to this type of evaluation in the short term is that it can be done very quickly, given adequate knowledge on the part of management. In the long run, this is equally apt to be a disadvantage, since it may encourage quick-and-dirty evaluations without time for consultation with the employee, and hence without an opportunity to correct or to forestall problems. For the concerned employee, the one-dimensional evaluation is inevitably unsatisfactory, unless accompanied by extensive discussion with a supervisor, since it neither explains the perceived weaknesses leading to an unsatisfactory evaluation nor reinforces the particular strengths which led to a good rating.

A similar problem exists with the ranking procedure which compares employees to each other rather than to an outside standard. Unless the supervisor takes time to explain the thinking behind the ranking, the employee is left with little or no useful information; the supervisor is less likely to take that time because relative ranking is a time-consuming procedure and because relative ranking is extremely difficult to explain to an employee without creating morale problems and hard feeling among colleagues.

Dimensionalized Ranking System

Slightly better, from the point of view of feedback to the employee, is a format known as dimensionalized rating scale, which breaks the job down into various components ("dimensions") and rates each one separately. This format allows the supervisor to distinguish, for instance, between quantity and quality of work, or to deal separately with research ability as opposed to contributions to reader services in the library. The dimensionalized rating scale also has the potential for a high degree of employee participation in formulating the specific job dimensions statements. A librarian who works with a supervisor in identifying various components before beginning the job has a better grasp of what is expected than one who simply reads a prepared job description. There are still two problems with this form of rating, however. The first is that few of the scales used allow for an indication of priorities among the various components. Thus, an inexperienced librarian may encounter severe problems when being reviewed for reappointment because of having devoted an inordinate amount of time to mastering the collection and providing first-quality reference service, for instance, at the expense of establishing a good liaison with the professorial faculty and doing research with a view to publication. The second problem with this or any rating scale based on something other than pure quantity is that relative ratings will vary considerably from one supervisor to another; one person's "acceptable" may be another's "average" or better.

From this point of view, one refinement of the dimensionalized rating scale, called a behaviorally anchored rating scale, offers some improvement. While still rating each component of the job using only a numerical or brief verbal designation, the rater has a set of definitions or standards to follow in selecting a rating. The definition statement for "excellent" faculty liaison work might include the concept of regularly visiting each member of the department, and sending individual notification of special interest items, whereas an inadequate faculty liaison rating might include waiting passively for faculty to come to the library with problems. With these descriptive anchors in full view, there is less tendency for the rater's individual expectations to interfere with a stable measurement process. The anchors also provide a starting point for discussions during the review process. For further explanations of these rating scales, see Schoen's discussion in *Supervision: The Management of Organizational Resources.*[7]

Management By Objectives

Evaluations based on rating scales can be made almost infinitely complex, but their basic character remains the same, and many academic libraries are turning instead to more sophisticated methods of performance review which focus first on objectives. The most well-known example of this is management by objectives (MBO), which depends heavily on teamwork and cooperation for success, starting with the establishment of goals for the overall organization. Schoen describes a simplified one-on-one version of MBO in which the supervisor and the subordinate together determine the subordinate's goals for a specific future period of time (one year is most common in academic libraries) and outline the methods to be used.[8] At the end of the period, they meet again to review the subordinate's actual accomplishments, to discuss problems, and to plan for the next cycle. This approach is excellent for many academic libraries because it encourages discussion, allows librarians to place their goals in the context of overall library operations, and fits easily into an annual schedule based on the academic year. An alternative approach uses a variable time frame based on the specific objectives to be met, with a built-in review at the end of each major project.

As Schoen points out, one of the strongest advantages of MBO is that, by definition, it forces goal-setting from the top of the organization down through the lowest levels, accompanied by discussion on specific objectives which must be reached as part of the pursuit of those overall goals. The high level of planning involved, however, brings with it a high level of paperwork, and necessitates spending a great deal of time in talking as well as doing. Other problems with MBO include the inevitable deviation in level of individual goals set from one supervisor-subordinate pair to another, leading to biased comparisons of effectiveness on paper, and also includes the problem of outside influences which may interfere with the employees' achievements through no fault of their own. Addressing these shortcomings to produce an equitable evaluation system requires still more time on the part of both management and staff.

Most MBO performance appraisal systems evaluate on the basis of stated objectives, but give little weight to the method in which those objectives are achieved.[9] This can be a serious omission in a library from the point of view of both public relations and budget. While it is extremely difficult to mandate behavior and attitude in a system which deals only with results, a slightly different approach to MBO allows greater control over operations by tying goals to financial resources. The Planning-Programming-Budgeting System (PPBS) is familiar to any library which has experimented voluntarily or involuntarily with zero-base budgeting. It follows the same principles as MBO, but with added financial controls.

Gannon breaks down PPBS into five steps:

1. Planning (define objectives)

2. Programming (outline plans to accomplish objectives, including resources needed and description of costs and benefits)

3. Budgeting (allocation of resources to programs selected as having highest priorities)

4. Working (completion of programs selected)

5. Evaluating (analysis of results).[10]

Some of the refinements offered by PPBS include emphasis on priorities as defined by the allocation of resources, enforced attention to cost-benefit ratios of alternate programs, and review of fiscal responsibility as well as goal achievement within each program.

Classification by Degree of Participation

For librarians as members of the faculty of an academic institution, the specific format used for performance appraisal may be less important than the degree to which they are involved in the evaluation and planning process. A scale of evaluation types could be formulated, starting with a purely top-down process at one end, where supervisors evaluate subordinates without consultation and announce the results to them with little or no discussion. At the other end of the spectrum is a self-appraisal method wherein employees evaluate their own progress, using a standard form or unformatted written report, and then take it to the individual supervisors for discussion. In the middle of the scale fall various degrees of consultation before, during, and after the commitment of the evaluation results to paper. There is also a school of thought which strongly disagrees with keeping any written record of evaluation. This view, however, must give way to the personnel policies of the campus, which may prescribe the inclusion of annual evaluation results in the dossier of any candidate being considered for reappointment.

Whether evaluation processes are classified by format or by method, it is most important to find the procedure which will work best in any given library situation. In the final analysis, the goal is to formulate a review process which will help to groom librarians from the beginning to fulfill their academic obligations while advancing their careers.

BEYOND EVALUATION

The ideal performance evaluation program would do more than look to the past: it would also be of crucial importance for the present and the future, by helping the library administration in three areas: monitoring ongoing activity, planning ahead, and motivating library faculty to excel both inside and outside the confines of the library organization. All three of these objectives can be achieved, but their success hinges not only on the format and style discussed above, but also on the timing of the evaluation process compared to the rest of the academic schedule.

Monitoring

The academic library, to a greater extent than some kinds of institutions, makes a very heavy commitment to people. A large percentage of management time (and, by the committee process, of all faculty members' time) is spent in the process of judging, selecting, training and reviewing library personnel. For a university library, much of this effort is directed toward bringing each librarian into the ranks of the tenured faculty to ensure a continuing and productive working relationship.

On some campuses, it will be six or seven years before the final determination is made; during that time the library has made a heavy investment in time and money. It is therefore vitally important that everyone in the personnel chain, from the beginning librarian up to senior administration, be kept informed as to what progress is being made and what problems are being encountered. In this respect, the performance evaluation program acts as an early warning system, indicating both the strengths and weaknesses of junior librarians, showing where they may have wandered from what the institution considers the most valid path toward tenure, as well as where they have shown potential not previously recognized. For the senior member of the faculty, a regular performance evaluation may turn up evidence of a new professional interest which may be explored to the mutual advantage of both the librarian and the library; it may also point up the beginning of frustration, boredom, or restlessness before they turn to bitterness and resentment.

For librarians and libraries to profit from the evaluation process, it should not be a one-way communication, but should allow librarians to express their view of the individual library and vice versa. Too often, however, while the communication takes place in both directions, it happens on a one shot-basis only:

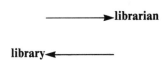

The librarian and the institution trade impressions briefly and formally, and then the paperwork is filed away and forgotten until the same time next year.

Ideally, the communication should be a continuous loop, providing constant feedback between librarian and library so that both may build on the discoveries and decisions of the past. It is when this occurs that the best kind of planning is possible.

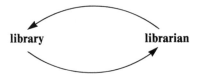

Planning

"Best," in this instance, assumes that a high degree of employee participation is desirable. By integrating planning with performance evaluation, the library can keep its staff informed and involved on many levels, from whatever formal five- or ten-year planning documents may exist for the library and the campus as a whole, to next year's budget and how it will affect library services.

Some degree of planning can be built into the evaluation process regardless of the style of the organization, be it top-down management where plans are handed down already finalized, or participatory management where the staff joins with the administration in discussions. Regardless of the context, most librarians find it easier to work when they know what is expected of them and what to expect from the organization, and why. The library which keeps everyone well informed of future plans so that staff can see where they fit into the overall scheme will have a more energetic and enthusiastic workforce than if the staff feels they "never know what is going on."

Similarly, the library administration needs and deserves to know about the plans of its faculty. By discussing the future as well as the past during performance review, a total picture can be formed of where library faculty members want to go next, and where they think the library should be heading. One of the most cogent reasons for looking ahead is purely practical: many projects require funding which must be requested well in advance of the desired date. If librarians are to be judged on their ability to meet stated goals and objectives, it is part of the library's responsibility to assist in providing the necessary backing. This is one of the advantages of PPBS over simpler forms of management by objectives, since it forces early discussion of resources needed as well as of tasks to be performed.

We should therefore insert a planning component into the evaluation feedback cycle, since planning is also a continuous process which builds constantly on the past while looking to the future.

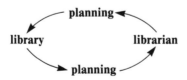

Thus far, the performance evaluation program has been seen as a useful tool for giving and receiving information, and for planning ahead, provided that the library faculty know what they need to achieve and are anxious to get on with it. What about the librarians who feel no desire to excel, but only want to "get by"—what, if anything, can the performance evaluation do for them?

Motivation

By now almost everyone is familiar with Maslow's hierarchy of needs, which theorizes that human needs can be classified into a sort of pyramid form, starting with basic needs at the bottom, and ascending to higher needs at the top, such that any one person is driven by the most basic need on the pyramid until that need is filled, after which the next need takes over as the driving force.[11] From the bottom up, the needs are physiological (food, shelter), followed by safety (protection, security), belonging (acceptance, friendship), esteem (from self and others), and finally, at the top of the pyramid, the need for self-actualization and fulfillment. The theory which evolved from this description of needs is that the only form of motivation which will work on any given person is the one which is aimed at his proper need level, neither higher nor lower. Thus, librarians who see themselves as badly underpaid may be willing to take uninteresting jobs for the sake of a good salary (financial security), but tenured librarians working at an acceptable salary may "turn off" because they find themselves unable to progress to more challenging work.

At the top of the pyramid, there may be a wide variation in what is necessary for self-fulfillment from one person to another. David McClelland's achievement motivation theory holds that while everyone has some need for achievement, some individuals have a much higher need than others, and in differing areas, which McClelland classifies as need for achievement, need for power, and need for affiliation.[12] Ascertaining which area is most appealing to employees, and on what level, can be extremely difficult, since they may not have any awareness of what is motivating them.

Another view of motivation which approaches from a different tack is called expectancy theory, because it hinges on the expectations of the individual worker. According to this theory, two conditions must exist in order for workers to be motivated: they must perceive a likelihood that effort on their part will result in successful performance (effort-performance linkage), and they must perceive a likelihood that successful performance will result in a desired reward. Rewards are divided into two types: intrinsic rewards which are related to the nature of the work itself (e.g., challenging, interesting), and extrinsic rewards which relate to general working conditions (e.g., salary, environment). To some extent, the extrinsic factors of expectancy theory parallel the lower need levels of Maslow's hierarchy, while the intrinsic factors relate more closely to the upper levels.

The common factor which runs through almost all writings on motivation is that it takes more than money to keep a worker going. Libraries abound with possibilities for enhancing output based on these theories, from personal gratification over helping a patron, to meeting the challenge of opening a branch despite a minimal collection and an even more minimal staff. Performance evaluation can be used, not only as an opportunity for positive reinforcement on achievements, but also to discuss possibilities for the future, to suggest new avenues for exploration, and new dimensions for the library and the individual. All of this, however, requires time, and while it may be one of the most important activities performed in the library, it may also be the most difficult to fit into the schedule and the most tempting to push aside.

Timing

While there is no one, "ideal" time to schedule performance evaluations, some general guidelines do exist. First, it has been frequently stated that performance evaluation and salary review should not be handled simultaneously.[13] It is difficult to have an open discussion of performance without the presence of defensiveness or hostility. When the question of salary is tied directly to the same discussion, it becomes virtually impossible.

Another complicating factor is that less experienced members of the staff may need more frequent reviews and consultations, perhaps even quarterly, while more senior members need at most an annual review. There is some question as to whether senior librarians need to be reviewed at all. It could be argued, however, that it is only a matter of common courtesy for each librarian to have a regular opportunity to engage in formal, two-way communication with the library management, however good the informal communications may appear.

A third factor, almost as time-consuming as the review process, is the annual report. In many libraries, shortly after the termination of the fiscal year or calendar year, each faculty member prepares a report outlining the accomplishments of the past year. This report is passed on to a department head, and so on through the section head, the unit head, and ultimately to the library director who reports in turn to the president of the university or one of his/her senior officials. The time from the beginning of the individual librarians' reports to the final submission of the report for the entire library system may be six months. Meanwhile, all normal activities are carried on, regardless of the contents of the reports.

Many librarians feel that the annual report should be used as the planning tool in which each librarian spells out the goals for the year ahead. There are some problems with this approach. First, some library faculty hesitate to commit themselves on paper without being able to gauge the reaction to their ideas. Many also feel that too detailed an outline of the coming year may limit their flexibility should a really interesting project pop up unexpectedly. There are even a few who deliberately aim low in their reports because of a fear of failure should they announce an overly ambitious plan of action. One other problem is that less than one year ahead is simply not enough time for planning where budgets and resources are concerned.

The ideal schedule, then, would fit the writing of the annual report, the salary review, and the performance review into a continuous cycle of dialogue between library and librarian.

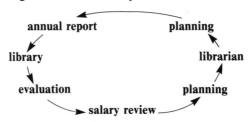

CONCLUSION

There is no perfect method of performance evaluation, and many pitfalls await the library which practices it in any form. In the long run, however, the planning and communicating which are necessitated by a good evaluation program are well worth the effort. They reduce uncertainty for both the organization and the individual, to the betterment of both.

REFERENCES

1. Ernest R. DeProspo, "Personnel Evaluation as an Impetus to Growth," *Library Trends* 20 (July 1971): 61.

2. Dimity S. Berkner, "Library Staff Development through Performance Appraisal," *College and Research Libraries* 40 (July 1979): 335ff.

3. James D. Thompson, *Organizations in Action,* (New York: McGraw-Hill, 1967), p. 159.

4. Marion G. Haynes, "Developing an Appraisal Program," *Personnel Journal* 57 (January 1978): 14ff.

5. Douglas McGregor, "An Uneasy Look at Performance Appraisal," *Harvard Business Review* 50 (May–June 1957): 89ff.

6. E.C. Keil, *Performance Appraisal and the Manager,* (New York: Lebham-Friedman, 1977), p. 4.

7. Sterling H. Schoen, *Supervision: the Management of Organizational Resources,* (Englewood Cliffs, NJ: Prentice Hall, 1979).

8. Schoen, p. 175ff.

9. Berkner, p. 337.

10. Martin J. Gannon, *Management: an Organizational Perspective,* (Boston: Little, Brown, 1977), p. 126.

11. Abraham H. Maslow, "A Theory of Human Motivation," *Psychological Review* 50 (1943): 370ff.

12. Gannon, p. 200.

13. Robert C. Hilton, "Performance Evaluation of Library Personnel," *Special Libraries* 69 (November 1978): 431.

Appraising Appraisal

Let's Put Appraisal Back in Performance Appraisal: Part I

by J. Peter Graves

A distinction must be made between performance appraisals and discussions about performance.

Maybe it sounds funny to suggest that we need to put appraisal back in performance appraisal. But, in fact, over the last 20 years, we have seen a systematic trend away from appraisal in performance appraisal.

In most articles, seminars and advertisements on the subject, performance appraisal is described as something that a manager "conducts," like a meeting. The focus is usually on the way to "conduct an appraisal" in a manner that is forward-looking, motivating, encouraging, and so on. Great emphasis is placed on the manager's interpersonal and counseling skills, such as active listening, empathy and openness. Further, it is universally suggested that such "appraisals" be conducted more frequently than once a year—preferably on an ongoing basis.

All this attention on the interaction between manager and subordinate on performance issues is fine, but it is not performance appraisal. What is needed is a clear distinction between performance appraisal and discussions about performance. "Appraisal" is defined by Webster's as "to judge the quality or worth of." Performance appraisal is a judgmental process of evaluating the performance of another. If and when the appraiser chooses to share the evaluation with the person evaluated, then we have a performance discussion or a feedback session.

J. Peter Graves is president, Strategic Decision Data, Inc., Redlands, CA. "Let's Put Appraisal Back in Performance Appraisal: Part I," by J. Peter Graves, copyright November, 1982. Reprinted with permission of *Personnel Journal,* Costa Mesa, California. All rights reserved.

DISCUSSION AND DOUBLETALK

Most of the current interest under the topic of performance appraisal is really about the performance discussion—its timing, frequency, content, the role of the manager and subordinate, etc. The effect of this interest and attention has been twofold. The first effect is that we now know how to much better conduct such a discussion, and practitioners are developing innovative programs for training managers in talking about performance with their subordinates.

The second result, however, is that far less attention is being placed on the appraisal process itself. In some instances, the process of evaluating performance is viewed as incompatible or inconsistent with good performance discussions. Since our understanding of the effective performance discussion is of relatively recent origin, compared with evaluation techniques, it is sometimes even assumed that frequent discussion is the new way to do appraisals, while rankings, ratings and forms represent the old way to appraise performance.

Some organizations, in their eagerness to appear to be up-to-date on the issue of performance appraisal, will avow that, "We only use performance appraisals for development in our organization," or "We don't rank or compare people around here." These kinds of statements ignore a fact of organizational life—organizations will always comparatively evaluate the performance of their members. Said another way, organizations will always rate the performance of their members from good to poor, and compare performance from better to worse.

Whenever the organization makes a personnel decision—a promotion, transfer, layoff, merit increase or demotion—a comparative, evaluative decision has been made. Since decisions are seldom made without information, one wonders where the data are coming from in organizations that only use appraisals "for development."

Our current infatuation with the performance discussion is causing increasing disparity between what organizations are doing about performance appraisals and what they say they are doing. To be sure, there is nothing out of the ordinary in discrepancies of this sort, except that in this particular situation, it can get the organization in trouble.

FEDERAL GUIDELINES ARE CLEAR

The principle reason for reconsidering the appraisal now is that the EEOC's uniform guidelines on selection and testing view performance appraisals to be as much a test as the paper-and-pencil variety. Organizations today must be able to defend the basis for personnel decisions. The weight of proving that a decision is job-related and not unfairly biased rests squarely on the performance data that are used.

Because of the attention being focused on personnel actions by EEOC concerns, the rules of the game have changed. Organizations can no longer afford the luxury of an appraisal process that is merely compatible with their climate and management philosophy. When required, an organization must also be able to retrace the entire decision process that resulted in a promotion, layoff or other such action. For decisions like these, that benefit some and not others (these are called zero-sum situations), managers need comparative data. Such information clearly identifies the high and low performers on the important criteria. Appraisals must demonstrably comply with the federal guidelines in two important respects: reliability and validity.

BUT IS IT RELIABLE?

Personnel specialists are adept at throwing about the words "reliability and validity" as if they were roughly synonomous—like "fuel economy and estimated highway mileage" when describing an automobile. But these appraisal words are not the same because they describe two very different aspects of evaluation or appraisal. To continue the automobile analogy, they are about as similar as "good fuel economy" and "impressive to the folks in Toledo." One is a characteristic of the automobile, the other of the setting in which it is used. The same is true of the reliability and validity of performance appraisal. Reliability is a characteristic of the method being used to gather data. The validity of a system is not a property of the method used, but of the setting in which it is used.

While there are many technical definitions of reliability, an easy way to judge the reliability of any evaluation is to answer a few simple questions, like the following:

1) Would you expect the ratings to be the same whether they were going to be used in feedback sessions or kept for confidential management use?

2) Would you expect the evaluations to look the same whether performed by a "Theory X" task-oriented rater, or a "Theory Y" people-oriented rater?

3) Would you expect the ratings to look the same whether performed by a manager trained in evaluation or one untrained?

4) Would you expect the ratings to be the same whether the appraisal was performed on Monday morning or Wednesday afternoon?

If you can answer "yes" to such questions, then the evaluations are reliable. If you have to answer "no"—that is, if situational factors, rater differences, or the confidentiality of the data can affect the ratings themselves—then the rating process is not very reliable.

THOSE VALIDITY ISSUES

Note that we haven't said anything about which criteria to use for evaluation, who should evaluate, nor how frequent the evaluations should be conducted. These issues all relate to the validity of an evaluation. These validity issues are currently very popular topics in articles and seminars on performance appraisal. We seem to know all the right questions to ask about validity, but we don't know when to ask them. Validity issues are meaningless without reliability, because an appraisal process must first be reliable before it can be valid. But reliability does not guarantee validity either.

For years we have been accustomed to questioning the reliability and validity of tests and measurements because psychologists have been producing generalized aptitude and intelligence tests with reliability and validity built in. Even today, tests designed for the general population, such as college entrance exams, must demonstrate both reliability and validity. But appraisal validity is job-related, and a valid appraisal is one that measures the right criteria to determine performance.

Since the issuance of the EEOC guidelines, it has become clear that only in the rarest instances can the validity of a general test or battery suffice for job-related validity in the legal sense. Job-relatedness also means situation specific, so no appraisal can be said to be validated unless reference is made to some specific job situation. What all this means is that an organization must be prepared to demonstrate that its appraisal system is reliable and valid for each job.

NONCOMPARATIVE METHODS

At first glance, there appear to be many alternative methodologies for appraisals. But as each one is considered in light of the requirements for legal and meaningful appraisal, the number of realistic alternatives narrows considerably. As each technique is discussed, the focus will be not on how to use them, but rather on their strengths and weaknesses relating to reliability and validity. Following customary practice, the various approaches will be considered in two categories: noncomparative or comparative. (Comparative methods will be discussed in the next article in this book, Part II.)

Noncomparative methods are so called because they consider the performance of an individual with little or no reference to the performance of others. In most cases, these procedures evaluate an individual's performance with reference to job requirements, job standards or negotiated expectations. Some approaches described in this section are not appraisal methods at all, but are included simply because the lore of contemporary performance appraisal usually includes them.

MANAGEMENT BY OBJECTIVES

Management by Objectives (MBO) was suggested by Douglas McGregor as an alternative to traditional appraisal. After 25 years of attempting to substitute MBO for appraisal, however, most organizations still view performance appraisal uneasily. It is not that MBO has failed, it is that MBO simply is not performance appraisal.

The many features of MBO have received exhaustive attention elsewhere, but a few points are distinct advantages pertaining to performance appraisal. First, it is a powerful means of clarifying job requirements and documenting those shared expectations. These documents then serve as the logical starting point for a later review of performance. Regardless of whether the philosophy of MBO is ever fully integrated in the organization, the process of systemizing previously informal expectations is a tremendous addition to discussions about performance. For this reason, MBO has been a favorite among the proponents of the performance discussion.

MBO is not appraisal because it is not evaluative. Nor is it intended to be; it is contrary to the philosophy of MBO for individuals to be compared or evaluated. The accomplishment of a stated objective is no more than that—just an accomplished objective. Before the accomplishment can be useful for management decision making, the accomplishment must be evaluated or appraised.

We are all familiar with the difficulty of trying to compare a challenging objective almost attained to the overattainment of an easy objective. The resolution of such a situation is a judgmental one. Such judgments must always follow MBO so managers will have the information they need for making decisions. That MBO itself provides none of this necessary information is its major weakness as an appraisal method.

CRITICAL INCIDENTS

Some organizations make a practice of recording in detail specific instances of on-the-job performance for later review. If done properly, the critical incidents are recorded and discussed descriptively rather than evaluatively.

Because it is not evaluative, and describes specific actions and behaviors, the critical incident method is a powerful support to the performance discussion. The manager and subordinate are then able to discuss the actual behaviors the subordinate engaged in when faced with problem situations. By discussing the critical incidents descriptively, the potential for defensiveness and disagreement is greatly reduced. Unlike Management by Objectives, the critical incidents are retrospective only, and provide little or no stimulus for discussing future performance.

While the critical incident approach provides the basis for a good performance discussion, somebody ultimately has to determine whether the subordinate performed effectively or not. If decisions on salary or promotion are pending, someone has to determine whether the subordinate performed better or worse than others. So another appraisal is necessary to translate the critical incidents into usable data for decision making.

In a very real sense, the MBO and critical incidents methods are just formalized means of documenting performance expectations and outcomes, rather than appraisals. This documentation is invaluable when discussing performance, but is inadequate when making and defending comparative decisions.

NARRATIVE APPRAISAL

Narrative appraisal is the first approach that can realistically be considered an appraisal, because it is evaluative as well as descriptive. The appraiser writes a narrative description of the individual's performance, using specific incidents where necessary, but also containing adjectives like "excellent," "unsatisfactory" and so on.

As mentioned above, critical incidents and objectives must first be evaluated before becoming useful for decision making. But, because the narrative appraisal is evaluative, it may, by itself, form the basis for noncomparative decisions. For example, if an individual must be terminated because of poor performance, a narrative appraisal may provide the necessary basis for the decision.

Compared to more structured methods to be described below, the narrative appraisal is much more flexible for the appraisers. Generally, they are free to write as much or as little as they desire. Given that appraiser attitude toward the appraisal process can be an important factor in the quality of results, this flexibility is an important asset.

One disadvantage is that the evaluative words in the narrative appraisal take on tremendous meaning to those who read the appraisal. Unfortunately, the real meaning of such adjectives is usually not available within a single narrative appraisal. An engineer who believed he was getting reasonably good performance reviews suddenly found himself caught in a 5% reduction in force. It turned out that the phrase he had been seeing in his appraisals—"quite good"—was just about the worst that the engineers in his organization were ever told about their performance.

Like many others, the engineer simply didn't understand how easily a code can develop among appraisers. The code words are much like the "giant," "economy" and "family" designations that food manufacturers use in their packaging. As long as you know the code, or can see the different sizes lined up together, each adjective has real and consistent meaning. Lacking such comparison, however, the reader understandably believes exactly what he reads.

To the extent that no serious action needs to be taken, many managers see nothing wrong in all this. With a bit of contorted logic, they can even persuade themselves that it is helpful to the subordinate. "What would happen," they reason, "if these lower performers were to learn where they really stand? It would be so demoralizing that it would render them useless."

While written narrative adds the evaluative dimension, it provides no comparative information. A termination for poor performance, mentioned earlier, is a noncomparative decision. But, if a person must be laid off because of budget cutbacks, we have a very different situation. Even though the same individual may be involved in each case, the layoff decision is a comparative one because the poor performer must be shown to be the poorest performer. For decisions that require a knowledge of who has performed better than others, more information than is provided by the narrative appraisal must somehow be obtained.

RATING SCALES

By far the most widely used appraisal method is the rating scale. Judgments about performance are recorded on a graphic scale, usually consisting of five to seven points, from low to high.

Sometimes, adjectives are used to define each scale point, such as: outstanding, very good, satisfactory, marginal or unsatisfactory. The scales are generally used for more than one dimension or criterion of performance. Thus, an appraisal form may have many different scales to complete, each representing a different facet of job-related performance.

These scales are easy to construct and score, easy to understand, and require minimal time for appraisers to complete. Because rating scales can be used with multiple criteria, instead of a single, global evaluation, the appraisal can be more carefully matched to the job description.

The principle weakness of the rating scale is its unreliability. Because it is simple and straightforward, raters check any point on the scale they wish. While this should mean that the evaluation will be sensitive and meaningful, it can also mean some or all of the following:

1) All persons could be rated outstanding when they really are not.
2) Raters can give higher ratings when they know that ratees will be shown the appraisals. (Research has shown this to be almost universally the case.)
3) A harsh rater can rate everyone lower than an average or lenient rater would.
4) If a salary decision has already been made, the ratings can easily be made to justify the salary action.

THE CONTROL GAME

This list of possibilities can go on and on. There is an equally long list of controls to prevent them from happening. Some organizations, to prevent all ratees from being rated high, establish minimum and maximum percentages for the number of ratings in each category. They may, for example, allow only 5% in the outstanding category, or require at least 2% in the bottom category. That would be fine, unless you had only 1% outstanding. Another 4% would be rated higher to fill a quota. Or what if you had a highly qualified group with 10% who are really outstanding? Such a rule would permit only half of the best performers to be accurately rated. This cure can be worse than the disease.

To overcome leniency and central tendency errors, some organizations have elaborate rater-training programs. Sometimes appraisals are required to be completed and filed before salary discussions begin, to prevent the decision from driving the appraisal.

The above are all examples of the way organizations typically try to control the lack of reliability inherent in the rating scale technique. But notice that they are all external controls—none of them are modifications of the rating scale itself to increase reliability. They add an expensive and burdensome mechanism to the administration of the rating process. All of the benefits of a simple, straightforward process would be eaten up by the control mechanisms; and you still wouldn't know if your efforts had improved the reliability, you could only hope they had.

BEHAVIORALLY ANCHORED RATING SCALES

The behaviorally anchored rating scales (BARS) is an approach to the rating scale that attempts to address some of the reliability problems mentioned above, but from the inside of the appraisal process—rather than with an external rule or constraint. The BARS uses the rating scale, but instead of adjectives at each scale point, behavioral anchors related to the criterion being measured are used. Figure 1 is an example of a BARS used to measure "perseverance" in a computer programmer's job.

By using observable behaviors instead of adjectives, the meaning of each point on the scale is clarified. The raters don't need to imagine what outstanding performance is—they can see an actual example in the behavioral anchor. BARS is also a boon to the performance discussion. Because behaviors are much easier to discuss than adjectives, the performance discussion can deal with specific activities that need attention.

FIGURE 1. Behaviorally Anchored Rating Scale (BARS)

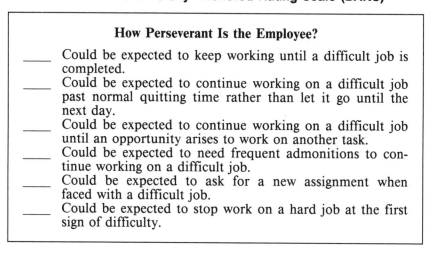

How Perseverant Is the Employee?

____ Could be expected to keep working until a difficult job is completed.

____ Could be expected to continue working on a difficult job past normal quitting time rather than let it go until the next day.

____ Could be expected to continue working on a difficult job until an opportunity arises to work on another task.

____ Could be expected to need frequent admonitions to continue working on a difficult job.

____ Could be expected to ask for a new assignment when faced with a difficult job.

____ Could be expected to stop work on a hard job at the first sign of difficulty.

The most glaring disadvantage of the BARS is the time and resources needed to develop meaningful behavioral anchors. After a careful job analysis has identified the dimensions of a job that should be evaluated, a complete set of behavioral anchors must be written for each dimension (and five to 10 dimensions for a single job are not uncommon). This task cannot be accomplished without the participation of the most important people—the high performing job incumbents and their managers. Also, since the job analysis performed for one job is not valid for another, the entire process must be repeated for every single job.

A ROSE IS A ROSE?

Even if the organization can muster the resources to develop the behavioral anchors, they quickly encounter a more disturbing problem. Some performance dimensions, they discover, cannot be reduced to specific behaviors. This is especially true with professional or managerial positions, where the exercise of judgment and discretion is required.

Suppose, for example, that a job analysis identified "evaluating the performance of subordinates" as an important dimension of a supervisors's job. It is hard to imagine what the behavioral anchors for this dimension might look like. "Evaluating" is a cognitive, judgmental task, not an observable behavior. (Note, again, that we are not talking about conducting a performance discussion.)

This dilemma is even more likely to occur as you move up the ladder of responsibility to senior managers and top professionals. The logic for this is unavoidable: If we could reduce the contribution of these valuable people to a set of behaviors, the task of executive and professional development could likewise be reduced to merely training a set of behaviors. Such is obviously not the case.

But there is an even more fundamental disadvantage. The argument that behaviors are better than adjectives is a strong one, but only if the behaviors are actually observed. Because it cannot be assumed that the person being appraised has exhibited one of the behaviors described in the anchors, they are frequently written not as behaviors, but in the form, "Could be expected to . . ." If no such behavior has ever been seen, then the raters are recording their expectations about behaviors that might occur if conditions were right. It can hardly be argued that guesses about possible behaviors are any more reliable than adjectives about past performance.

Despite these weaknesses of the behaviorally anchored rating scale method, it is a strong favorite among personnel professionals and writers on the subject.

REFERENCES

Guion, R.M. *Personnel Testing* (New York: Mc-Graw-Hill, 1965).

Kingstrom, Paul O., and Allen R. Bass. "A critical analysis of studies comparing behaviorally anchored rating scales (BARS) and other rating formats." *Personnel Psychology*. Vol. 34 (1981), pp. 263–289.

McGregor, Douglas. "An Uneasy Look at Performance Appraisal." *Harvard Business Review* (May–June 1957), pp. 89–94.

"Uniform Guidelines on Employee Selection Procedures." *Federal Register*. Vol. 43. No. 166 (Aug. 25, 1982).

Let's Put Appraisal Back in Performance Appraisal: Part II

by J. Peter Graves

Arguments for a comparative approach are simple and powerful.

Last month [see previous article], Part I of this article discussed performance methods that examine or evaluate performance with no direct reference to the performance of other individuals. Instead, evaluations are made with reference to objectives, or performance standards, or desired behaviors. Part II will examine methods of appraisal that compare the performance of one person to the performance of another.

Arguments for a comparative approach are simple and powerful. The simple part of it is that organizations do it anyway, all the time. Whenever personnel decisions are made, the performance of the individuals being considered is ranked and compared. People are not promoted because they achieve their objectives, but rather because they achieve their objectives *better* than others. Most personnel decisions are zero-sum in nature and do not involve just a single person. A single person may be promoted, but others are considered and not promoted. It is also clear from court tests of appraisal systems that evidence for not promoting a person is just as important as the evidence to promote.

To make these comparative decisions, managers need comparative data on performance, which they will get from the formal appraisal system or somewhere else. Even in organizations that roundly proclaim that ranking and comparisons destroy teamwork and self-esteem, the managers will have all the comparative data they need to make personnel decisions. We'd like to hope (and so would the federal government) that the comparative evaluations used by these organizations are reliable and valid, but they are more likely to be informal and undocumented.

If the formal appraisal system fails to provide managers with the data they need, they will use informal methods. The real question is not whether the organization rates or ranks the performance of its members, but whether they will be open and explicit—or obscure and subtle—about the methods and criteria used. The real irony is that organizations that enthusiastically embrace MBO-type "appraisals," because they are "developmental," are only pushing the comparative appraisals into the smoke-filled rooms and the informal bull sessions.

The second reason (the powerful one) for using comparative as opposed to noncomparative methods is that they are far more reliable. This is because reliability is controlled by the rating process itself, not by rules, policies, and other external constraints. If an appraiser using a noncomparative method wishes to avoid controversy, or lies, or misunderstands the instructions, or simply can't think straight, this will all affect the appraisal, but there is no way to know that this is happening.

If comparative methods are used, some or even all of these sources of unreliability can be completely controlled. The comparative approach simply requires raters to make remarks about one person's performance that are consistent with what they are saying about another's.

COMPARATIVE RANKING

Ranking is the most widely used method of comparative evaluation. All individuals in a given category are ranked from highest to lowest based on their performance. Such an evaluation can be done by a single individual, but is usually done by a group of raters.

One advantage is that ranking is obviously a simple and straightforward procedure. It takes little formal instruction and capitalizes on the natural tendency to rank individual performance from highest to lowest. The direct result is exactly the type of comparative data needed for personnel decision making. No extrapolation or intermediate calculations are necessary to arrive at a consistent picture of relative performance. (As we shall see, this gives rise to a major weakness, too.) The only limitation on the numbers of individuals who can be ranked is simply the number of individuals supervised by the rater.

Because ranking directly produces the complete comparative picture, it can be manipulated very easily. If a rater wants a ratee to look different than his or her performance actually warrants, the rater need only move the ratee's name up or down the ranking. When more than a single rater is used, this manipulation often takes the form of social or political pressure as the raters assemble their judgments into a consensus.

Another weakness is that it is usually possible to use only a single, global criterion of performance. This raises serious validity questions because it reduces performance to a single index. Job analyses, on the other hand, almost always identify multiple dimensions of performance.

Another disadvantage is that ranking order data reveal little about the intervals between the individuals listed in the ranking. Can you realistically assume that everyone is equally spaced from the highest performers to the lowest? It is often surprising, and not a little unsettling, what compensation specialists do with simple, rank-order data. Percentiles are quickly calculated and quartile groups are delineated as if the difference between persons seven and eight were exactly the same as between 21 and 22.

Serious problems can also result when rankings are combined. Frequently, rankings from small groups are combined into departmental rankings, which may be further combined with other departments. (Even if this is not done explicitly, changing rank data into percentiles and then equating percentile scores achieves exactly the same thing.) There are no acceptable means to do this without making unwarranted assumptions about the performance of various groups. There are obvious political overtones as well, when rankings are merged across organizational boundaries. Conscious manipulation of ranking data is commonplace, for example, when departments jockey for shares of a limited salary increase pool.

PAIRED COMPARISONS

With this method, the rater compares the performance of a pair of individuals. The rater's task is to choose the individual whose performance is better on a particular quality or dimension. Every possible combination of everyone being rated is presented to the rater. The relative position of the ratees in the final ranking is determined by the number of times one individual is preferred over another.

The principle advantage of the paired comparison over the straight ranking is that the consistency of the raters' judgments will be visible. For example, when a rater says that Person A's performance is better than Person B's, B is better than C. When the rater adds that C is better than A, the rater is doing more than recording a preference; the rater is also documenting an inconsistency. The practical value of this process is that the paired comparison is far more difficult to manipulate. This is especially the case as the number of ratees increases. Most raters quickly realize that being honest and candid is the safest way to maintain the consistency of their decisions with the paired comparison.

Another advantage of the paired comparison is that every comparison between ratees is actually made. Pairwise decisions are implied by the straight ranking method, but, in practice, those in the middle of a rank order often do not receive the attention given those on the top and bottom. The paired comparison assures equal attention to all ratees and increases the overall reliability of the evaluations.

A main disadvantage involves the number of ratees included. As the number of ratees increases, the number of possible pairs increases very fast. With 10 ratees, the rater is faced with 45 pairs, but with 20 ratees, the combinations jump to 190. At 30 ratees, not by any means an unusual size group to be evaluated, a rater would have to complete 435 pairs. The unreliability caused by fatigue and boredom would quickly erase any benefits of using the paired comparison.

Another weakness surfaces when the pairings are scored. While the paired comparison can be effectively used with multiple raters, every rater must know and evaluate each ratee to avoid a serious flaw in the way the paired comparisons are scored. When raters are only able to evaluate a subset of the total ratees, the scoring procedure is biased toward the better-known ratees. Well-known, above-average ratees are ranked higher than less well-known peers of equal performance. Well-known, below-average ratees are ranked lower than their less well-known equals. This bias toward notoriety is an artifact of the scoring procedure for the paired comparison, and is not "washed out" with a large sample of sizes.

The forced-choice nature of the paired comparison does not allow for an "equals" decision. The rater is forced to choose one or the other, even when the two appear equal in the rater's mind. Further, the rater has no way of recording the degree of difference between ratees. Sometimes there will be large differences in the performance of the two ratees; other times there will be slight, but meaningful differences. With the paired comparison, the rater will have an either-or choice. Because of this inflexibility, the final ranking will only show ordinal position, and will provide no information on the differences between individual performances. Thus, paired comparisons will suffer the same weaknesses mentioned earlier about the intervals in the straight ranking method.

THE SCALED COMPARISON

The scaled comparison is an entirely new methodology for appraisal. Also known under the commercial name of the Objective Judgment Quotient (OJQ), the scaled comparison has been in use for more than 10 years in the public and private sectors. The scaled comparison represents the first really new technology in evaluation since the introduction of the Likert-type scales more than 40 years ago.

Like the paired comparison, the scaled comparison requires the rater to compare the performance of two individuals on a certain criterion. But there the similarity ends because moderate differences can be noted on the rating form used for this method. For instance, if the rater thought A's performance was much better than B's, the space on the rating form nearest A's name would be checked. If B's performance was seen as much better than A's, then the space nearest B's name would be checked. If they were seen as equal, a middle space would be checked. Moderate differences could be indicated with the intermediate spaces.

Unlike other comparative methods, the scaled comparison is not limited to a single global criterion of effectiveness. Every important dimension of a job can be separately measured and weighed if some criteria are more important than others; a one-to-one match between the job analysis and the appraisal can be made.

Another advantage is that because multiple criteria are usually employed, the ratings will not result in a single number. This makes it possible to speak of strengths and weaknesses in performance instead of a position in a one-dimensional rank order. Also, the scaled comparison is not restricted by large numbers as is the paired comparison. Groups as large as 2,800 individuals have been evaluated at the same time without the process becoming burdensome to raters.

The scaled comparison does not require that one rater know all or even most of the individuals to be evaluated. Many raters, each familiar with but a subset of the total group of ratees, may participate. All of the evaluations from the various raters are combined into a consensus that shows the relative position of all ratees. Small groups of ratees are combined computationally into larger groups without the difficult, and often political, merging of rankings across divisions or departments.

In addition, the scaled comparison uses multiple raters. This is viewed as an advantage, but it can also be a disadvantage as well. Multiple raters are required because the scaled comparison is a means of consensual data gathering. Thus, the result is not the opinion of a single rater, but rather is the consensus of five to 10 raters who know the individual being evaluated.

The consensus also offers greater control over bias and manipulation than even the paired comparison. As mentioned earlier, the paired comparison allows the evaluation of the raters' decisions by "comparing them to themselves"—that is, by seeing whether raters are being logically consistent from one decision to the next. In addition, the scaled comparison allows the comparison of an individual rater's judgments to the consensus, to see how that rater's views differ from those of the other raters. This represents increased control over appraisal manipulation, and, more importantly, it permits the discovery of unique viewpoints at the same time that a consensus is obtained.

Finally, the scoring of the scaled comparison does not just result in a rank order on each criterion. Rather, the data show intervals between ratees as well as rank position. If two ratees were judged to be equal by the raters, they would appear equal in the results. If the highest performer were "head and shoulders" above the second best, the scaled comparison would preserve that perceived difference. The practical value of interval data over ordinal (rank) data is that they reflect the real distribution of performance—whether normal (bell-shaped), skewed, flat, or bimodal.

SOME DISADVANTAGES

While mentioned above as an advantage, the requirement for multiple raters may also be a disadvantage. In organizations in which the immediate supervisor has traditionally been the only appraiser, management might feel that nobody else knows as much about an individual's performance. Except under unusual circumstances, this is rarely the case. What is very likely, however, is that managers in this situation may be reluctant to share the job of evaluation with others. In the case of the scaled comparison, this reluctance is often softened as the raters begin to appreciate its control over manipulation and bias. But many organizations simply may not have the climate that permits multiple raters under any condition.

Another disadvantage is that the scaled comparison is not an appraisal "system"—it is just a data-gathering process. The organization using it must build the system around it, from the job analysis, which identifies the evaluation criteria, all the way to the performance discussion that logically follows the appraisal. Such a total system is a requirement for any valid appraisal, but it may come more neatly packaged with some methods discussed earlier.

Finally, management may not want strong comparative data about performance. Some organizations have definite, though probably unstated, policies that certain personnel decisions are to be made without respect to measured performance. Such unwritten expectations often apply to relatives of key executives, protected EEO groups, and situations where seniority counts more than performance. A valid, nonmanipulable appraisal method would simply get in the way, constraining managers to act contrary to their real intentions. While this might not be an attractive picture of organizational decision making, it is reality in many organizations.

PERFORMANCE APPRAISAL AND THE PERFORMANCE DISCUSSION

Is the scaled comparison just a new tool for managers to get what they need from appraisals? If employees are uncomfortable finding out where they stand in a simple rank order, do they like it any better knowing the gaps between themselves and their co-workers? Does the scaled comparison really make it easier to talk to employees about their performance?

Much attention has been paid to the employee reaction to knowing where they stand relative to their peers. Blame for the apparent negative reaction has unfortunately been placed on the appraisal method, with the reasoning that using a noncomparative method would avoid the negative reaction. But it is not that simple, for we know that every organization uses some comparative process, either formally or informally. The real problem lies with the validity of the performance data and how those data are presented to employees.

It is important, first of all, to realize that negative reactions to appraisals do not just come from those being evaluated. Appraisers are cynical about their own methods, too, and are just as uncomfortable about defending the results as appraisees are about hearing them. It was this discomfort that McGregor said causes a manager to feel he is "playing God" with appraisals.

Experienced managers know that most appraisal methods work like the old shell game. Every appraiser, and most appraisees, knows that there is neither trick nor magic to making the pea appear under the right shell. Unless raters really enjoy such games, the forms and procedures quickly become a burden. Part of this burden is due to imperfect methodologies, as I have already discussed. But a significant part is due to basic differences in the reasons for performing appraisals.

In many respects, the reasons management needs performance appraisal are incompatible with why the individual employee needs it. Managers need (and the law now encourages) comparative performance data for making comparative decisions—decisions that are zero-sum in nature. Managers need these data in a form that clearly identifies the high, medium, and low performers.

WHAT THE EMPLOYEE NEEDS

The individual, however, needs nothing of the sort. In fact, Thompson and Dalton have shown that when comparative or ranking data are too obvious, or "too public," it negatively affects the morale of all, even those at the top of the list. The emphasis here is not on whether the ranking information is known, but the degree of public knowledge about performance. (Some information, of course, will always be available by simply noting who gets promoted, let go, and so on.)

It is wrong to assume that the problem is that someone used a zero-sum appraisal method. That is analogous to saying that the reason you had an automobile accident is that you got out of bed that morning. Sure, you could have avoided the accident by not getting up. But you can't avoid getting out of bed any more than organizations can avoid comparing the performance of their employees. On the other hand, organizations can avoid mishandling the sensitive performance data they collect.

The individual employee needs information about his or her performance that clearly and realistically identifies strengths and weaknesses. In addition to being a review of past performance, the data should also stimulate a dialogue between manager and subordinate that looks forward to the next appraisal period, with an eye to growth and development.

But we know that if the review doesn't go well, the discussion of future performance won't go at all. And the review seldom goes well if the appraisal process is unreliable or invalid. Since most appraisal methods are both, it is not surprising that Meyer, Kay and French suggest that *two* discussions take place—one to review past performance and the other to consider future plans. Still others have suggested that past performance plays no role at all in a performance discussion; only future goals and objectives are important. These "solutions," however, simply create two separate processes—one for decision making and one for performance discussions.

ONE GOOD SYSTEM

We don't need two systems; we need one appraisal process that provides believable information about performance. So believable, in fact, that during the discussion, no time at all is spent asking who (did this to me), where (did these data come from), why (do we have to do this at all), how (were the results calculated) or when (can I talk to my lawyer). The only question ought to be, "How do those who know me on the job view my performance in all the different areas of my responsibility?"

Answering this question does not require that the individual be shown a ranking of his or her peer group. That would have the "too obvious" effect mentioned earlier, and would be demoralizing for even high performers. What is needed is a clear and credible statement of strengths and areas for needed improvement, not a single number or a bunch of numbers. And, at the same time, the confidentiality of everybody else's appraisals must be guarded. If the review of past performance meets these conditions, the discussion will smoothly lead to the next question, "Where do we go from here?"

A good comparative appraisal method can fill both management's need for performance data and the individual's need for meaningful performance feedback. Such is hardly the case even with the best of the noncomparative approaches. The scaled comparison represents a means of bridging the gap between comparative appraisals and the performance discussion in three ways:

1) The data can't be manipulated.
2) The data reflect a consensus rather than a single viewpoint.
3) The data measure all the meaningful criteria.
4) The data are also the same appraisal that management uses for decision making.

For many of the above reasons, the scaled comparison has been received favorably by collective bargaining units, and some employee groups have requested that management use it for their appraisals. When the scaled comparison is used, much of the skepticism surrounding the appraisal process begins to dissipate.

For their part, managers responsible for appraisals favor the scaled comparison for the following reasons:

1) It can't be manipulated by raters to force a desired outcome.
2) It achieves a consensus without political pressure.
3) It permits rating of the raters on appraisal ability.
4) It provides them with data for decision making and performance feedback.
5) It doesn't require consultants or specialists.

As a result, the managers feel less like they are "playing God" when they appraise their employees. They also begin to view the appraisal as a powerful and essential tool, rather than a burdensome requirement.

REFERENCES

McGregor, Douglas. "An Uneasy Look at Performance Appraisal," *Harvard Business Review* (May–June 1957), pp. 89–94.

Meyer, H.H., E. Kay, and J.R.P. French. "Split Roles in Performance Appraisal," *Harvard Business Review* (Jan.–Feb. 1965), pp. 125–129.

Thompson, Paul H., and Gene W. Dalton. "Performance Appraisal: Managers Beware," *Harvard Business Review* (Jan.–Feb. 1970), pp. 149–157.

Appraising the Performance Appraisal

Are they for judging performance, developing personnel—or both?

Consulting psychologist Harry Levinson tells the story of the newly appointed executive who was told to get a floundering division into the black. This he accomplished with alacrity, only to find himself passed over for promotion because top management felt that his managerial style had been too high-handed. The problem, Levinson says, was that the executive expected to be judged on results, while his superiors judged him on the means by which those results were achieved.

Levinson's story may be apocryphal, but it illustrates one of the major problems plaguing human resources specialists: how to get the mixed signals out of performance appraisal. Although few experts say that appraisal systems should ignore whether specific job goals are achieved, most are wrestling with ways to assure that performance appraisal does more than simply determine salaries. They want a system that will pinpoint specific managerial behavior that should be reinforced or discontinued, serve as a personnel development tool, provide realistic assessment of an employee's potential for advancement, and—a particularly hot issue in the 1980s—stand up in court as a valid defense in discrimination suits.

Finding expertise. Developing such systems is no easy task. "We've struggled with performance appraisal more than with any other process in the company," says Bill N. Rutherford, human resources vice-president for Sun Co. Selig M. Danzig, program manager for human resources systems development at General Electric Co., wonders whether "looking for a truly effective system is the same as pursuing the Holy Grail." Many companies are seeking expert help to get their systems on the right track. "Over the last three years I've done nearly 70 [assignments to set up] performance appraisals, where

I used to do no more than six a year," notes Daniel E. Lupton, a principal at Towers, Perrin, Forster & Crosby Inc.

The experts agree only on what a performance appraisal should not be. Last July industrial psychologists had a field day mocking the White House's much publicized, abortive attempt to evaluate its staff. The White House instructed evaluators to rate subordinates numerically on such nebulous traits as stability and brightness. The critics regarded this as so subjective and weighted toward personality as to be useless at best, and damaging at worst. The White House appraisal form did leave some space to list the individual's major strengths and weaknesses, but it in no way encouraged programs to improve performance.

While the experts agree that the White House system placed personnel theory back into the 19th century, there is no unanimity over what constitutes 20th century state of the art.

- Donald G. Carlson, vice-president at Booz, Allen & Hamilton Inc., says that "it is inane to think that performance appraisal should not be linked to salary," while Donald W. Jurgensen, director of personnel and industrial relations at Dover Corp.'s Elevator Div., says that he "encourages people to separate salary discussions from appraisal."

- Sun's Rutherford believes a valid appraisal "should be done by an objective third party," while GE's Danzig insists that "the data are resounding—the immediate manager is the most appropriate person to do the appraisal."

- Consultant Levinson believes that behaviorally anchored appraisal systems—particularly those using the critical incident method, which asks supervisors to record examples of employee behavior as they occur—are the only effective systems. But George Chinnici, marketing administrative manager at William H. Rohrer Inc., claims that "if you give an employee specific, achievable objectives he'll [automatically] change his behavior to meet the objectives."

Nearly every current research study focuses on methods to judge behavior rather than results. Although companies complain that the critical incident concept casts the supervisor in the role of spy, a few have found it a valid tool to create a broader behavioral system. Corning Glass Works recently used the technique to pinpoint behavior that should be included in its performance appraisal form. The result was a 76-point form on which managers rate subordinates on such items as whether they object to ideas before they are explained or whether they involve their own subordinates in decision-making.

Such systems are costly to devise, however. Even consultants who tout behavioral appraisals over result-oriented systems admit that the costs are prohibitive unless the performance appraisal program covers a vast number of people. "It could cost as much as $3,000 to develop a behaviorally anchored system for a job category," notes Marvin Rafal, head of Personnel Measurement Systems Inc., a New York consulting firm. "If it's a job with lots of people—such as an entire sales force—it makes sense. But it's silly to do it for, say, 12 forklift operators."

Training evaluators. Even when development cost is not a major objection, training supervisors to appraise behavior intelligently can be difficult. Corning had to send 3,800 managers to two-day seminars just to get its system in place. Some psychologists question whether training to appraise job performance is even possible. GE's Danzig recently engineered an in-house survey in which managers discussed their experiences appraising a particular subordinate, and the same subordinate discussed what it felt like to be appraised. Danzig wound up with more than 3,000 responses that shot down the myth that formally-trained managers made better appraisers. "Subordinates didn't recognize any difference in the way managers held meetings," he insists.

Robert S. Atkin, an assistant professor at Carnegie Mellon University's Graduate School of Industrial Administration, came up with similar results when he recently surveyed attitudes toward appraisal at a large Pittsburgh company. "Everyone felt he had the interpersonal skills necessary to do a good appraisal and that his boss didn't," Atkin recalls. "Most people still come out of a performance review reasonably convinced that their boss doesn't know what they do."

A number of human resource specialists see that perception as a valid one, and they are trying to build dual evaluation into their systems. TPF&C's Lupton encourages his clients to ask the evaluator's supervisor to provide a second opinion on each appraisal. In true "physician-heal-thyself" fashion, he has introduced a second-level review concept into TPF&C's own appraisal system. "Supervisors were not spending enough time on appraisal, and our old [single-evaluator] system didn't compensate for differences among appraisers," he explains.

Wider involvement. To Sun's Rutherford, simply adding one more opinion does not go nearly far enough. To obtain a performance appraisal on one select group of executives, he sounded out their subordinates, peers, and bosses. "Performance appraisal is really about telling people how they are perceived," he maintains, adding that the immediate superior's view of the subordinate's work and image is often too narrow. Rutherford hopes to create a similar comprehensive appraisal program for approximately 200 high-level Sun executives by the end of this year. He believes it will take much longer than that for the system to filter down to lower levels.

Not surprisingly, few companies are as ambitious as Sun or GE in developing new approaches to appraisal. But quite a few are looking to hybrid systems that are neither overly costly to develop nor difficult to administer. These would include more than simple checklists of personality traits for supervisors to rattle off, and combine the best of both job-result and behavioral appraisals.

By far the most common are the type of goal-setting and review systems that Rohrer's Chinnici espouses. As recently as three years ago, Rohrer rated employees as either outstanding, satisfactory, or marginal, and nitpicked over such issues as whether they came to work on time. "We didn't get into what the real expectations were," he says.

Similarly, V.N. Anderson, sales vice-president for E.R. Squibb & Sons Inc., introduced a goal-based system for his sales force in April. "Our performance reviews had always been historic," he explains. "Now we're looking to the future, making the appraisal system provide employees with tools to help them perform better." For example, if a sales representative's over-the-counter drug sales are low, the appraisal process would establish a quota of in-store presentations for him or encourage him to meet six new store clerks each month.

Evaluating appraisers. Such systems put a large part of the developmental onus on the appraising manager, of course. The manager is motivated, proponents of the goal systems say, by the realization that his superior's appraisal of his own performance will take into account how well he or she evaluates and develops his [or her] own staff. At Dover Corp.'s Elevator Div., appraisers are expected to list the most important tasks their subordinates perform and evaluate how well they do them, describe strengths and weaknesses in relative detail, and lay out specific agendas to improve performance in the employee's current job and prepare him or her for promotion. It is a formidable task, but personnel director Jurgensen notes, "The form evaluates the appraiser as well as the appraisee." Jurgensen's staff reviews more than 400 appraisals each year, and the company's president looks at close to 100. "Supervisors know they are 'graded' on the appraisals, and it makes them think and express themselves in ways that are almost competitive," Jurgensen says.

One factor favoring the goal-setting appraisal technique is that its own objectives are built in. Many attempts at appraisal bog down, psychologists say, when the system developers are not quite sure what they want to accomplish. "A good part of the problem with existing systems," notes Booz's Carlson, "is that people don't know why they're doing them—whether it is to make compensation decisions, to do succession planning, career planning, or instant promotion decisions." GE's Danzig states it another way: "The appraisal process can be improved significantly if you decide whether it is there to satisfy the manager's needs or the subordinate's. You can't ask a manager to be a judge and mentor at the same time." He notes that an appraisal system geared to career development should probably give the subordinate an opportunity to participate in filling out his or her own appraisal form. An appraisal designed essentially for salary increases can be conducted solely by the supervisor without the employee's participation.

The blank sheet. The perfect appraisal system has not been developed, largely because no one yet knows how to factor out human error. The behavioral systems run the risk of a "halo effect"—supervisors basing a summary judgment on one or two dramatic quirks or habits of the employee. Goal-oriented systems often ignore external factors—for example, a windfall order that helps a salesman exceed a quota or adverse economic conditions that prevent him from fulfilling a quota. Even the much-maligned checklist systems, in which employees are rated on specific traits, run the risk that supervisors may feel they must give all their subordinates high ratings.

Perhaps Arthur W. Alexander, vice-president and director of personnel at Schlumberger Ltd., sums up the problems best. He and the company's chief operating officer have made a big point of discussing the importance of performance appraisal at general management meetings, and the systems used in his company seem to have an enviable mix of concrete goals and behavioral evaluations. "We've tried to whittle away at the third-grade report-card evaluation of 'works and plays well with others,' but we still do not have the best forms," he says. "The best form would be a blank sheet of paper."

Appraising the Performance of Performance Appraisal

by Derick W. Brinkerhoff and Rosabeth Moss Kanter

This article provides a critical examination of formal performance appraisal systems in organizations. It argues that the role, effectiveness, and validity of appraisal data are limited by a number of organizational factors: the purposes of the appraisal (both avowed and covert), the characteristics of the tasks for which the appraisal is performed, and the location in the structure of the organization of both appraisers and appraisees. The authors conclude that data from formal performance appraisal systems should never be utilized alone and uncritically, without full consideration of the context in which the appraisal is being performed and used. Ed.

All organizations, whether in the private, public, or nonprofit sectors, face the problem of engaging the energies of their members in the task of reaching their goals. Solving this problem requires that organizations devise means to influence and channel the behaviors of their members, correcting deviations and rewarding competent performance. Performance evaluations and appraisals constitute one of the major tools employed in the organization *control* process.[1]

Since the connection between individuals and organizations is not static, and people may move into and out of or through a sequence of positions as the need arises, organizations also face the problem of deciding whom to assign to roles and then justifying those decisions to the people affected and to others. Thus, some kind of

Derick W. Brinkerhoff is a consultant and graduate degree candidate at Harvard University, Cambridge, MA. Rosabeth Moss Kanter is a professor at Yale University, New Haven, CT. Their article, "Appraising the Performance of Performance Appraisal," is reprinted from *Sloan Management Review* 21 (3) (Spring 1980): 3–16, by permission of the publisher. Copyright © 1980 by the Sloan Management Review Association. All rights reserved.

appraisal of performance is also a critical element in *human resource allocation* and management.

The notion of appraising individual performance against predetermined standards for the purpose of sanction or job allocation is an undeniable part of the nature of bureaucracy itself—that is, of modern, complex, formal organizations. Bureaucracy, as Weber posited the ideal type, replaces a diffuse relationship where people are subject to the arbitrary whims of authorities with a specific, contractual bond where demands are clearly laid out and objective standards developed for testing compliance with those demands. Thus, at the same time that performance appraisal of some kind is a tool in organizational control and decision making, it can also be seen as a way of rationalizing and clarifying the employment relationship and protecting the individual from arbitrary discipline or the effects of nonperformance-based favoritism. But appraising performance is also nonbureaucratic in that it assumes that individuals do not automatically pass through a series of graded career steps without review.

We find it natural, then, that profit-making organizations are the leaders in the development of formal performance appraisal systems. In the private sector, control and resource allocation issues are paramount; the employment contract is highly rationalized; and except in some unionized jobs, promotion is not formally automatic but is the result (supposedly) of deliberate decision making. But recent public interest in personnel allocation decisions (e.g., EEO and other employee rights and concerns) has also led to pressure on all organizations to rationalize their employment relationships and to objectify the sanctioning and allocation process. Increasingly the private, governmental, and nonprofit worlds face the same pressures for productivity, accountability, rationalized human resource allocation, and EEO compliance, and thus, we can predict a growth in the use of formal systems of performance appraisal modeled on the private sector's experience.

Just as the term "organizational performance" subsumes a wide diversity of concepts and activities, so does performance appraisal. Evaluations range from official, prescribed meetings between an evaluator and evaluatee to casual, chance occasions where an evaluator observes work activities and indicates his or her assessment with an informal comment. While informal, random appraisals are important parts of organizational life, we will restrict our discussion to the more formalized end of the evaluation spectrum.

Despite the obvious need for formal systems of performance appraisal and the rapid rate of their adoption, there has been relatively little critical examination of what we know about their effectiveness and their limitations. This article surfaces the major factors that have an impact upon the appraisal process. It becomes clear through our analysis that the more a system of performance appraisal is asked to do, the less satisfactory the results are. It is also clear that

PA works best for some kinds of roles and positions and not as well for others, raising the issue of whether one can completely substitute formal procedures for other kinds of human judgment. Finally, we conclude that knowledge of a number of key organizational factors is necessary.

Organizational reality is a dense fabric of technical, social, and psychological threads woven together in interlocking patterns. The PA process, as a part of that reality, cannot be properly understood if separated from those patterns. Thus, we must look at them and at their importance for performance appraisal. We identify three critical factors influencing performance appraisal: purpose, task characteristics, and organizational structure.

PURPOSE

Just as investigating issues of organizational effectiveness requires delving into questions of "effectiveness of what?"—so too must we ask "performance appraisal for what?" Clutterbuck singles out decisions regarding purpose as the most important factor in designing a PA system, because the stated purpose for which performance evaluations are used influences appraisal outcomes.[2]

Basically, performance appraisal has served two purposes: the first is evaluation (as the term "appraisal" implies), and the second is developmental.[3] The evaluative function of PA refers to assessment of the extent to which progress toward goals, which we can define as desirable end states, has been furthered by the appraisee's efforts. This purpose of PA is fundamentally backward (or historically) oriented; past performance is reviewed in light of results achieved. PA for evaluation has traditionally served as the basis for allocating promotions, transfers, and salary increases. This can also turn into allocating terminations, as when one large company decided to reduce its work force several years ago. Its PA system required managers to "grade on a curve," giving out only so many 1 ratings (the highest), 2 ratings, 3 ratings (acceptable), and so forth. The 4s and 5s were immediately terminated. Then managers were asked to break down their 3-rated employees into three categories, and the company cut the lowest-rated group.[4]

PA is intended to enable organizations not only to make decisions about individuals but also to compare candidates on some apparently "objective" basis. It responds to the need for documentation in the case of firings as well as justifications in the case of promotions, so that regulatory agents, employees, and other members or constituents will perceive the organization as "fair." For the reasons discussed below, however, the achievement of objectivity and fairness in practice has proved elusive.

PA's developmental function is forward-looking, aimed at increasing the capacity of organization members to be more productive, effective, efficient, and/or satisfied in the future. For developmental purposes PA facilitates appraisee improvement in relevant job skills, career planning, employee motivation, and effective coaching and information exchange between managers and subordinates. These developmental aspects of PA have been positively linked to employee effectiveness.[5]

When used developmentally, performance appraisal generally involves the following elements: (a) separate assessments by the manager and the subordinate; (b) a face-to-face discussion of these assessments, often with a third party (such as a personnel officer) present to mediate and offer an outside view; (c) a chance for the subordinate to declare his or her interest in other jobs or training programs via self-nomination processes formally included in PA; (d) an action plan or "contract" between manager and subordinate about further steps to develop the subordinate; and (e) in large corporations, increasingly, collection of data about worker skills and career goals in a central information bank. Note that developmental PAs require by their very nature that managerial ratings be shared with employees and that information is relatively open and accessible so that, in some cases, employees can even argue for a different rating. But there is no necessity that evaluative PAs be known by employees, and some organizations do keep this information secret.

A certain amount of overlap exists between these two purposes, as the following examples demonstrate. Organizations with a sales function often use PA systems to provide comparative standings, like batting averages, that form the basis of future targets for individual members of the salesforce. This function of PA is backward-looking in the sense of evaluating past performance so as to establish standards, and yet at the same time is forward-looking to the extent that these standings are intended to serve as incentives for future performance improvement through generating peer competition as well as the desire to beat one's own past record.

Another example of the melding of these two purposes is the use of PA as a means to identify potential problems before they become serious. This "remedial education" function entails reviewing past performance in order to detect signs of future difficulties that could result in lowered performance later on. PA here is basically a monitoring device that makes sure that employees know what they are accountable for, clarifies problem areas, and assures mutual understanding of responsibilities. Thus, when an organization wants to change the behavior of its employees or introduce a new set of procedures, it can simultaneously communicate this to employees and underline the importance by including the areas as items on formal performance appraisals. Some companies have recently done this in the equal employment opportunity (EEO) area, including performance related to EEO compliance in every managerial or supervisory performance appraisal.

There is an additional overlapping but also overarching purpose for PA beyond the measurement of individual performance and potential: to ensure that *managers* are performing a critical managerial function by making certain that they are paying close attention to defined aspects of subordinates' work. Thus, a formal system of performance appraisal is also a control tool with respect to managers to indicate their accountability for the behavior and effectiveness of their employees. In some companies performance appraisal data from particular work groups are scrutinized by higher-level management as an indication of how well the supervisors of those work groups are carrying out *their* functions. Too many low ratings (or sometimes, too many high ratings) can be viewed as evidence of inadequate supervisory behavior. The former points to a manager who may be too hard on his or her subordinates, while the latter suggests one who may be excessively lax in applying company standards.

The importance of attending to purpose becomes clear when we look at the results of research on the use of PA for the two functions. Historically, PA systems have emphasized the evaluative function. With the trend in management theory toward attention to human relations, participation, and job satisfaction, appraisal systems have incorporated more and more of the developmental functions into the PA process. This has resulted in confusion over what PA is supposed to do—evaluate performance or improve it.[6]

It is clear that when a company uses PA to make termination decisions, whatever developmental thrust the system is intended to have is lost, and both managers and subordinates will do whatever they can to defeat the stated goals and protect their own territories and jobs. Thus, it is not surprising that a classic study by Meyer, Kay, and French found that combining the two purposes in one appraisal led to nonfulfillment of the intended developmental functions of the PA process.[7] Based on their findings, they recommended: (1) separating evaluation and salary administration issues from efforts to improve performance, (2) involving employees in setting specific performance targets, (3) increasing coaching activities, and (4) avoiding negative criticism.

A striking example of the impact of purpose on performance appraisal results is found in an experiment carried out in an educational setting.[8] Six different groups of performance evaluators rated the same professor on teaching effectiveness. Three of the groups were informed beforehand that the instructor was to be rewarded—either promoted, offered tenure, or given a salary increase. The other three groups were told that he was to be punished—put on probation, laid off, or immediately dismissed. The experiment found that the evaluators generally rated the instructor contrary to the stated purposes of the appraisal. When told that the purpose was to determine whether the instructor should be rewarded, they gave him a poor rating, apparently to keep him from receiving the reward or because those receiving rewards must be seen as highly deserving. Conversely, when the stated purpose was to determine whether the instructor deserved punishment, the raters gave him a higher evaluation in order to prevent punishment. Thus, some people will invoke high standards when there is no cost and when rewards must be deserved but will behave protectively of others, lowering their standards when the others are threatened. The experimenter concluded that a single performance evaluation should not be used for different purposes, and recommended the use of multiple appraisals. It is clear that good data for developmental purposes will not be generated when the punishment potential of evaluation is also present.

The study by Meyer et al. examined the effects of PA purpose on ratees; Gallagher's study investigated the effects of purpose on raters. While correct in their attention to the split roles PA plays in organizations, both of these studies, and others like them, fail to take into account the impact of task and organizational variables on the PA process. They also focus on technical and social psychological issues in designing a PA system and ignore a number of larger political issues. Depending on who gets the data and what state the system is in at the moment, a supposedly neutral, "rational," "objective" tool, intended in part to protect and reward, can, once in place, be used to threaten or punish.[9] Therefore, efforts to act upon the findings of these studies and implement their suggestions have tended to create evaluative appraisals, technically "accurate" and cloaked in developmental rhetoric, which do little to motivate performance and much to breed cynicism on the part of evaluators and evaluatees alike.

Furthermore, because the narrow focus in much of the literature concentrates attention upon the individual ratee, the rater, and the rating instrument, the wider system-justifying purpose of PA has been glossed over. The need to justify organizational decisions is an important source of impetus behind PA. Demonstrating that judgments made by the organization are logical, objective, and fair can be a crucial factor in employer-employee relations. This is certainly a critical part of union contracts, and it is also an impetus behind a variety of drives for employee rights which would include giving access to PA data by allowing employees to examine their own personnel files.[10] In the current environment with heightened pressures for equal employment opportunity (EEO) and affirmative action (AA) in all sectors, PA's justificatory function has become increasingly significant.[11] This function of PA provides documentation for hiring, promotion, and firing decisions; legal protection from discrimination suits; and proof of fairness in compliance with regulations. Yet, it is still not clear that the data from formal performance appraisals serve as the true basis for promotion and salary decisions in all cases nor that PA processes themselves are always objective and fair.[12] The point is the *appearance* of fair procedure rather than the *proof* of it.

Thus, the confusion about purpose does not center only on whether PA is to evaluate employee performance or improve it. Besides these individual-level concerns, PA also is called upon to fulfill the system-level purpose of justifying organizational personnel decisions. It is little wonder that organizational PA systems, torn among three potentially conflicting purposes, have sometimes been viewed by those in organizations with a combination of disillusionment, distrust, and derision.

TASK CHARACTERISTICS

Three characteristics of tasks have strong impact on the PA process: complexity, clarity, and predictability.

Complexity

Dornbusch and Scott note that "the more complex the task, the more complex is the evaluation process required. If the task entails many activities and there are numerous properties of interest in connection with the activities or outcome, then the process of arriving at a valid and reliable performance evaluation is likely to be complicated."[13] For this reason, the most technically accurate evaluations have generally been limited to jobs with relatively simple content and for which there are unambiguous measures.

One approach to dealing with task complexity is to apply job analysis techniques. Job analysis breaks a job into component parts, eliminates redundancy of measurement through the use of factor analysis, and develops a rating scale. Morse and Wagner used this technique to develop a means to evaluate managerial effectiveness.[14] They listed 106 item statements describing specific managerial behavior and activities based on interview data. Through pilot testing and factor analysis the list was reduced to a 51-item measurement instrument that was clustered around six functional categories: (1) managing organizational resources, (2) organizing and coordinating, (3) information handling, (4) providing for growth and development, (5) motivating and conflict handling, and (6) strategic problem solving.

Overall, however, organizations that go to such lengths to develop scientifically based evaluation systems for complex and high-level jobs number in the minority. More common is the practice of using assessments of an individual's past accomplishments (e.g., degrees held, previous employment) as an indicator of future performance, coupled with the use of some standard appraisal format in order to justify salary decisions. The current productivity climate, however, may mean renewed efforts to develop measures for complex tasks. This is likely to be the case in the federal government in the wake of the Civil Service Reform Act.[15]

Clarity

Another characteristic of tasks that influences the PA process is knowledge and/or agreement on what is to be done: that is, clarity concerning task goals. Tasks with specific, clear-cut objectives upon which organization members and their relevant constituencies can agree lend themselves to operationalization and measurement that form the basis for relatively straightforward evaluation of performance.

However, tasks characterized by diffuse goals pose problems for performance appraisal. Such goals provide little help in determining what to measure and/or what standards of evaluation to employ. Because of their vague qualities, conflicts and disagreements become commonplace.

The situation that arises in organizations seeking to achieve diffuse and vaguely stated goals is the familiar one of goal displacement. For organization members, the tasks for which they are evaluated become the goals. Thus, for example, the task of the policeman becomes the achievement of high arrest rates; that of the employment agency worker, high job placement rates; or that of the college professor, extensive publication records.[16]

The implications of this task characteristic for performance appraisal can be compared to a self-fulfilling prophecy. Whether or not the PA truly represents an organization's tasks, over time those that it does represent will in fact become its tasks. Dornbusch and Scott sum up this problem by noting that "when organizational objectives are diffuse, a rigid, quantitative approach to evaluation may create as many serious problems for goal attainment as a lax procedure in which few serious attempts are made to evaluate the contributions of participants."[17]

Predictability

Predictability is particularly relevant for evaluations based on outcomes. In the case of predictable tasks, the relationships between quality of performance and amount and/or quality of outcome are relatively constant. Typing a letter, filing reports, or sorting fruit are all examples of predictable tasks where examination of outcomes provides a fairly accurate picture of performance.

Unpredictable tasks, on the other hand, do not allow accurate assessments of performance on the basis of outcomes. Such tasks are common in areas where knowledge of cause and effect relations is incomplete and where appropriate standards for assessing performance are ambiguous.[18] Indeed, Kanter has argued that as uncertainty in a job increases (e.g., difficulties of measuring results, time lag between action and results), so does the tendency to fall back on social characteristics in deciding who should occupy these jobs.[19] There is far less reliance on nonperformance characteristics where tasks are more highly routinized and can be broken down into component elements and analyzed. Thus, it is precisely the *difficulty* of doing objective appraisals of performance in high uncertainty areas (such as new tasks, risky ventures, and higher-level management strategic decisions) that results in the appearance of bias through reliance on subjective factors, such as trust and social similarity or historical factors unrelated to current performance (such as appropriate prior experience). Demonstrating the difficulty of setting standards in high uncertainty jobs, the president of one major corporation reputedly wrote down as the performance standard for his job: "The Chairman thinks I am doing a good job." Since uncertainty tends to rise with organizational "heights," it is precisely at the most "exclusive" levels of organizations that PA cannot help reduce "exclusion"—i.e., selection of people on subjective grounds. It is also at the most critical direction-setting levels that PA cannot help increase control and accountability.

In high uncertainty areas it is also difficult to attribute outcomes to single acts because of the complex relations among a number of potential causal factors. An obvious example comes from the medical profession. Observing two healthy patients following treatment by different doctors gives little indication of the doctors' performances. A variety of elements external to the quality of the doctors' performance could have had an impact on outcomes—e.g., the specific diseases involved, the prior health of the patients, the physical facilities available, the quality of nursing staff, the extent to which the patients followed the doctors' orders. In fact, studies of outcomes for patients in hospitals have attributed most of the variance to institutional characteristics rather than the skill of physicians, but physicians still often take the credit.[20]

In the case of unpredictable tasks, assessment of performance has often taken the form of evaluation of procedures, with attention paid to "due process." Establishment of due process in such cases is usually accomplished by setting standards based on the activities of other, comparable organizations.[21] Organization members engaged in unpredictable tasks but subject to demands for accountability have generally responded by attempting to gain control over the standard-setting process, as is evidenced by the efforts of professional associations (such as the AMA) to resist third-party evaluations and by the rise in white-collar and professional unionization.[22]

ORGANIZATIONAL STRUCTURE

Because the PA process is not an independent, isolated set of activities but is structurally linked to a variety of other features and processes of the organization, it is important to consider some of these structural characteristics. This section examines five organizational features that have a direct impact on performance appraisal systems: task interdependence, observability of task performance, the structuring of the authority system, power differentials, and the nature of communicated appraisals.

Task Interdependence

Complex organizations are composed of functionally specialized units whose activities and outputs combine to achieve some common goal. Though members of these units have responsibility for specific tasks, at some point these tasks reach an interface with either those of other members of the same unit or those of other units. Task interdependence characterizes this interface.

Despite the fact that most people familiar with organizations would readily admit that many work tasks are interdependent, there is a tacit assumption behind a majority of performance appraisals that the appraisee is the sole determinant of his or her performance. This is especially true of PA as applied within the Management by Objectives (MBO) framework.[23] As a result, the appraisee can be placed in the situation of being evaluated for performance over which he or she has little control. The following examples serve to illustrate: the R&D engineer whose design project is evaluated poorly when the production department failed to implement it properly, the waitress whose supervisor rates her slow in serving customers when the kitchen takes a long time in preparing food, or the foundation administrator who is criticized when a grantee fails to follow through on a proposal. Rarely do those engaged in PAs also appraise the *organization* and ask whether employees were given the tools or resources to get their jobs done.

Observability of Task Performance

Organizational arrangements and the nature of the task place limits on the extent to which performance can be observed. Some tasks are, by their nature, difficult to observe—for example, research. Others, though observable, take place under circumstances that make inspection difficult or extremely costly (e.g., school teachers isolated in their classrooms and salespersons or social workers in the field).

Even in situations where barriers to observability are slight, certain psychological considerations enter in. The sense of excessively close supervision inherent in highly visible task situations can actually be detrimental to performance.[24] People need to know that their *contributions* are recognized but not necessarily the processes by which they made them. In fact, most people tend to resist constant surveillance of their work activities, and sometimes protest such observations as in the recent case of the American Telephone and Telegraph Company employees who staged demonstrations against "over-supervision."[25]

Thus, it is important to differentiate between task and outcome. Some highly visible outcomes are the product of relatively unobservable tasks and vice versa. Therefore, depending on whether a given PA system focuses upon process or results, good or bad performance ratings for the same job become a possibility. This problem is further complicated when adding task interdependence to the equation as well. In addition, one could hypothesize that those doing highly observable tasks are more likely to be appraised (implicitly or explicitly) on such task criteria as reliability rather than outcome or results criteria because of measurement ease, resulting in a recurrent bureaucratic problem: focus on means, not ends.[26]

The sampling problems related to task observability have received some degree of attention in technical discussions of performance appraisal.[27] Foremost, perhaps, have been efforts to deal with the so-called "halo effect" and the "recency effect."[28] These terms refer respectively to: (1) the tendency of an evaluator to remember most clearly a worker's best performance, and (2) the tendency to recall his or her most recent performance.

The task visibility characteristic is also important to the criteria-setting component of PA. In the history of the use of appraisals, there has been a trend toward basing evaluation criteria more on observable behaviors than upon "invisible" personality traits, such as industriousness and dependability.[29] While this is an attempt to replace potentially biased subjective assessments with apparently objective criteria capable of predicting future performance, it raises a number of critical questions. To carry out such behaviorally based appraisals, tasks must be open to observation. But observation has the negative consequences identified above. And if people resist observation, it is a safe bet that high-power organization members have more capacity to do this than lower-power members. This is the case because: (a) high-power members tend to have jobs whose content is inherently less observable than many low-power members (e.g., managing versus making widgets); and (b) they tend to have more discretion over how, when, and where they work, making observation more difficult. So as with the uncertainty-predictability issue, higher-level managers are more easily insulated from PA, and even if it is carried out at those levels, it is not clear it has much impact.

The Structuring of the Authority System

The structure of the organizational authority system affects the PA process through its impact on who is involved in PA components. To the extent that different people, at different levels within the organization's hierarchy and possessed of varying degrees of authority, are responsible for allocating tasks, setting criteria, sampling performance, and evaluating, the probability of clear understanding of the PA system, satisfaction with the system, accuracy of appraisal, and smooth functioning is reduced.

A study by Borman examines one aspect of the influence of authority structure on PA: who has authority to set performance criteria.[30] He set up an experiment in which two groups devised performance criteria for, and evaluated performance in, the job of secretary. Secretaries made up one group, and their bosses, one level higher, composed the other group. Borman found that each group developed different job behavior dimensions for use in setting criteria. He also found that when the bosses evaluated secretarial performance using the criteria they had developed, inter-rater agreement was greater than when they used the criteria the secretaries had devised. The same pattern held when the secretaries became the raters, using first their own and then the bosses' performance criteria.

Power Differentials

Closely related to, but by no means necessarily contiguous with the impact of authority systems is the capacity of organizational power differentials to affect the workings of the PA process. We have already mentioned how the higher levels of management can be insulated from PA, and how in unions or professional associations, some organizational members, mainly professionals, have been able to gain control over the extent to which their work is subject to scrutiny. This control is a function of power rather than authority.

Kanter looks at the amount of power present in various job positions and examines its relationship to work orientation, supervisory style, and career advancement.[31] She defines power as possessing the access to information and resources needed to get things done—credibility and clout—rather than the ability to coerce someone into doing something. Her research shows that managers who are powerless tend to act in domineering, controlling, and often punishing ways. They tend to reward mediocrity rather than talent, because talent is too threatening. In addition, subordinates do not see them as desirable bosses. And other decision makers in the system may discount them, not trusting their judgments about their employees.

These findings have several implications for the PA process. Powerless raters are less likely to be able to use PA effectively for developmental purposes and may have a tendency to use it punitively. While most evaluators no longer look upon their role as "playing God" with their subordinates, no amount of human relations technique can change the fact that evaluations represent the exercise of power and authority by superiors over subordinates.[32] Subordinates will try to discover what kinds of performance "really" count (as opposed to what is said to count) and to direct their efforts accordingly.

In addition, while frequent appraisals enable employees to correct aspects of performance that may get them into trouble later, refusing to give accurate feedback to employees is a good way to hurt their career chances. Here bosses use their power in a prejudicial way. Kanter discovered in one company that the first women in the salesforce were often allowed to fail by the reluctance of their managers to give them critical feedback in a timely fashion so that they could learn. Instead some women never heard that there were any problems in their work until they were transferred out of sales.[33]

Finally, powerless raters, who tend to be rules-minded and see their own jobs in terms of "putting in time" rather than performance, are less likely to evaluate subordinates accurately. With their nit-picking approach to supervision, they lack the motivation to carry out the PA process with sufficient care to facilitate employee development.[34]

But power issues cut two ways, and supervisors may be made to feel powerless by resistant workers as well as by controlling managements.[35] Supervisors may be tempted, under such circumstances, to give higher performance ratings to employees just to keep the peace, or to fail to insist that all standards be met. After all, "holding back" or subtle foot-dragging is one form of negative power that even the lowest-echelon workers possess, and they can often make life miserable for their supervisors. The supervisors, in turn, may "bribe" them with higher performance ratings, thus allowing power dynamics to undermine the validity of the PA system.

For example, in the engine testing department of a large automobile manufacturing plant that we observed recently, industrial engineers had established performance targets for the number of engines to be tested. These targets, however, were never reached because informal work group norms, backed up by threats and physical harassment, kept potential "rate busters" in line. Thus, supervisors were never able to get workers to meet official standards, and, in turn, their management did not hold them accountable for lesser results. In practice then, much power was held by the workers, and no formal control system could make a difference, nor did these particular workers have to be "protected" from arbitrary authority.

The Nature of Communicated Appraisals

The final organizational feature with important consequences for PA is the nature of communication around evaluations. We can consider this in terms of "when," "how," and "what" dimensions.

The question of when to communicate appraisals to performers has been subject to a variety of answers. Frequently communicated evaluations are advocated as a means to (1) provide evaluatees with immediate and accurate feedback, (2) reduce the halo and recency effects that plague appraisal accuracy, (3) limit the level of concern and anxiety for appraisers because each evaluation would be one of many, and (4) reduce employee motivation to argue over a specific rating.[36]

On the other hand, frequent evaluations can be seen as indicative of excessively close supervision and can result in a stifling work climate where employees feel they have little discretion in their work. This can contribute to an atmosphere of powerlessness and to the negative organizational consequences that flow from such a situation.[37] Thus, it is clear that a balance needs to be struck between timely feedback and over-surveillance. One way of achieving this balance is to conduct frequent appraisals for new employees, and as they learn and grow they can be given more autonomy and less observation.

The "how" and "what" dimensions are closely related. These two have received perhaps more attention in the PA literature than anything else. Unfortunately, most of this literature treats these dimensions in narrow terms of technique and tends to ignore or gloss over the factors discussed in this article.

Of the components of the "how" dimension, few have been as widely discussed as the issue of ratee participation in the PA process. (All of the technical literature on PA assumes that employees will have some access to the data. However, we wish to note that this assumption may bear little relationship to the true picture in organizations, and it is not known how much appraisal data of a formal sort are kept secret.) Rater-ratee collaboration in setting the goals for appraisal is particularly central to PA systems based on MBO.[38] Greller states that the most important factor in conducting a successful appraisal interview is the creation of a sense of ownership by the appraisee.[39] This sense of ownership is generated through collaborative goal setting and PA communication oriented toward problem solving.

Besides participation, the other main component of the "how" dimension of PA is the communication style employed in the appraisal interview. The Meyer et al. study found that a critical approach to evaluation generated defensiveness in the appraisee and tended to result in lowered performance following the appraisal.[40] In response to this and similar findings, most PA interviews follow a joint problem-solving approach that downplays the evaluative aspects of the process.[41] This kind of approach provides for a balance between positive and negative feedback, a characteristic that Fletcher and Williams found important for effective appraisals in their study of British civil servants.[42]

Finally, the "how" issue also encompasses the matter of the communication vehicle and, thus, the ability of the manager or supervisor (the rater) to reflect honest views. The literature cited above tends to take for granted the face-to-face appraisal interview as a preferred form, just as it assumes ratee access. But the social psychology of organizational life suggests that the validity of data obtained when rater must confront (and be confronted by) the ratee may be suspect. In one large company, employee relations staff sometimes laughed at the appraisals they saw because they would often have independent information that an employee rated "outstanding" was constantly complained about by his manager. Similarly, Kanter identified the problem of the unwillingness of some male managers to criticize female subordinates to their face.[43] Furthermore, managers may also withhold negative judgments from employees when they know they must continue to "live with" those employees and count on their cooperation. So a variety of audience effects enter in and shape what finally is written on an appraisal form. For some purposes, then, anonymity may be preferable, sometimes on both sides, despite the "openness" tenet conveyed in much applied behavioral science literature today. But it is almost gratuitous to say this, because the direction of employee rights in organizations suggests a tendency toward more, rather than less, open access to personnel data and review of personnel decisions.

The "what" dimension of communicated evaluations covers a wide variety of components, the details of which extend beyond the scope of this article. Broadly, the following observations can be made. As noted above, assessments based on personality traits have been shown to be less effective than those that rate job-based behaviors.[44] Task-oriented appraisals are most successful in improving performance when they evaluate accomplishment in the light of specific, challenging goals; concentrate on behaviors that the appraisee can change and on outcomes over which he or she has control; and provide feedback that is neither completely positive nor overwhelmingly negative.[45]

ORGANIZATIONAL FACTORS IN PA

This discussion of the factors that influence performance appraisal has brought out the contingent nature of PA data. What emerges from a given PA system depends upon purpose, task features, and characteristics of organizational structure. Basically, PA data may tend to be unreliable or misleading for the organizational and social psychological issues just outlined. But the bulk of the appraisal literature, with its technical focus on scientifically developed rating instruments rationally applied, fails to confront the realities of practice that contribute to this unreliability.

The preceding sections lead us to the conclusion that PA systems and the data contained within them can take on a life of their own in organizations in the sense that they can affect organization members in unintended ways that are often beyond both the perceptions and control of their designers and operators. In practice, these systems are heavily influenced by "nonrational" human components of organizational life. Constrained by the characteristics of the job being done, shaped by perceptions of who gets the data and what they will do with them, and subject to multiple interpretations of intent, PA only remotely resembles an impartial tool in the service of rational organizing principles. Performance appraisal as a concept has its roots in the Weberian notion that a rational, rules-based explication of the employer-employee relationship frees employees from the potentially arbitrary whims of a superior and channels their performance in appropriate directions. Ironically, though, performance appraisal in practice may be limited by capricious dependencies, since technical discussions ignore the uncertainties and power dynamics that figure in organizational reality.

It is difficult for us to provide specific recommendations in this area, since our purpose is to reintroduce complexity into a system that has sometimes been treated too simplistically. However, let us suggest some general directions.

Data from formal performance measures tend to be most reliable when:

— The purpose of the appraisal is clear;
— Tasks are simple;
— Goals for the tasks are clear;
— Outcomes are predictable;
— Tasks are relatively independent;
— Task performance is observable;
— Criteria for performance are set by those later assessing performance;
— Appraisers feel secure in their own jobs and have no personal stake in hurting the performer.

This suggests that single measurement systems based on formal checklists and ratings by the supervisor should be confined only to those more routinized tasks in organizations that can meet these criteria. As uncertainty grows—or complexity, interdependence, power concerns, and/or multiple appraisal purposes grow—then so should the number of additional features and sources of data added to appraisal systems.

For example, when tasks are highly interdependent, add a series of ratings of the overall *work context* in which the person performs: adequacy of resources, cooperation from others, timely information from managers, etc. These context ratings should then be factored into the individual appraisal for all people in that setting.

When goals and objectives for the work are unclear, keep some aspects of the performance appraisal general and open-ended to provide room for nonmeasurable goals and to avoid redefining the job in terms of satisfying only quantifiable goals.

When power issues can affect the reliability of PA data, reduce dependency on a single rater and add additional third-party observers who are not personally involved in the situation and who have no stake in particular outcomes.

In short, we recommend that data from formal performance appraisal systems never be utilized alone and uncritically, without full consideration of the organizational context in which the appraisal is being performed and used. We also recommend that the purpose of a PA system be clear and focused with no hidden agendas, such as eventual terminations for those with low scores. The type of appraisal used—and the sources of data—should also be appropriate to the specific work setting. There is probably not "one best method" for the whole organization.

Furthermore, recognizing that people in higher-level positions can insulate themselves from PA more easily than those in lower-level positions, and can be insulated from evaluation by the low task observability and greater uncertainty of outcomes, we recommend that lower-level people be given more tools with which to protect themselves from unfair or punitive appraisals. Wherever possible, they should be measured less on directly observed performance than on achieved results. They should participate in setting the standards. And they should have recourse to a third-party hearing if the PA data appear "unfair."

Finally—and this is perhaps our most important recommendation—the impact of the PA process back on the people using it and subject to it should be examined before a PA system is implemented and periodically thereafter (a kind of "appraisal of appraisals") so that decision makers can continue to shape the process toward desired ends.

This paper was originally prepared for the Program on Non-Profit Organizations, Institution for Social and Policy Studies at Yale University.

REFERENCES

1. See V.R. Buzzotta and R.E. Lefton, "How Healthy Is Your Performance Appraisal System?" *Personnel Administrator* (August 1978): 48–54.

2. See D. Clutterbuck, "Helping Managers Improve Performance Appraisal," *International Management,* November 1976.

3. See W.J. Kearney, "Performance Appraisal: Which Way to Go?" *MSU Business Topics,* Winter 1977, pp. 58–64.

4. See also B.A. Stein, "Organizations in Trouble: Two Vignettes," in *Life in Organizations: Workplaces as People Experience Them,* ed. R.M. Kanter and B.A. Stein (New York: Basic Books, 1979).

5. See G.R. Oldham, "The Motivational Strategies Used by Supervisors: Relationships to Effectiveness Indicators," *Organizational Behavior and Human Performance,* February 1976, pp. 66–86.

6. See P.R. Kelly, "Reappraisal of Appraisals," *Harvard Business Review,* May-June 1958.

7. See H.H. Meyer, E. Kay, and J.R.P. French, Jr., "Split Roles in Performance Appraisal," *Harvard Business Review,* January-February 1965.

8. See M.C. Gallagher, "More Bias in Performance Evaluation?" *Personnel,* July-August 1978, pp. 35–48.

9. See Stein (1979).

10. See D.W. Ewing, *Freedom Inside the Organization: Bringing Civil Liberties to the Workplace* (New York: Dutton, 1977).

11. See: S.T. Beacham, "Managing Compensation and Performance Appraisal under the Age Act," *Management Review,* 1979, pp. 51–57; R.C. Ford and K.M. Jennings, "How to Make Performance Appraisal More Effective," *Personnel,* March-April 1977, pp. 51–57; D.B. Schneier, "The Impact of EEO Legislation on Performance Appraisals," *Personnel,* July-August 1978, pp. 24–35.

12. See R.M. Kanter, *Men and Women of the Corporation* (New York: Basic Books, 1977), p. 182.

13. See S.M. Dornbusch and R.W. Scott, *Evaluation and the Exercise of Authority* (San Francisco: Jossey-Bass, 1975), p. 145.

14. See J.J. Morse and F.R. Wagner, "Measuring the Process of Managerial Effectiveness," *Academy of Management Journal,* March 1978, pp. 23–35.

15. See J.M. Sugarman, "Observations on the Construction and Use of Performance Appraisal Systems" (Washington, DC: United States Office of Personnel Management, April 1979).

16. See: G.T. Marx, "Alternative Measures of Police Performance," in *Criminal Justice Research,* ed. E. Viant (Lexington, MA: D.C. Heath, 1976), pp. 179–193; P.M. Blau, *The Dynamics of Bureaucracy* (Chicago: University of Chicago Press, 1963); P.M. Blau, *The Organization of Academic Work* (New York: John Wiley & Sons, 1973).

17. See Dornbusch and Scott (1975), p. 148.

18. See J.D. Thompson, *Organizations in Action* (New York: McGraw-Hill, 1967).

19. See Kanter (1977).

20. See W. Richard Scott et al., "Organizational Effectiveness: Studying the Quality of Surgical Care in Hospitals," in *Environment and Organization,* ed. M. Meyer (San Francisco: Jossey-Bass, 1978).

21. See Thompson (1967).

22. See M.R. Yessian, "Delivering Services in a Rapidly Changing Public Sector," *American Behavioral Scientist* (July-August 1978): 829–859.

23. See M.L. McConkie, "A Clarification of the Goal Setting and Appraisal Processes in MBO," *Academy of Management Review,* January 1979, pp. 29–40.

24. See Kanter (1977).

25. "The Dissatisfaction at AT&T," *Business Week,* 25 June 1979, pp. 91–97.

26. See: A.W. Gouldner, *Patterned Industrial Bureaucracy* (Glencoe, IL: Free Press, 1954); J.G. March and H.A. Simon, *Organizations* (New York: John Wiley & Sons, 1958), pp. 44–45.

27. See J.B. Miner, "Management Appraisal: A Capsule Review and Current References," *Business Horizons,* October 1968, pp. 83–96.

28. See Ford and Jennings (March-April 1977).

29. See J.P. Campbell, M.D. Dunnette, R.D. Arvey, and L.V. Hellervik, "The Development and Evaluation of Behaviorally Based Rating Scales," *Journal of Applied Psychology* (1973): 15–22.

30. See W.C. Borman, "The Rating of Individuals in Organizations: An Alternate Approach," *Organizational Behavior and Human Performance* (August 1974): 105–125.

31. See Kanter (1977).

32. See D. McGregor, "An Uneasy Look at Performance Appraisal," *Harvard Business Review,* September-October 1972.

33. See Kanter (1977).

34. See T. Decotiis and A. Petit, "The Performance Appraisal Process: A Model and Some Testable Propositions," *Academy of Management Review* (July 1978): 635–647.

35. See R.M. Kanter, "Power Failure in Management Circuits," *Harvard Business Review,* July-August 1979, pp. 65–76.

36. See Ford and Jennings (1977).

37. See: Kanter (1977); Kanter (July-August 1979).

38. See: McConkie (January 1979); R.R. Ball, "What's the Answer to Performance Appraisal?" *Personnel Administrator* (1978): 43–47; R.L. Taylor and R.A. Zawacki, "Collaborative Goal Setting in Performance Appraisal: A Field Experiment," *Public Personnel Management* (May-June 1978): 162–171; J.B. Lasagna, "Make Your MBO Pragmatic," *Harvard Business Review,* November-December 1971.

39. See M.M. Greller, "Subordinate Participation and Reactions to the Appraisal Interview," *Journal of Applied Psychology* (1975): 544–549.

40. See Meyer et al. (January-February 1965).

41. See L. Wallace, "Nonevaluative Approaches to Performance Appraisals," *Supervisory Management,* March 1978, pp. 2–9.

42. See C. Fletcher and R. Williams, "The Influence of Performance Feedback in Appraisal Interviews," *Journal of Occupational Psychology* (June 1976): 75–85.

43. See Kanter (1977).

44. See Kearney (Winter 1977).

45. See: E.A. Locke, "Toward a Theory of Task Motivation and Incentives," *Organizational Behavior and Human Performance* (1968): 157–189; Kearney (Winter 1977); Fletcher and Williams (June 1976).

Rating the Raters Improves Performance Appraisals

by Mark R. Edwards and J. Ruth Sproull

Most performance appraisal systems provide no feedback for appraisers

Who could drive a car without performance feedback? No one. Anyone who tried could expect to have an accident and possibly destroy the car. To provide the requisite feedback, cars as well as planes, cameras, computers and other machines of our information-sensitive era come complete with gauges, dials, bells and even voices to advise us when our behavior is out of line.

Nearly every task we do provides information and reinforcement to ensure that we stay on target and can, wherever appropriate, improve our performance. In the absence of feedback, how can good or bad performance be validated? How can improvement occur? Quite simply, it cannot. There is no ability to measure, and hence no control over, actions which are taken blindly (*i.e.,* without the benefit of feedback).

Every basic management textbook has a section on measurement or control. It therefore is surprising that what many consider the most important task in human resource management, performance appraisal, most often is accomplished blindly (without feedback) by appraisers.[1] No textbook or current literature on single rater performance appraisal systems offers a practical means for providing useful feedback to appraisers. Supervisors render performance ratings as if they have a gift for hitting a target (or of avoiding errors)—blindfolded. Appraisers receive no information about their rating errors.

Mark R. Edwards is assistant professor and director of the Creative Institute, College of Engineering, Arizona State University, Tempe, AZ. J. Ruth Sproull is an attorney in Phoenix, AZ. Their article, "Rating the Raters Improves Performance Appraisals," is reprinted from the August 1983 issue of *Personnel Administrator,* copyright 1983, The American Society for Personnel Administration, 606 North Washington Street, Alexandria, VA 22314, $40 per year.

These errors may result from their misunderstanding of performance criteria, their misinterpretation of rating instructions or their personal biases. A brief survey of EEO law and employment discrimination cases suggests that most organizations have little control over the fairness or validity of their performance measurement process.[2] This article examines the state of current appraisal methods and offers a means for achieving significant improvement through innovations in appraiser feedback.

CURRENT APPRAISAL PRACTICE

Existing performance appraisal systems have been scrutinized in recent years by management researchers. For example, Lazer and Wikstrom reported on the national survey conducted by The Conference Board which examined the performance appraisal systems for 293 major industrial firms.[3] Approximately 75 percent of the firms reported that middle management appraisals were reviewed by the appraiser's immediate supervisor. However, not one firm reported using a method that provided any information regarding the biases of managers who appraised people or the accuracy of the appraisal process itself.

Other researchers, Stinson and Stokes, reported on the United States Bureau of National Affairs survey in which fewer than 10 percent of the companies polled expressed confidence in their performance appraisal systems.[4] One of their major concerns was the possibility of bias on the part of the individual appraiser. Similarly, it can be expected that women in a predominantly male firm, for example, would have considerable misgivings about an appraisal system that relied totally on a single evaluation by a sole (probably male) supervisor. By contrast, the use of rater feedback as well as multiple raters diminishes potential biases and adds objectivity to the performance appraisal system.

Another researcher, Edward Lawler, estimated that most organizations—99 percent—do not validate their performance appraisal systems.[5] He predicted that, if confronted with an EEO case filed by one or more employees, any of these organizations would find it difficult to defend due to their poor performance evaluations. The single supervisory performance appraisal may be rife with human biases—especially if the appraiser receives no information on personal rating behavior.

Yet another researcher, N.B. Winstanley, identified major sources of potential error in performance appraisal as follows: rater, method, ratee, job, context and the interaction between each of them.[6] Winstanley believes most organizations are "flying blind" in that they do not know what their appraisals are doing for or to the organization. He has concluded that "the current state of performance appraisal and the practical, legal and ethical implications are—to put it mildly—disturbing."

Extensive research on performance appraisal, as well as perception and information processing, has verified the intuitively known fact that people are extraordinarily diverse in their respective rating abilities. Some individuals are more consistent, more lenient or more biased than others.[7]

Rater training would appear to provide a logical way to overcome the deficiencies of rater inaccuracy. Indeed, 60 percent of the companies in the national Conference Board survey reported some form of training for appraisers. From his review of observer training programs, Spool concluded that behavior can be observed more accurately by observers who have been trained to minimize rating errors.[8] Unfortunately, accuracy of behavior observation may differ from accuracy of performance appraisal, which has been defined as the degree to which ratings are relevant to or correlated with true criterion scores.[9]

Only three published studies regarding rater training for performance appraisal have used accuracy as a dependent measure.[10] Results in each study indicate that performance rating accuracy is not improved as a function of rater training. In fact, Bernardin and Pence reported that rater training may temporarily lower certain biases such as leniency and halo but rater training can actually lower the accuracy of performance ratings. Their explanation is that rater training creates new response sets and thereby decreases rating accuracy. Researchers have reported significant problems with:

- individual variation in rating performance;
- ability to improve rater accuracy through training; and
- performance appraisal systems lacking in feedback to the appraiser (which, surprisingly, to date have not been seriously challenged but may face future legal penalty).

RATER FEEDBACK

Rater feedback may be provided immediately or years later, in concrete terms or through subtle cues. For example:

- Concrete feedback given immediately.
- Every employee given an outstanding rating is a white male.
- Subtle feedback, given years later.
- Every person in a corner office is a white male.

Rater feedback may in rare instances be objective, based on differences from a specified distribution or a consensus judgment.

Rater feedback is most often subjective, as is typical in the case where a next higher level (second level) supervisor "reviews" the ratings made by the immediate supervisor.[11]

Peter McGuire concluded that subjective, second level review of performance appraisals has failed because the employee's immediate supervisor, the appraisal writer, has tried (usually unsuccessfully) to satisfy two different readers: the employee (subordinate) and the reviewing (second level) superior.[12] The immediate supervisor's fear of negative feedback from the second level superior may result in appraisals that do not meet the needs of either the superior or the subordinate who is being appraised.

It is also probable that the second level supervisor would have difficulty providing constructive feedback to the rater. It is unlikely that a single second level supervisor would identify biases such as halo or leniency from reviewing the appraisal of an individual ratee. Hence, feedback on performance ratings tends to be subjective and virtually worthless to the raters. The discussion between the immediate supervisor-rater and his superior (in second level reviews of appraisals) typically focuses on the ratee's behavior and interaction with the rater upon being advised of the appraisal results, rather than the biases in the rater's appraisal.

Another intra-firm method of identifying general trends in performance evaluations is an audit of all appraisals by department, section and appraiser. This may allow early identification of some systematic appraiser biases. For example, if no women in one department received a high appraisal, feedback to the manager might help uncover the reason for the apparently poor performance. The problem could be the manager's perception (bias) or lack of managerial support or training for the women in the group. Feedback regarding general tendencies for any specific groups could then provide a catalyst for change in management methods that might forestall charges of discrimination.

More useful, however, for improving performance appraisals, than any time-delayed feedback system is immediate, objective rater feedback. Two methods have been described in the literature which allow, in theory or in practice, respectively, for immediate, objective rater feedback. They are mixed standard scale (MSS) format, a modification of a behaviorally anchored rating scale (BARS), and the Objective Judgment Quotient (OJQ) process.

MIXED STANDARD SCALE (MSS)

Blanz and Ghiselli proposed the MSS format to minimize halo and leniency errors common in traditional BARS.[13] The MSS, like any BARS, for each rating dimension, provides three rating choices (in general, low, medium or high) for the rater. In other respects, however, the MSS differs from a traditional BARS. For example, in the MSS all items are presented in random order and raters must respond without knowing whether a low, medium or high rating for a particular item has a positive, neutral or negative correlation to performance. (In other words, the rater is not supposed to know whether his choice—low, medium or high—on a particular item has a positive, neutral or negative dimension as it relates to the ratee's performance.) In the MSS, raters are required to choose one of the following three responses for each item: the ratee's performance is lower (or poorer) than the item description (–); the ratee's performance fits the item description (0); the ratee's performance is higher (better) than the item description (+).

Saal and Landy reported that the MSS format is superior to BARS in reducing halo and leniency errors.[14] Blanz and Ghiselli believe this reduction in biases occurs because the MSS disguises dimensions and the ordinal relationships among the items; the rater cannot detect an order of merit in the items.

The MSS format provides for error counts that can be used to identify rater errors and ambiguous dimensions. The erroneous ratings could be used to provide important feedback to the raters. Unfortunately, no reports of rater feedback using the MSS have been published.

If the MSS format were used with multiple raters, even more rater errors would become obvious upon comparison of each individual rater's opinions with those of the group (a summed consensus) for the various ratees. It would then be possible for the firm to give the greatest credence to those ratings which are close to the consensus (multiple rater) judgment. Most importantly, individuals whose ratings were consistently different from the consensus could receive feedback about those differences. Again, these advantages are only theoretical since there have been no reports of the MSS being used with either multiple raters or rater feedback.

The MSS format in theory provides an opportunity for rater feedback. In practice, the process of evaluating rating differences among raters would be extremely time consuming or require extensive programming if computer analysis were available. Bernardin and Pence also warn that disguising the items' dimensionality and the logic of the MSS scoring system results in rater frustration and low rater acceptance. The authors noted that the U.S. Army abandoned its use of forced-choice rating scales because the raters found the "hidden ball" of disguised dimension ratings so unacceptable that they concentrated on ways to beat the rating system.

Another method of providing immediate, objective rater feedback that has been tested extensively in applications with such firms as Bank of America, Nestle and R.J. Reynolds is the Objective Judgment Quotient (OJQ) process.[15]

OBJECTIVE JUDGMENT QUOTIENT (OJQ)

The OJQ system is a measurement tool developed to solve the problem of identifying and weighing criteria for job analysis. OJQ provides a simple numeric solution to this dilemma: how can a firm collect, organize, combine and present its judgmental data without distorting or eliminating important information?

OJQ rating dimensions, related to job performance, are determined in a manner similar to the BARS or MSS methods. Instead of having open ended scales like the BARS and MSS, the OJQ scaled comparison looks like, but overcomes, many of the difficulties of the paired comparison (where the ratee's performance is paired with and evaluated as low, medium or high against one item at a time). The greater advantage of the OJQ scaled comparison is its algebraic solution (rather than the typical statistical solution to paired comparisons). This allows for construction of an extremely reliable multiple rater consensus judgment and a scaled rank order output, using far fewer comparisons than required for standard paired comparison methods.[16] A scaled comparison rating is shown in Figure 1.

It is unnecessary to make every possible comparison between all ratees when an algebraic solution to the scale is used. Hence, where OJQ is used, the fatigue factor associated with paired comparisons does not diminish the psychometric advantages of the scaled preference format.

OJQ also eliminates most of the distortion due to the "popularity" (*i.e.,* the most well-known persons are rated higher) which typically results with conventional statistical methods. The OJQ process reduces distortion and achieves a consistency among rater judgments which is dramatically superior to paired-comparison or other ranking methods.

The OJQ process results in reports, presented in a standardized format, to management, the ratee and the raters. First among these reports is "ranking with criterion," which lists all persons rated in rank order together with their ranking scores on the particular criterion.

The OJQ process also results in the following standard reports: the summary report, which alphabetically lists the scores of all personnel appraised; the individual profile, which provides a graphic representation of an individual's scores compared to the others in the group; and the rater inconsistency report, which identifies the number and the direction of rater inconsistencies (as compared to the consensus judgment). Of these, the report providing rater feedback on significant (usually set at 20 percent) inconsistencies or deviations from the consensus is particularly valuable and made possible because:

● Each rater's rating is used in determining the consensus for the scaled ranking.

- Each rater's individual rating is then compared to the multiple rater consensus for that individual to determine if there is more than a 20 percent deviation between the consensus and the individual rater.

Figure 1
Scaled Comparison Judgments

	Much Better	Slightly Better	Equal	Slightly Better	Much Better	
Rater: I.M. Macho					Date: November 15, 1982	
			Performance Criterion: **Quality of Work**			
Alice Dunn	: ____	: ____	: ____	: ____	: _X_	Tom Kanes
Brenda Saal	: ____	: ____	: ____	: ____	: _X_	John Trane
Brad Farr	: _X_	: ____	: ____	: ____	: ____	Brenda Saal
Victor Barnes	: ____	: _X_	: ____	: ____	: ____	Alice Dunn
Allen Mann	: ____	: _X_	: ____	: ____	: ____	Linda Keyes
Maxwell Thomas	: _X_	: ____	: ____	: ____	: ____	Linda Keyes
Diane Bell	: ____	: ____	: ____	: ____	: _X_	John Trane

NOTE: *Ratings (from the top to bottom) indicate I.M. Macho believes the following about work quality displayed on the job:*

> *Tom Kanes is "much better than" Alice Dunn;*
> *John Trane is "much better than" Brenda Saal;*
> *Brad Farr is "much better than" Brenda Saal;*
> *Victor Barnes is "slightly better than" Alice Dunn;*
> *Allen Mann is "slightly better than" Linda Keyes;*
> *Maxwell Thomas is "much better than" Linda Keyes; and*
> *Diane Bell is "much better than" John Trane.*

An example of an OJQ "rater inconsistency" (analysis-of-inconsistencies) report appears in Figure 2.

As reflected in Figure 2, an OJQ rater feedback report demonstrates four key elements:

1. The significant disagreements the rater has with the multiple rater consensus (MRC) score. The MRC score is depicted in the far left- and right-hand columns of the "analysis of inconsistencies" listing, while Mr. Macho's rating is shown in the center (see Figure 2). In the first example Mr. Macho is depicted as having rated Tom Kanes "much better than" Alice Dunn. The MRC score for Kanes was only 46 while Dunn's score was 84.

Figure 2
Rater Feedback Report

Rater: I.M. Macho
Rating Group: Financial Staff
Group Size: 66
Rating Date: November 15, 1982
Criterion 7 - Quality of Work
Analysis of Inconsistencies

MRC	Macho		MRC
84	Alice Dunn	Tom Kanes	46
86	Brenda Saal	John Trane	34
66	Brad Farr	Brenda Saal	86
46–7	Victor Barnes	Alice Dunn	84
58	Allen Mann	Linda Keyes	84
60	Maxwell	Linda Keyes	90
	Thomas		
87	Diane Bell	John Trane	84

Rater I.M. Macho has a total of 51 inconsistencies (ratings which deviate more than 20% from the consensus)(only seven of these inconsistencies are displayed in this example).

*Scaled comparisons positions used: : 45: 12: **10**: 18: 34*

Total Judgments = 120 (42.5% inconsistent)

Decision index = 83 (This means that I.M. Macho made strong, decisive judgments. He tended to mark the outside position of the scaled comparison ratings).

The analysis of inconsistencies in Figure 2 shows, reading from the top, that according to I.M. Macho's rating: Tom Kanes is much better than Alice Dunn (Dunn 84; Kanes 46); John Trane is much better than Brenda Saal (Saal 86; Trane 34); Brad Farr is much better than Brenda Saal (Saal 86; Farr 66); Victor Barnes is slightly better than Alice Dunn (Dunn 84; Barns 46); Allen Mann is slightly better than Linda Keyes (Keyes 90; Mann 58); Maxwell Thomas is much better than Linda Keyes (Keyes 90; Thomas 60); and John Trane is much better than Diane Bell (Bell 87; Trane 34).

2. The percentage such disagreements (inconsistencies) bear to the number of choices made. In Figure 2, 43 percent of Mr. Macho's ratings were significantly different from the MRC.
3. A Decision Index which measures the decisiveness of the rater in terms of his having marked positions away from

center on the rating forms. Mr. Macho's score of 83 indicates he is a very decisive (although inconsistent) rater.

4. The number of times each position of the scaled comparison was marked by a rater and the total of the scaled preferences made. People who prefer to avoid making decisions or are indecisive often have many ratings in the center. Mr. Macho had only 10 ratings marked in the "equal to" position and 46 + 34 in the two extreme "much better than" positions.

Useful rater feedback appears in the format displayed in Figure 2. This type of rater feedback is a standard output received by each rater on each dimension evaluated using the OJQ performance appraisal process and similar feedback could be derived from other types of objective rater analysis.

An analysis of inconsistencies report, such as that used in the OJQ process, is a sophisticated application of the Delphi method. Raters who disagree significantly with the consensus on a particular criterion may have information which is not available to the other raters. Examining such disagreement may force recall of "critical incidents" which strongly influence judgment. Also, if use of a particular criterion such as "communication skills" leads to numerous rating inconsistencies, the description of the criterion or its use can be changed or even eliminated to improve reliability.

Figure 2 portrays only a small sample of Mr. Macho's 120 rating judgments on the criterion "communication skills." He also made about 120 judgments (scaled comparisons between individual associates) on each of seven other job-related performance criteria. He may have been selected as a rater by as many as 30 associates although only nine associate-ratees are shown in the example.

The most critical rating feedback is Mr. Macho's very high inconsistency rate. Of comparison judgments made on the performance dimension "communication skills," Mr. Macho was inconsistent with the MRC on 51 out of 120 ratings (*i.e.,* 43 percent of the time). This is a highly irregular result. Experience has shown that most raters are objective and consistent when using the OJQ technique. Typically, 90 percent of all raters render ratings which are inconsistent with the MRC less than 10 percent of the time. However, it may be the few relatively deviant raters who are very decisive, yet inaccurate, that undermine fairness in performance measurement systems.

Figure 2 shows that Mr. Macho is not only a deviant rater but also, that he is biased against women. At every opportunity, in the sample of rating opportunities shown, Mr. Macho rates men better than women even though the MRC results show the opposite to be true. While a few inconsistencies might indicate that a rater has special information, systematic rating tendencies like those displayed by Mr. Macho evidence discrimination or bias. Even though research has suggested that the MRC may not always be accurate, unquestionably composite judgments are a better estimate of an employee's true value than individual judgments.[17]

OJQ rater feedback has the important advantage of identifying systematic rating tendencies (favorable or unfavorable) if they exist. In addition to evidencing group-based bias, a rater may demonstrate many inconsistencies on one criterion and few on the others, indicating the rater's confusion about one of the critera. Specific training can be designed to remediate rater errors, biases or confusion that, in a single rater appraisal system, would go unnoticed.[18] A reduction in systematic biases among raters means performance appraisals are more accurate and fair—something of great significance to the employees being rated as well as governmental enforcement agencies such as the EEOC. Experience with successful OJQ performance appraisal systems at large firms like R.J. Reynolds, Nestle and Florida Power and Light indicate the value of rater feedback.

Employees become involved in the decision process that affects them the most as they choose their own raters and serve as raters for others. Effective participative management requires rater feedback about rating behavior. Raters who see their own rating behaviors can often assess their own training needs. Systematic rating inconsistencies provide targeted training need identification for management.

REFERENCES

1. Latham, Gary P. and Wexley, Kenneth N. *Increasing Productivity Through Performance Appraisal,* Reading: Addison-Wesley, 1981.

2. Field, Hubert S. and Holley, William H. "The Relationship of Performance Appraisal System Characteristics to Verdicts in Selected Employment Discrimination Cases," *Academy of Management Journal,* 25(2), pp. 392–406.

3. Lazer, R. and Wikstrom, W. *Appraising Managerial Performance.* The Conference Board, 1977.

4. Stinson, John, and Stokes, John. "Manpower: How to Multi-Appraise," *Management Today,* June (1980), pp. 43–53.

5. Lawler, Edward E., III. "Administering Pay Programs...An Interview with Edward E. Lawler, III," *Compensation Review,* First Quarter, 1977, pp. 8–16.

6. Winstanley, N.B., "How accurate are performance appraisals?" *Personnel Administrator,* August (1980), pp. 55–58.

7. Borman, W.C., "Individual Difference Correlates of Rating Accuracy Using Behavior Scales," Presented at American Psychological Association, 85th Annual Convention, San Francisco, August 30, 1977.

8. Spool, M.D., "Training Programs for Observers of Behavior: A Review," *Personnel Psychology,* No. 31 (1978), pp. 853–888.

9. Dunnette, M.D., and Borman, W.C., "Personnel Selection and Classification System," *Annual Review of Psychology,* Vol. 30 (1979), pp. 477–525.

10. Borman, W.C., "Effects of Instructions to Avoid Halo Error on Reliability and Validity of Performance Evaluation Ratings," *Journal of Applied Psychology,* Vol. 60. No. 3 (1975), pp. 556–560; Borman, W.C., "Format and Training Effects on Rating Accuracy and Rater Errors," *Journal of Applied Psychology,* Vol. 64, No. 2 (1979), pp. 410–421; and Bernardin, H. John and Pence, Earl C., "Effects of Rater Training: Creating New Response Sets and Decreasing Accuracy," *Journal of Applied Psychology,* Vol. 65, No. 1 (1980), pp. 60–66.

11. Glueck, William F. and Kilkovich, George T. *Personnel: A Diagnostic Approach,* Third Edition, Plano: Business Publications, Inc., 1982.

12. McGuire, Peter J., "Why Performance Appraisals Fail," *Personnel Journal,* Vol. 59, No. 8 (1980), pp. 744–762.

13. Blanz, F., and Ghiselli, E.E., "The Mixed-Standard Scale: A New Rating System," *Personnel Psychology.* Vol. 25, No. 2 (1972), pp. 185–199.

14. Saal, F.E., and Landy, F.J., "The Mixed Standard Rating Scale: An Evaluation," *Organizational Behavior and Human Performance,* Vol. 18 (1977), pp. 19–35.

15. Edwards, Mark R., "Improving Performance Appraisal Through the Use of Multiple Raters," *Industrial Management + Data Systems,* July-August, 1981, pp. 13–16.

16. Bartlett, Thomas E. and Linden, Leonard R., "Evaluating Managerial Personnel," *OMEGA, The International Journal of Management Science,* Vol. 2, No. 6 (1974), pp. 815–819.

17. Libby, Robert and Blashfield, Roger K., "Performance of a Composite as a Function of the Number of Judges," *Organizational Behavior and Human Performance,* 21, 1978, pp. 121–129.

18. Edwards, Mark R. and Goodstein, Leonard D., "Experimental Learning Can Improve Performance Appraisals," *Human Resources Management,* Spring, 1982, pp. 18–23.

A Final Word about Appraisal in Libraries

Another Look at Performance Appraisal in Libraries

by G. Edward Evans and Bendict Rugaas

Libraries around the world share many similarities in spite of different cultural and institutional settings. One similarity that many of them share today is the need to function in an environment of limited resources, both human and physical. Certainly, the cause of this problem is the world economic condition, and libraries, like other institutions and individuals, must attempt to make their limited financial resources stretch further and further. As a result, libraries have had to set priorities, cut back on a number of activities and/or stop or slow expansion programs. However, effort is devoted to at least maintaining, if not improving, the quality and types of services available to library patrons.

One method of maintaining quality and quantity of service in the face of diminishing purchasing power is to have more efficient and productive staff. Even without pressure to increase overall productivity, many libraries establish a base line for assessing individual staff members' performance. American libraries—in fact the majority of academic libraries[1]—employ a highly formalized system, with annual or semi-annual appraisal forms being filled out by supervisors to assess the performance of each staff member they supervise. Although no solid data are published on the number of public and school libraries using a formal appraisal process, probably all of those that are a part of a merit system are involved in annual appraisals.

One concern of administrators, supervisors, employees, management consultants, and teachers of management is and has been per-

G. Edward Evans is associate dean, Graduate School of Librarianship and Information Management, University of Denver, Denver, CO. Bendict Rugaas is director of libraries, Royal University of Oslo, Norway. Their article, "Another Look at Performance Appraisal in Libraries," is reprinted from *Journal of Library Administration* 3 (2) (Summer 1982): 61–69. Copyright 1982 by The Haworth Press, Inc. Used by permission of The Haworth Press, Inc., 28 East 22 Street, New York, NY 10010.

formance appraisal and what to do about it. Indeed, performance appraisal is assumed to be a fact of administrative and supervisory life. Management and personnel administration textbooks all make at least some reference to the process, while most of them devote one or two chapters to the topic, and entire books have been devoted to the theory and practice of conducting performance appraisals.[2,3] Both ALA[4] and ARL[5] have issued collections of performance appraisal forms and guidelines in the last few years, and literally dozens of journal articles appear each year on the subject (for example, in 1979, some 93 articles were listed under the heading of performance appraisal in just *Business Index* and *Library Literature*). The following quotations typify statements about performance appraisal:

> The productivity of all individuals is measurable to some extent. If an objective measurement is impossible, a subjective measurement is attempted, perhaps comparing one individual with another. The measurement of individuals *is vital* to good personnel administration and management and *it must be accepted* as part of employment.[6] (Emphasis added)

> The rating or evaluation of one person by another is as old as mankind itself. It is a natural phenomenon in the sense that individuals continually judge others by what they say, what they do, and how they affect other people. This process applies not only to work situations, but also to all facets of life.[7]

> All libraries should have some formal plan for regularly appraising each employee. Each individual wants to know just how he is evaluated by his supervisor. He may have had a few words of praise for some above average activity or criticism for a mistake, but he must have an objective measurement of his overall performance.[8]

> Appraisal questions are generally avoided. The superiors may tend to hold back until the employee is due for a regular performance appraisal. They then fill out the required forms and schedule appraisal interviews with their subordinates. During the interview, past performance is reviewed. The superior justifies the evaluation. Often the employee is surprised about how he or she is characterized and rated. The meeting is tense and emotional, often fraught with explanations and defensiveness. Frequently developmental objectives are never discussed.[9]

According to theory, what should performance appraisal do for the supervisor, the employee, and the organization? Based on an extensive review of the literature, it is possible to identify the following beliefs about the nature and function of formal performance appraisal systems in American organizations:

1. The process is essential to good management.
2. The process is natural or normal.
3. The process is the only reasonable method available for assuring at least minimal performance.

4. The process is the only valid basis for granting or withdrawing employee economic benefits.
5. The process is the primary means of maintaining control of staff productivity.
6. The process is essential for growth and well-being of the individual employee.
7. The process is an important element in an effective system of motivation.
8. The process is essential in work orientation programs.
9. The process is or can be an objective assessment of an individual's strengths and weaknesses.
10. The process is primarily directed toward the subordinate.
11. The process is continuous and reflects a careful analysis of the individual's daily performance.
12. The process is equally effective whether carried out by a supervisor or the employee's peers.
13. The process is concerned with all aspects of an individual's work, not just the performance of the assigned duties.
14. The process is useful in assessing an employee's future and potential progress in the organization.
15. The process is essential in planning organizational personnel needs for the present and the immediate future.
16. The process is important in counseling and suggesting areas of improvement that the individual should achieve if the individual hopes to gain more responsible positions either in the organization or outside it.

This a long and impressive list of functions for one process to accomplish. And if the process is conducted by a supervisor in terms of an individual, and if this is the normal procedure, it is inevitable that personalities will enter the picture and probably color the evaluations. Should this happen, the performance and productivity aspects may be lost in a maze of personality issues irrelevant to the work situation.

Although the literature review indicates a complex set of beliefs about the value and nature of personnel appraisal activities, it is possible to identify two general goals that can be achieved by means of performance appraisal: administrative and behavioral. On the administrative side, the process can supply the documentation on which to base decisions regarding individual employees (promotions, salary increases, transfers, and in extreme cases, demotions or dismissals). Behavioral goals relate to the question of how well the individual performs assigned tasks, and what can be done to improve performance. Although it is possible to make a case that the two goals are really the same, such an approach merely compounds an already highly complex situation. In theory, one process should be able to accomplish both goals. Also according to theory, formal performance appraisals should have a direct positive relationship to productivity: the closer the monitoring and greater the feedback on performance, the higher the productivity should be. Such does not seem to be the case. In fact, it might be argued that the process has just the opposite effect.

A comprehensive review of the literature attempting to locate answers to the question "do productivity measures pay off for employee performance?" concluded that the data available were insufficient to answer the question, even in a tentative manner. The report indicated a fairly large body of literature about the process of conducting an appraisal, comparison of different techniques, use of forms and their content, and so forth. However, very few studies addressed the question of the result of conducting the process. "Applications of productivity measurement to personnel management are beginning to be made as a consequence of more emphasis on organizational development and MBO, but we found no evaluation of such personnel practices. Nor are there scientific experimental studies of the impact on productivity of existing personnel practice."[10] In essence, the emphasis has been on administrative goals rather than on the behavioral goal of increased productivity. My own literature search confirms the report's finding—to date, no article, book, or report has been found that provides data about the effect of performance appraisal on productivity. The closest that one comes to finding such data is in studies of employee attitudes about the appraisal process.

A 1953 study about worker attitudes toward performance appraisal as well as how it was conducted found that 74% of the 340 persons questioned felt the process had little or no effect as far as improving their performance (35% little value, 39% no value).[11] More recently, 1980, an article entitled "Do Public Servants Welcome or Fear Merit Evaluation of Their Performance?" appeared in *Public Administration Review.*[12] The researchers were concerned with determining "whether public employees consider the creation of a 'good' performance appraisal system to be both a laudable and practical undertaking."[13] They noted that many of the respondents indicated that an appraisal system was in existence in their agency and that it *did not* promote better performance. Even with the word "good" modifying the word "performance," only 82% of respondents agreed with the question "many people believe a good performance appraisal system can improve individual performance. Would you agree?" One interesting note is a sharp drop in support of the question as the length of service in the agency increased: 91% agreement from those employed less than a year to 76% for those with more than 10 years service.[14] It is important to note that none of the questions asked related to personal performance but were about an abstract "individual" appraised by a "good" system.

We believe that two points are important about the above discussion. First, we have no direct evidence about the performance outcome of conducting performance appraisals. Second, in the United States there is an assumption that the process, in particular a "good" one, will lead to better performance. Perhaps we do not need the process at all.

Our interest in performance appraisal and the questioning of the need for the process started seven years ago. In 1973, Evans received a Council on Library Resources fellowship to study the training of librarians and library paraprofessionals in the Scandinavian countries. He used a highly structured interview schedule asking a variety of questions (or as one Dane said, 10,000 questions) about the educational programs and their "value." Several of the questions related to evaluating a person's performance as a student, as a professional on the job, or as a teacher in a library school. After the second week of interviewing he spent some time tabulating the responses. A disturbing pattern, or rather a lack of pattern, became apparent for all questions relating to performance appraisal. Some people did not answer the questions, or people in the same organization gave almost opposite answers to questions about how performance appraisals were done. The cause of this outcome was unclear; Evans thought perhaps it was a language problem. Fortunately, not long after that, he interviewed a Danish librarian who had worked in an American library for over five years. She responded to the first question about performance appraisal with "I know what you are asking, but we don't do that." After further questioning, she made it clear that "we" referred to Scandinavians, *not* simply the library where she worked.

With this idea in mind, as impossible as it seemed to be, Evans added several questions that modified the original items. At the end of the three months of interviewing, it appeared that none of the Scandinavian libraries used a formal appraisal process. In discussing the issue with Rugaas, Evans and Rugaas decided to investigate the role of performance appraisals and work performance. Over the next six years they did this with the basic finding that performance appraisal, as we know it in the United States, does not exist in Scandinavian libraries. Another finding is that Scandinavians think it strange that we do this "thing," just as Americans find it incredible that Scandinavians don't.

As a result of these experiences, whenever Evans is asked to speak to a group of American librarians about a management topic of his choosing, he selects performance appraisal. He has two purposes in selecting this topic: (a) to let people know about alternatives to conducting formal appraisals and that it is not inevitable; and, (b) to collect some data about librarians' attitudes about the process. Since 1975, he has discussed the subject at nine different meetings with 407 persons. At each meeting, each person is asked to answer 5 questions:

1. Is formal performance appraisal necessary for good supervision?
2. Do you feel confident and "comfortable" in conducting a performance appraisal?

3. Do you think the system provides a factual assessment of the employee's performance?

4. Do you think the process has a positive influence on the employee's job performance?

5. Do you think the process can help improve or correct an employee's job performance?

	Percentage YES	and NO
Question 1	90.6	9.4
Question 2	16.7	83.3
Question 3	47.1	52.9
Question 4	13.0	87.0
Question 5	2.7	97.3

It appears that this group of 407 persons, although predominantly feeling that performance appraisal is important, seems to have little or no confidence in the ultimate value of the process. Certainly the fact that less than 3% felt that the process can help improve or correct an employee's job performance indicates doubts about how well the process achieves the behavioral goals. That, combined with the low affirmative response (13%) to the question about positive influence may be why only 16.7% of the people said they felt confident in conducting appraisals.

As noted, one cannot make too much out of these data since the samples were self-selected—the survey was done as an aside to a presentation/discussion at regional meetings of special interest groups or staff meetings, and the process was not designed as a structured research project. These data seem to reveal: librarians may have very deep concern about the value of performance appraisal, they were surprised to learn that libraries in some countries achieve very high performance from staff members without engaging in performance appraisals, and, perhaps having two goals for performance appraisal may be one too many. Several other writers[15,16] on this subject have suggested that one goal for the process would be a more realistic approach. However, no one seems to question the need for such a system, yet it may not be necessary—if the Scandinavian pattern is a model of what happens without such appraisals.

The data collected in the above informal manner are not that far removed from those reported by Van Zelst and Kerr. They are close enough, given the differences in the approach to collecting the data, to warrant a formal study of the attitudes of librarians about the value of performance appraisal in terms of behavioral goals. There is an opportunity to conduct a cross-cultural study of attitudes of librarians (in this case, academic librarians) about performance appraisal in the United States and Scandinavia. (A study is being planned as a joint project by the University of Denver, Graduate School of Librarianship and Information Management and the Norwegian State Library School.)

Saul Gellerman made a suggestion about behavioral aspects of performance appraisal that seems especially sound in light of data collected in the informal survey.

> Unless a 'weakness' is perceived by a consensus of observers to be easily correctable by relatively minor conscious effort, little is to be gained by pointing it out. The manager may vent displeasure, the subordinate may be mortified, and the weakness will probably persist. The wiser course is to say nothing, and either to tolerate the weakness or, if it seriously impairs job performance, redesign the job or transfer the employee. (Remember, we are considering persons whose overall performance is satisfactory and for whom our primary goal is development.)[17]

To some degree, this may be what is done in Scandinavian libraries, although this is yet to be determined. It is not an accepted common practice in United States libraries, where formal appraisal systems existed. Based on the information collected, our guess is that it is a common practice of supervisors, but because the practice is not "accepted" or given formal approval by top management they feel somewhat guilty about not pointing out weaknesses. In part, the practice, if it is common, arises because of the potential for conflict between supervisor and employee, thus making it easier to "tolerate small weaknesses."

According to David Peele,[18] the British have still another approach to performance appraisal. Drawing on E.V. Corbett's[19] work and his own experience in both countries, he shows what the differences are, and suggests that Americans use some elements of the British system that would result in a less formalized system. The British system appears to be halfway between the highly structured American system and the very informal Scandinavian approach. Although Peele does not directly question the need for an appraisal, he does show that variations exist, and each seems to work equally well. Or, perhaps it is more accurate to say that no clear evidence exists that any system helps improve staff performance.

No matter what the goal(s) may be for the process, staff members need a clear explanation of what those goals are and how to accomplish them. Anyone with experience in examining a large number of performance evaluation forms is struck by the fact that the vast majority of the staff are rated "average" or above average—a rather interesting phenomenon (where is the lower half of the statistical curve?). Some academic libraries state in their personnel policies that a person must be excellent to be hired and outstanding to move up to the next rank; later advancements in rank require the person to be rated as superior, exceptional, and distinguished.[20] With such a system, is it a wonder that few people ever get rated less than excellent, or that people begin to doubt the value of such an appraisal system as a true assessment of ability or a means of promoting greater productivity? All too often, only the administrative goal is achieved because the staff see this as the sole purpose of the process and really have no training in using the system to achieve the behavioral goals such as improvement of an individual's performance or for growth and development.

In summary, a review of the literature and the informal data collection indicates that a formal performance appraisal is considered essential for good management in the United States—essential because it provides a means of control over employee job performance and, thus, over individual and organizational productivity (behavior goals). It also carries with it what many managers and supervisors believe to be a powerful sanction for failing to achieve a satisfactory performance and level of productivity (administrative goals). That sanction is the granting or withholding of economic rewards, opportunities for advancement and promotion, and in the case of totally unsatisfactory performance, dismissal from the organization. What is assumed is there is a direct relationship between conducting performance appraisals and maintaining or improving an individual's contribution to the organization (productivity). One does *not* find in the literature any articles that supply evidence that the assumption is valid. Nor does one find, other than indirectly, any questioning of the need for such a system. Yet, as we have seen, at least one working alternative exists to the highly structured American system in Scandinavia and possibly a less structured approach in use in Great Britain.

Thus there is a need for extensive research in this area. This article is filled with "it seems," "it appears," "perhaps," which reflects the current lack of evidence about the following areas: (a) the effectiveness of performance appraisal practices; (b) influence of performance appraisal on work relationship (superior/subordinate and peer); (c) relationship between performance appraisal and productivity; and, (d) the cost benefit of conducting performance appraisals. Each of the areas could be further subdivided into a number of smaller more manageable research topics. We hope a number of persons will begin to investigate these areas in general and specifically in terms of libraries. As noted before, the Graduate School of Librarianship and Information Management at the University of Denver, and the Norwegian Library School hope to secure funding to examine one very small portion of this highly complex subject.

NOTES

1. M. Johnson. "Performance Appraisal of Librarians-A Survey," *College and Research Libraries* 33(September 1972): 359–67.

2. R.G. Johnson. *Appraisal Interview Guide* (New York: AMACOM, 1979).

3. J. Budde. *Measuring Performance in Human Services Systems* (New York: AMACOM, 1980).

4. College Libraries Section (Association of College and Research Libraries, American Library Association), *Performance Appraisal - 1–80. CLIP Notes: College Library Information Packets* (Chicago: ALA, 1980).

5. Association of Research Libraries Office of Management Studies, *SPEC Kit 53 - Performance Appraisal in ARL Libraries* (Washington, DC: ARL, 1979).

6. E. Chapman. *Supervisors' Survival Kit: A Mid-Management Primer.* 2nd ed. (Palo Alto, CA: Science Research Associates, 1975), p. 94.

7. R.D. Steuart and J.T. Eastlick. *Library Management,* 2nd ed. (Littleton, CO: Libraries Unlimited, 1980), p. 97.

8. K. Stebbins and F. Mohrhardt. *Personnel Administration in Libraries,* (Metuchen, NJ: Scarecrow, 1966), p. 121.

9. J. Rizzo. *Management for Librarians: Fundamentals and Issues* (Westport, CT: Greenwood Press, 1980), p. 228.

10. Georgetown University Public Services Laboratory. *Do Productivity Measures Pay Off for Employee Performance?* (Washington, DC: Public Services Laboratory, 1975), p. 46.

11. R.H. Van Zelst and W.A. Kerr. "Working Attitudes toward Merit Rating," *Personnel Psychology* 6(October 1953): 159–72.

12. N.P. Lovrich, P.I. Shaffer, R.H. Hopkins and D.A. Yale. "Do Public Servants Welcome or Fear Merit Evaluation of Their Performance?" *Public Administration Review* XX (May-June 1980): 214–22.

13. *Ibid.,* p. 216.

14. *Ibid.,* p. 217.

15. S. Gellerman. *The Management of Human Resources* (New York: Holt Rinehart, 1976).

16. D. McGregor. "An Uneasy Look at Performance Appraisal," *Harvard Business Review* 35(May-June 1957): 89–94.

17. Gellerman, *Management of Human Resources,* p. 173.

18. D. Peele. "Evaluating Library Employees," *Library Journal* 97 (Sept. 15, 1972): 2803-2807.

19. E. Corbett, "Staffing of Large Municipal Libraries in England and the United States: A Comparative Survey," *Journal of Librarianship* 3 (April 1971): 81–100.

20. University of California, Los Angeles. *Promotion in the Librarian Series.* Los Angeles, University Research Library, 1979.

Performance Problems: A Model for Analysis and Resolution*

by Ann Allan and Kathy J. Reynolds

There are many reasons why individual library employees may fail to carry out their responsibilities successfully. Just as there are numerous causes of performance discrepancies, so there exists a wide range of potential solutions from which the library manager must choose in attempting to alleviate the problems. Herein proposed is a systematic procedure for analyzing performance problems in the library. This procedure is intended to minimize costly misjudgments and guide the manager toward those remedial steps most likely to contribute to successful resolution of the performance problem.

Today with austerity budgets and personnel cutbacks, one observes an intensified interest in performance accountability and a concern for maximizing the return on dollars invested in library personnel. One integral means of addressing this concern is to review hiring procedures to ensure that one's library is benefiting from systematic and thorough search and screening techniques that result in the employment of persons most qualified to hold particular positions within a system. Yet no matter how diligent one may be in striving to assemble a dedicated team of high-caliber personnel, performance discrepancies will occur and, on occasion, given employees will fail to carry out adequately their responsibilities. The reasons why such perfor-

Ann Allan is associate professor of library science, Kent State University, Kent, OH. Kathy J. Reynolds is media specialist, Midview Middle School, Grafton, OH. Their article, "Performance Problems: A Model for Analysis and Resolution," is reprinted with permission from *The Journal of Academic Librarianship* 9 (1) (May 1983): 83–88.

*Based on the paper presented by Dr. Allan at the ALA Annual Conference, Dallas, Texas, 1979.

mance problems develop are many and diverse, as are traditional responses by library managers.

In *Analyzing Performance Problems,* Robert Mager and Peter Pipe propose a systematic procedure for identifying, analyzing, and resolving such discrepancies. The intent here is to provide, after extensive modification, an adaptation of the Mager-Pipe design as illustrated in the flowchart (Figure 1) and to demonstrate its relevance to the library environment.[1]

A performance discrepancy exists when there is inconsistency between that which is required or expected of a given employee and that which actually takes place. On rare occasions, one encounters the overproductive employee, such as the secretary who is so well organized and so attentive to sheltering one from all unscheduled interruptions that one's daily routine lacks spontaneity and flexibility. Much more common, however, is the case of the underproductive employee, such as the bibliographic searcher of low output, or the person whose work is poor in quality, such as the cataloger who consistently misjudges subject analysis.

In either case, the first step toward resolving the problem is to describe clearly the nature of the performance discrepancy (A). It has been said that a problem well stated is a problem half solved. Conversely, a problem poorly defined may never be solved. There exists a natural tendency to bypass this vital first step in one's eagerness to arrive at a solution as quickly as possible. For example, it is not uncommon to hear a manager say, "We have a training problem." Yet training, in this sense, is not the problem; it is, instead, one of many possible remedies. While it may be that training will turn out to be the best method for alleviating the performance problem, the manager who speeds to that conclusion without carefully defining the discrepancy and analyzing its cause(s) may invest considerable time and resources and still remain on "square one," having made little progress toward resolving the situation. Therefore, an objective description of the performance discrepancy is the integral initial step in the analytical process.

Once the nature and extent of the problem is determined, one must assess its relative importance (B). What would happen if the situation were ignored (C)? Not all discrepancies are worth eliminating. A few years ago, a cataloger in a large academic library related the following account of an incident which took place in her department. She and a colleague were carrying on an admittedly non-job-related discussion when the director of libraries walked into their office and pointedly declared, "If you ladies would stop talking, we'd be number one instead of number three in OCLC's statistics." Ignoring the ill-advised brusqueness of his approach, one still has to question whether the criticism was really deserved. If the department was ranked number three, chances are they already were doing an outstanding job and the director's expectations were, at the least, unrealistically demanding, if not self-

FIGURE 1
Model for Analyzing and Resolving Performance Problems

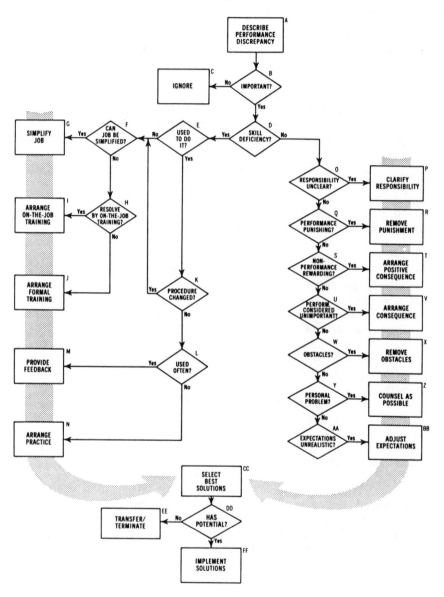

aggrandizing. Make an objective appraisal: is the targeted performance problem critical enough to justify the time, effort, and resources one will have to invest to resolve it successfully?

Assuming that a clearly defined performance discrepancy has been identified and that its resolution is important to the harmonious and/or productive functioning of the library, it must be determined if the problem is or is not the result of a particular skill deficiency (D). Is the employee not performing satisfactorily simply because he does not know how? Or does he basically understand the process for accomplishing the task, but lack the proficiency that comes with experience? Would he be able to do it if his life depended upon it? If the answer to the last question is "no," then a skill deficiency does indeed exist. This is a pivotal juncture in the analytical process, for "yes" or "no" judgments on the question, Is there a skill deficiency? will lead to quite divergent courses of responsive action.

YES, THERE IS A SKILL DEFICIENCY

Let us consider first the case in which a performance problem traceable to a skill deficiency has been isolated and successful resolution is important to the productive functioning of the organization. At this point, one should ask whether the task or procedure is one that the employee used to carry out satisfactorily (E). There is a big difference between the paths a manager might take (1) to resurrect a skill that obviously once existed, and (2) to correct a situation in which the employee was *never* able to perform the task adequately. If the latter circumstance is evident and the worker never possessed the necessary skill, one may choose to follow one (or more) of three courses, namely: (1) simplify the job procedure (G), (2) provide on-the-job training (I), or (3) arrange formal training (J).

Generally, the first alternative—simplifying the job procedure—requires the least investment in terms of time and resources and should, therefore, be given first consideration as a possible solution. Consider the case of the file clerk who, although bright and generally accurate in carrying out his assigned duties, could not remember the exceptions to the basic rules and, as a consequence, made frequent errors when, for example, filing chronological entries. The clerk was one day provided with a guidesheet, summarizing the most common filing idiosyncrasies, to carry as he worked. By changing the details of the job (i.e., by providing a guidesheet rather than insisting that the clerk commit the exceptions to memory), filing errors were virtually eliminated with no deleterious effect upon productivity. As in this example, one will occasionally find it as efficient and much less time-consuming to simplify the job procedure rather than impose more elaborate correctives. In fact, close examination of the activity may reveal procedures that have long been in need of updating and revision.

If, on the other hand, training is deemed necessary to remediate the skill deficiency, a choice must be made between formal and on-the-job modes. When possible, on-the-job training may be simpler, less expensive, better tailored to individual need, more graciously accepted by the employee, and at times more effective than formalized training. There is, for example, general agreement that bibliographic searching in online databases and even in manual systems is most successfully taught on the job. Whether on-the-job training or more formalized training methods (workshops, coursework, in-house or cooperative in-service programs, etc.) are used, it is important to ensure that the specific skill that needs upgrading is isolated and addressed. To illustrate, at a recent Dialog update session, a trainer was asked to analyze why a particular person's searching time was so lengthy. After brief observation, the trainer said, "Do you know what you need? A typing course!" The searcher did not need another Dialog update session, nor did he need more training in search strategy. To have put him through such instruction would have been a waste of time. Training a person to do something he already knows how to do is not going to raise the level of performance.

Let us back up a moment to the point where we identified a skill deficiency and asked, "Is this something the employee used to do satisfactorily?" (E). If, instead of our original "no" response, we know that the worker did perform the task capably at one time, then we must determine whether the procedure or methodology has changed in such a way as to outdate the worker's skills (K). A prime example exists in many technical services departments which have undergone dramatic changes within the past decade. Revised cataloging rules and newly automated systems are examples of conditions under which changes in the requirements of the job may outrun the employee's efforts to keep pace. When such a situation exists, once again it must be determined whether the procedure can be modified to enable the employee to meet job requirements or whether on-the-job or formal training activities are necessary.

Conversely, when a worker fails to exhibit a skill which was evident in the past, even though the job procedure has not changed significantly, examine how frequently that skill is used (L). A skill which is not regularly practiced may fade or even disappear. When this is the case, periodic practice or some form of skill maintenance program may be advisable (N). The more critical the skill is, the more money involved, the greater the necessity of regular practice. A response to this type of need is the development of subsets of online reference databases (such as ONTAP ERIC, ONTAP CHEMNAME), on which an employee may sharpen searching skills at reduced hourly rates.

Another situation may occur in which the employee used to carry out a given assignment capably, the procedure has not changed, frequency of use has not diminished, yet a skill deficiency has surfaced. In such a case, it may be that the worker is not receiving sufficient feedback as to the quality of his work. It is said that "practice makes perfect," but this is only true when one understands what he is doing and does it correctly. Otherwise, practice is simply a means of entrenching poor performance. Inconsistencies in the OCLC database present a vivid example for all to see of catalogers not receiving necessary feedback. The implementation of AACR 2 provides an excellent opportunity for upgrading feedback in cataloging departments. Not only should department heads be sampling the output of their staff, but also an atmosphere of comradeship should be fostered in which employees are encouraged to share their questions with one another. Under any circumstances, when performance suffers and there is reason to believe that the employee is quite capable of accomplishing that which is expected of him, one should check to see whether that person is receiving the necessary feedback as to the quality of his work (M).

If, upon reaching this point in the analytical process, one is still unable to pinpoint the likely cause of the performance discrepancy, chances are the problem is not traceable to a skill deficiency as originally thought. Therefore, we will now back up to the fork in our flowchart and examine alternative possibilities when the anwer is "no" to the question, Is there a skill deficiency?

NO, THERE IS NOT A SKILL DEFICIENCY

At this juncture in the analysis, we have identified and described the nature of the performance discrepancy and further decided that, for whatever reasons, its resolution is important to the healthy functioning of the library. When responding negatively to the question, Is there a skill deficiency?, one is essentially stating that the employee could perform the required task successfully if he had to do so or if he wanted to do so. In other words, he understands the process and is physically and intellectually capable of accomplishing the assigned duties. Whereas remedial responses to problems traceable to skill deficiencies normally include training or instruction of some sort, responses to non-skill-related performance problems generally center on performance maintenance:

> Rather than modify the person's skill or knowledge (since it's likely that he already has the ability), you will have to modify the conditions associated with the performance, or the consequence or result of that performance. Rather than change what he *can* do,

change something about the world in which he does it so that doing it will be more attractive, or less repulsive, or less difficult.[2]

Too often one overgeneralizes and considers all non-skill-related performance problems to be the result of poor attitude. How often one hears the following statements: "He simply doesn't have the right attitude." "She just doesn't care." One could not say that such statements are never justified, for often they are. Perhaps this is a good point to reemphasize the critical importance of matching the right person with the right job during the selection process. Not only must one be wary of hiring unqualified or poorly motivated candidates, but one must also guard against placing an overqualified worker in a position which fails to capitalize upon the employee's abilities and ambition. Such a mismatch of job to worker often results in low morale and high rates of absenteeism.

Clarity of Job Description

Let us examine some possible explanations for performance discrepancies that are *not* traceable to skill deficiencies. One situation which is not uncommon and is usually associated with newly hired or recently transferred employees is the lack of clarity regarding job responsibilities (O). Perhaps the new reference librarian simply never knew that his duties included the preparation of periodic bibliographies, which ceased to appear after his hiring. Is a clearly detailed job description available and is the employee familiar with it? Does that job description need updating and revision so as to reflect more accurately what is currently required of the worker? The way to eliminate the confusion over job responsibility is simply to meet with the employee and take those steps necessary to remove the ambiguity (P).

Punitive Consequences

Could it be possible that good performance may have punitive consequences for the employee (Q)? If a worker has done such an outstanding job of weeding the annual report file he is next asked to tackle the clipping file, followed by the old magazine collection, one can well imagine what may happen to his level of performance. The employee is likely to perceive that his quality work is bringing him nothing but more of the same drudgery. Some form of positive consequence should be provided so that the employee will know that his initiative and efficiency are indeed recognized and appreciated (R). In the above case, one means of providing positive incentive would be to intersperse such tedious and monotonous tasks with assignments which should prove more challenging and stimulating to the employee, thus minimizing the potential for worker dissatisfaction and declining productivity.

Another example of commendable performance generating negative results is seen in the case of the "rate buster"—the employee who works so productively and efficiently that he incurs the resentment of his coworkers. Peer pressure *not to perform* can be very powerful and is present in many institutions and departments. Where such influences exist, steps should be taken to reduce or eliminate the negative effects and create positive or desirable consequences. Such counterbalancing inducements might include the potential for promotion, financial incentives, or the opportunity to participate in decision-making activities. Most importantly, a productive employee should be kept aware of the fact that his outstanding work is a valuable contribution to the functioning of the library and is sincerely appreciated.

Rewards of Nonperformance

A third possible explanation for a non-skill-related deficiency is that nonperformance may be in some way rewarding to the employee (S). Everyone has encountered at one time or another the petty bureaucrat who derives his satisfaction from stipulating rules and regulations, burying people in paperwork, and watching them wither in frustration. Sad to say, such personalities are not unknown to library staffs, and the problems they create can be difficult to eradicate. The challenge is to make an employee realize that good performance will bring greater rewards and satisfaction than will nonperformance (T). This is sometimes not an easy mission, for we may be dealing with long-ingrained personality traits and perhaps with a person who lacks self-confidence in his own ability to carry out his job responsibilities successfully. One may try counseling, monitoring, positive feedback, teaming an employee with a more positively directed coworker, and perhaps provide even more tangible rewards in an effort to upgrade a worker's attitude. Lack of constructive response from an employee may mandate harsher consequences, such as probation, transfer, or termination.

Performance Matters

Another question one might ask is, Is it clear to all concerned that good performance really matters? (U). If an employee feels that a task is not worth doing, it will tend not to get done. Paperwork is a good example—reports turned in late, haphazardly, or in error. To illustrate, the manager of acquisitions in a mid-sized academic library was known to complain regularly about the head of the searching unit, who each month submitted statistical reports which were largely illegible. Finally, in frustration, the manager sent the reports back to the head of the searching unit, asking him to do them over. By arranging a negative consequence (i.e., requiring that the reports be redone), the manager made it clear that performance did indeed matter. We need seldom resort to such negative consequences (V), however, if instead we provide means for periodic feedback, keeping employees aware that ongoing successful execution of one's responsibilities is an important link in the library's chain of operation.

One should also check for obstacles which may hinder performance (W). Common examples include the constantly ringing telephone; inconveniently located, poorly labeled, and undependable equipment; inadequately maintained supplies or tools; improperly lighted work areas; or uncomfortably furnished facilities. Perhaps an employee has been assigned job responsibilities without the means or authority for fulfilling those responsibilities. Where such obstacles are discovered, they will have to be removed (X), or job expectations will need to be adjusted accordingly.

Personal Problems

Occasionally, a non-skill-related performance discrepancy can be traced to a personal problem that the employee is experiencing (Y). An example of a job-oriented personal problem would be the case in which an employee is so disgruntled over some aspect of a work situation that performance is adversely affected. Or perhaps a personality conflict, between the employee and a supervisor, for example, exists. While unfortunate, such clashes are occasionally unavoidable wherever large groups of people work together over long periods of time. When such situations arise, it is advisable to examine the affair from several perspectives. Does the conflict center on only one or two persons, or are there other employees involved as well? What are the facts? When did the problem begin and what are the causes? Perhaps the situation can be resolved by counseling, by bringing two or more employees together in a face-to-face meeting, or through mediation or negotiation (Z). As in all cases, the choice of remedial action must be dependent upon the particular nature of the problem.

A parallel situation exists when a performance discrepancy is traced to a personal problem of other than job-related origin. The most prominent examples are domestic, financial, drinking, or health problems that carry over and affect work. Such externally generated problems can be among the most difficult of those with which the library administrator must deal, since the causes are largely outside the scope of his or her authority. Dependent upon the particular needs and resources of both the employee and the library, remedial steps might include (1) provision of in-house counseling, (2) arrangement for outside help for the worker (e.g., through a community service agency such as Family Services, Alcoholics Anonymous, or the Legal Aid Society, or through private counseling services), or (3) provision for a leave of absence.

Finally, could it be that expectations regarding employee performance are simply unjustifiably demanding (AA)? Recall the earlier example of the director of libraries who was dissatisfied because his catalogers were only third in OCLC's statistics. A similar problem may occur when a newly hired worker is expected to step in and fill shoes left by a seasoned and highly efficient former employee. It is always wise to step back and evaluate honestly whether the level of performance one demands is fair and realistic and, if not, to adjust expectations accordingly (BB).

Be careful not to overlook the possibility of multiple causes for a particular performance discrepancy. To illustrate, perhaps an employee feels that his good performance is resulting in punishing consequences and yet cannot communicate his frustration to his supervisor because of friction between the two. Where there are two or more contributing factors for a given performance problem, one needs to break that problem down into its causal components and, as necessary, adopt multiple remedial steps.

ASSESSING THE SITUATION

Once the cause or causes of a performance discrepancy have been isolated and the best possible solutions identified (CC), the overall feasibility and potential of the situation must be assessed (DD). Some remedial actions may clearly be inappropriate due to limitations in resources. It is also necessary to weigh the more overt costs of resolving the performance problem (in terms of time, effort, and money) against the potential costs of doing nothing (continued inefficiency, high turnover, dissatisfied patrons, resentful staff members, and absent employees). Only when all these factors have been considered and a practical and likely solution has been identified does one move from the process of analysis to the task of implementation (FF). If, however, one reaches the point of assessing possible solutions and must reject them all as beyond one's resources or impractical, it is then advisable to reexamine the performance problem as well as the solution(s) to determine whether one or both can be pared down to more manageable proportions and then addressed on that scale.

It is also wise to make an objective appraisal of the employee's potential: does he have what it takes to fulfill the responsibilities of the position, provided that the required remedial steps are arranged?

If not, the unavoidable consequence may be transfer or termination (EE). Such a course of action is seldom more pleasant for the manager than for the worker. Few wish to concede that an individual in their employ, perhaps even someone whose hiring they once supported, is beyond occupational redemption. Even fewer enjoy the responsibility of notifying the employee once that decision has been made. Yet good money can be thrown after valuable time in a futile effort to nurture an employee who simply lacks the physical or intellectual capacity or attitudinal dedication ever to meet the requirements of the position. Failure to take decisive measures in such recurring situations can result in whole departments full of walking performance discrepancies.

Most performance problems in the library, however, are resolvable through implementation of more positive alternatives. To that end the foregoing discussion is dedicated. While the analytical design may not relieve all aggravations in this area of managerial responsibility, it does provide a framework for systematic problem solving which minimizes costly misjudgments and serves to guide both manager and employee toward successful resolution of performance problems.

REFERENCES

1. Robert F. Mager and Peter Pipe, *Analyzing Performance Problems, or "You Really Oughta Wanna"* (Belmont, CA: Fearon, 1970). The original model by Mager and Pipe has been changed significantly from O through BB (performance discrepancies not traceable to skill deficiencies). In E through L and CC through FF the flow has been revised.

2. Ibid., p. 47.

Bibliography

Allenbaugh, G. Eric. "Coaching...A Management Tool for a More Effective Work Performance." *Management Review* 72 (May 1983): 21–26.

Advocates that a manager's goal be to develop the self and others to perform at optimum levels by focusing on making strengths productive. Provides a critique of appraisal processes as background for coaching, seven principles of coaching, and clear articulation of skills for effective coaching. Stresses that each contact with an individual is an opportunity for coaching, especially through continuous feedback through dialog.

Baker, H. Kent, and Holmberg, Stevan R. "Stepping Up to Supervision: Conducting Performance Reviews." *Supervisory Management* 27 (April 1982): 20–27.

Discusses five aspects of effective appraisal systems: goals should be measured, evaluation should integrate work with results, reviews should be objective, the system should be understood, and appraisal programs should be constructive. Traditional systems have operated on evaluating personality. However, the most effective systems measure performance against predetermined verifiable objectives. For the appraisal interview, the evaluator should be prepared, set the atmosphere, ask for self-evaluation, discuss total performance, formulate development plans, summarize, and provide documentation.

Beer, Michael. "Performance Appraisal: Dilemmas and Possibilities." *Organizational Dynamics* 9 (Summer 1980–Winter 1981): 24–30.

States that, when it is a pleasure, performance appraisal is easy; the ease is related to communication and the reward systems related to appraisal. However, appraisal generates conflict, even in the most ideal situation. Conflict generates ambivalence and avoidance, defensiveness and resistance in both appraisers and the appraised. Recommendations are: keep appraisal and development activities separate; choose appropriate performance data to evaluate; separate performance and evaluation of potential; recognize individual differences in system design; and include upward appraisal and self-appraisal. Also provides concrete guidance for preparing and conducting the interview.

Beer, Michael A., and Ruh, Robert A. "Employer Growth Through Performance Management." *Harvard Business Review* 54 (July/August 1976): 59–66.

Describes Corning Glass Works's experience with MBO and its development of "Performance Management System (PMS)" for its 3,800 staff.

Claims four distinctions for PMS: recognizes manager's triple role as manager, judge, and helper in dealing with subordinates; emphasizes development and evaluation; measures against self; and integrates results of MBO. PMS is made up of three parts: MBO, performance development and reviews, and evaluation and salary review. Authors present a mid-70s record of an intensive approach to performance appraisal in one industrial setting.

Belohlav, James A., and Popp, Paul O. "Employee Substance Abuse: Epidemic of the Eighties." *Business Horizons* 26 (July–August 1983): 29–34.

Cites 70% of the adult American population as alcohol users but notes lack of precision in defining the extent of alcohol abuse in the work force. Also cites a 1979 study showing 6% of employees with a drug abuse problem. Documented areas affected by substance abuse are related to absenteeism, accidents, and medical insurance rates. Alcoholics are reported to have a 16% higher absentee rate than the regular work force. One estimate claims that 15% of health claims paid are related to alcohol abuse. Discusses need for clear personnel policies to deal with substance abuse, especially in light of federal regulations.

Brache, Alan. "Appraising Appraisals." *Management World* 13 (February 1984): 36–37.

Suggests the following reasons for "manager dread" of performance appraisals: lack of clarity about objectives, lack of comfort appraising employees, lack of definitions and standards, a perception of total subjectivity concerning the appraisal exercise, a lack of comfort with the appraisal interview, and anxiety over honest appraisals. Posits obvious corrections.

Bushardt, Stephen C., and Schnake, M.E. "Employee Evaluation: Measure Performance, Not Attitude." *Management World* 10 (February 1981): 41–42.

Suggests that managers make judgments in three areas: pay, promotion, and transfer. A common occurrence for managers is evaluating attitude rather than performance. Three problems exist in evaluating attitudes: the possibility of making false assumptions, the inability to measure attitude, and the difficulty in changing attitudes. Adds that the real issue is behavior (performance of prescribed task).

Clewis, John E., and Panting, Janice I. *Performance Appraisal: An Investment in Human Capital.* Washington, DC: College and University Personnel Association, 1985.

Provides a good overview aimed specifically at the academic community. Gives balanced, summarized data on characteristics of performance standards, appraisal interviews, and performance improvement plans.

Continuing Education Committee, College Library Section, Association of College and Research Libraries. *Clip Notes: College Library Information Packets, #1–80 Performance Evaluation.* Chicago: American Library Association, 1980.

This collection of library-specific performance evaluation instruments provides good mid-level library samples of policy statements and forms, as well as an annotated bibliography that provided early 80s guidance for libraries. Should be reviewed by academic library administrators in any evaluation of performance appraisal instruments. One source for a simple, but useful, student assistant evaluation form.

Edwards, Mark R., Borman, Walter C., and Sproull, J. Ruth. "Solving the Double Bind in Performance Appraisal: A Saga of Wolves, Sloths, and Eagles." *Business Horizons* 28 (3) (May–June 1985): 59–68.
Addresses the twin dilemmas of supervisors who are sole evaluators and who are simultaneously performance coaches. Offers the concept of Team Evaluation (TE), based on a sample of 1,600+ raters in large companies. Provides identification and probable cause of six basic rating inaccuracies and lists training needs for raters. Concludes with a discussion of the trend toward separating performance considerations from salary questions, affirming the team (TE + MS) method.

Fletcher, Clive. "What's New in...Performance Appraisal?" *Personnel Management* 16 (February 1984): 20–22.
Fletcher discusses the skill and willingness of individuals to evaluate their own performance. He suggests that there are some situations where self appraisal works best. Those situations where it does not work as well tend to involve authoritarian supervisors. He offers an explanation concerning causes for poor performance and the source of the causes. If you explain your own poor performance factors, you are using external attribution if you blame situational or circumstantial factors. Your explanation of another person's behavior, based on characteristics of that person, is a use of internal attribution. His goal is to achieve lessening of bias in the appraisal experience through greater understanding of attribution of causes of behavior and more effective use of self appraisal in the process.

Fombrun, Charles J., and Laud, Robert L. "Strategic Issues in Performance Appraisal: Theory and Practice." *Personnel* 60 (November–December 1983): 23–31.
Reports on a conceptual framework for the role that a well-designed appraisal system can provide and survey results from a sample of *Fortune 1300* firms. Deals with the generic functions of the human resource system: selection, appraisal, the setting of rewards, development. Concludes from the survey that more careful attention must be given to design in the appraisal system in order to gain a more valid measure of performance. Also shows the need for integration of the appraisal system into the total human resource system: selection, appraisal, reward determination, and development.

"Guidelines for Performance Evaluation of Professional Librarians." *The Newsletter* (California Library Association) 27 (November 1985).
Appears to be the first state association-endorsed statement of criteria for the evaluation of the performance of professional librarians. It provides for evaluation in five areas: professional development; professional contributions; organization responsibility; community involvement; and area of specialization. The document is aimed at public, school, special, and academic librarians.

Ilgen, Daniel R., et al. "Supervisor and Subordinate Reactions to Performance Appraisal Sessions." *Organizational Behavior and Human Performance* 20 (December 1981): 311–30.

Describes research conducted with 60 pairs of supervisor-subordinates on performance feedback sessions using an MBO-operated system for evaluation. Research relates to the implementation of the MBO system in a wood products company. Analysis confirmed that employees consistently overrate performance. Responsibility for some of this was placed on supervisors who fail to be specific enough in their expectations. Also, supervisors tend to overestimate the quality of feedback they are giving and to limit it to the annual performance rating.

Kaye, Beverly L. "Performance Appraisal and Career Development: A Shotgun Marriage." *Personnel* 6 (March–April 1984): 57–66.

Both performance appraisal and career development are terms and processes that have been used long enough that there is a strong sense of familiarity with the terms, regardless of the effectiveness of the systems the terms represent. Both of these human resource systems require full understanding of how the system works, and both require willing participants for effective utilization of the systems. Superficial familiarity is detrimental to effectiveness. Kaye suggests that joining the two systems is a marriage of convenience and common sense. Performance evaluation and career development can be mutually reinforcing. Where they are successfully combined and reinforcement occurs, the union is a productive one for both employer and employee.

Latham, Gary P., and Steele, Timothy P. "The Motivational Effects of Participation versus Goal Setting on Performance." *Academy of Management* 26 (September 1983): 406–17.

Cites 10 classic studies that "assess the effectiveness of participation and goal setting on performance," dating to 1948. This 11th study, in a pajama-producing plant, demonstrated increased productivity levels related to employee goal acknowledgement and participation in job design. This article is a detailed report on the study/experience.

Levinson, Harry. "Appraisal of What Performance?" *Harvard Business Review* 54 (July–August 1976): 30–46ff.

Suggests that the critical issue in performance appraisal is the need for a dynamic job description, which includes summaries of emotional and behavioral aspects of the task to be performed. Four factors should be considered in forming a dynamic job description: ability of employee to handle aggression, manage affection, manage dependency needs, and obtain ego fulfillment from the job. Provides a program for managers to deal with their experiences and feelings about their functions and responsibilities in the appraisal process.

Linkins, Germaine C. "Department Head Evaluations: The Virginia Tech Library Experience." *Journal of Library Administration* 5 (Winter 1984): 53–60.

Describes a system in place since the 1970s for library faculty evaluation at Virginia Tech that provides for detailed analysis of the past year and goal setting for the next year. System implemented in Virginia Tech library was aimed at upward evaluation of department heads. Two concerns became evident early in the process: how to ensure anonymity in the evaluation process and who should participate in evaluation. The latter concern was addressed by limiting evaluation to faculty participation. Notes time necessary for effective implementation of this approach.

McMillan, John D., and Doyle, Hoyt W. "Performance Appraisal: Match the Tool to the Task." *Personnel* 57 (July/August 1980): 12–20.
Emphasizes that, to achieve maximum benefits, the purpose of the appraisal requires careful definition and, in fact, separate appraisals may be required for different purposes. Timing of the appraisal often is not considered adequately. Discusses the strengths and weaknesses of the most common appraisal methods: trait checklist, MBO, and free form. States that it is uncommon for companies to use "responsibility rating," a system where rating is job description task-specific, dependent on well-written job descriptions.

Moravec, Milan. "Performance Appraisal: A Human Resource Management System with Productivity Payoffs." *Management Review* 70 (June 1981): 51–54.
Provides a description of the method and levels of responsibility at Bechtel for employee task orientation, training, and evaluation. The role and responsibilities of the manager as clear communicator are emphasized. A good "how we do it good at ..." approach that refrains from being condescending.

Morrison, Ann M., and Kranz, Mary Ellen. "The Shape of Performance Appraisal in the Coming Decade." *Personnel* 58 (July/August 1981): 12–22.
Morrison and Kranz set out the legal protection provided by performance appraisal, the collection of data for human resources planning, and the increasing expectation of the work force in decision making. They project the needs for performance appraisal through the current decade. Because of these factors, and others, they suggest that conflicts will exist in the future between

- individual freedom/goal setting and centralized planning
- costs vs. value of data collected via performance evaluation and other human resource systems
- need for clear relationship of career development, job enrichment, and performance appraisal.

Nix, Dan H. "Getting Ready for the Appraisal Interview." *Supervisory Management* 25 (July 1980): 2–8.
Covers material ranging from "pre-interview gut-level scales" to performance and relationship scales that analyze present and project performance and supervisor/supervisee relationships. The focus is on providing aid to the supervisor to reduce anxiety.

Pascale, Richard Tanner. "Zen and the Art of Management." *Harvard Business Review* 56 (March/April 1978): 153–62.
Describes the difference between having enough data to make a decision and enough data to act on that decision. Points to the major difference

between American and Japanese approaches: one announces, then accomplishes; the latter accomplishes, then announces. There continues to be evidence that achievement and recognition are correlated.

Personnel Administrator 29 (March 1984).
Discusses performance appraisal in this special issue. Articles deal with the suggestion that some compensation/benefits (e.g., one-time-only bonus) could be awarded to boost morale without permanently affecting compensation. Presents the usual data in discussing the shortcomings of appraisal systems versus the ideal contribution they should make to employee development and company productivity. Considers a situational approach to appraisal, acknowledging that the personal needs of the employee dictate the employee's response to appraisal, and posits idea to use different appraisal systems to meet those needs and increase productivity. Promotes a system that analyzes rater's appraisals to determine effectiveness of rater. Issue provides a good overview of the subject.

Rice, Berkeley. "Performance Review: The Job Nobody Likes." *Psychology Today* 19 (September 1985): 30–36.
Presents the state of the art in popular literature. Reflects clear research, leading one to wish that it was documented with end notes or a bibliography. Provides a solid description of BARS (behaviorally anchored rating scales), their use in current industrial settings, and the evidence of greater reliability of rating results. Rice is cited by Zemke just three months later, an indication of the vitality of performance evaluation literature.

Sashkin, Marshall. "Appraising Appraisal: Ten Lessons from Research Practice." *Organizational Dynamics* 9 (Winter 1981): 37–50.
In light of recent regulatory and judicial decisions, Sashkin provides 10 guidelines for the evaluation of an appraisal system. Each is clearly illustrated with concrete examples. Unique to Sashkin are the questions dealing with the problem-solving focus of appraisals and clear differentiation of judge and counselor roles for appraisers. The bibliography, in essay format, is instructive.

Schuler, Randall S. "Taking the Pain Out of Performance Appraisal Interviews." *Supervisory Management* 26 (August 1981): 8–12.
Illustrates, through examples of dialog, positive aspects of the interview process; uses Elisabeth Kubler-Ross's five stages of reaction to change—denial (shock), anger, bargaining, depression, acceptance—as a basis for understanding reactions. This journal is one of the best in the field, especially for practical approaches leavened with humor.

Wells, Ronald G. "Guidelines for Effective and Defensible Performance Appraisal Systems." *Personnel Journal* 61 (October 1982): 776–82.
Provides clearly written guidance on legally defensible characteristics of performance appraisal. These include: job relatedness; subjective criteria (including initiative and industriousness); performance expectations; clear standards; uniformity; regular schedules for evaluation; and documentation. Also discusses characteristics of appraisers, the need for communication flow, training, and managerial responsibility.

Yankelovich, Daniel, and Immerwahr, John. "Let's Put the Work Ethic to Work." *Industry Week* 218 (September 5, 1983): 33–35.
Yankelovich and Immerwahr describe the "limited commitment" model of production productivity, which is a product of the industrial revolution, and the "scientific management" of production via the assembly line. In this model, productivity was independent of individual creativity and motivation. The shift in America toward white-collar/service sector occupations, new technologies being applied to manual production tasks (what Yankelovich identifies as new values), and a healthy work ethic all contribute to the opportunity to enhance and take advantage of the American work ethic. Based on data collected by the Public Agenda Foundation, the authors offer four suggestions:

1. performance incentives should encourage the work ethic;
2. standards should reinforce intrinsic worth and meaning of work;
3. a distinction should be made between job satisfaction enhancement and production increases via job improvements; and
4. the administrative hierarchy should be flattened.

Zemke, Ron. "Is Performance Appraisal a Paper Tiger?" *Training* 22 (December 1985): 24–32.
Zemke reiterates the sense of disillusionment with performance appraisal as an issue which has held the attention of personnel management in industry. Zemke, as one of the authority names in training circles, can get away with repeating the questions of the past including differing valuation of appraisal by managers and employees, reluctance to rate, and lack of objective data/results. Zemke summarizes the usual reasons given for the failure of performance appraisal and provides an excellent summary of Thomas H. Patten's *A Manager's Guide to Performance Appraisal* (Free Press, 1982). He concludes by reinforcing the following concepts: stick to objectives; scale rate a few key performance factors; conduct an essential discussion of rating by both parties; provide for an overall rating; and, of necessity, obtain both parties' signatures. Performance evaluation is moving into its fifth decade with mixed reviews about its vitality, but resignation about its necessity.

Zorn, Theodore E., Jr. "A More Systematic Approach to Employee Development." *Supervisory Management* 28 (June 1983): 2–12.
Provides a step-by-step guide to implementation of career development into the evaluation process. A bit elementary.

Index

Compiled by Debbie Burnham-Kidwell

023.9
P416   Performance evalua-
                  tion

DATE DUE

000 463   000 000